CRIMINAL EVIDENCE FOR POLICE

CRIMINAL EVIDENCE FOR POLICE

Fourth Edition

Paul B. Weston
Professor Emeritus
School of Health and Human Services
Division of Criminal Justice
California State University, Sacramento

Kenneth M. Wells, J.D.

Marlene E. Hertoghe, J.D.

 PRENTICE HALL, Englewood Cliffs, New Jersey 07632

Library of Congress Cataloging-in-Publication Data

Weston, Paul B.
    Criminal evidence for police/Paul B. Weston, Kenneth M. Wells,
    Marlene E. Hertoghe.—4th ed.
        P. cm.
    Includes bibliographical references and index.
    ISBN 0-13-304635-4
    1. Evidence, Criminal—United States.   I. Wells, Kenneth M.
    II. Hertoghe, Marlene E.   III. Title.
    KF9660.W38   1995
    345.73'06—dc20   94-33197
    [347.3056]   CIP

Production Editor: *Janet M. McGillicuddy*
Acquisitions Editor: *Robin Baliszewski*
Director of Manufacturing & Production: *Bruce Johnson*
Manufacturing Buyer: *Ed O'Dougherty*
Editorial Assistant: *Rose Mary Florio*
Formatting/page make-up: *Janet M. McGillicuddy*
Printer/Binder: *R. R. Donnelley*

©1995 by Prentice-Hall, Inc.
A Simon & Schuster Company
Englewood Cliffs, New Jersey 07632

Printed in the United States of America

10   9   8   7   6   5   4   3   2 1

ISBN 0-13-304635-4

Prentice-Hall International (UK) Limited, *London*
Prentice-Hall of Australia Pty. Limited, *Sydney*
Prentice-Hall Canada Inc., *Toronto*
Prentice-Hall Hispanoamericana, S.A., *Mexico*
Prentice-Hall of India Private Limited, *New Delhi*
Prentice-Hall of Japan, Inc., *Tokyo*
Simon & Schuster Asia Pte. Ltd., *Singapore*
Editora Prentice-Hall do Brasil, Ltda., *Rio de Janeiro*

For Kenneth M. Wells, 1925–1989, a talented trial attorney,
a progressively successful public official,
a gifted teacher, and a great co-author.

Contents

CHAPTER 4

Testimony   40

CHAPTER 5

Witnesses   61

CHAPTER 9

Direct Versus Circumstantial Evidence   118

CHAPTER 10

The Exclusionary Rule   128

CHAPTER 11

Evidence: Arrests, Searches, and Seizures   152

CHAPTER 12

Confessions and Admissions   167

CHAPTER 13

Discovery and Disclosure   178

CHAPTER 14

Evidence of Electronic Surveillances   185

Illustrations

Preface

One new chapter and two major chapter segments highlight the Fourth Edition of *Criminal Evidence for Police*. New Chapter 2, Briefing Cases, details legal research and the how-to of writing case summaries. The new segment of Chapter 5, Witnesses, is about the child sexual abuse victim-witness. And new in Chapter 8, Articles and Exhibits of Evidence, is the promise and problem of videotaping evidence.

There is also a thorough updating of material from the past edition, new cases, additional copy, and fresh comment.

As a learning resource, the Case Studies section at the end of each chapter has been enhanced by adding a new section, Miniprojects. This new material suggests areas of inquiry linked to a chapter's court cases/decisions. Additional discussion questions have been developed to encourage readers to work with the suggested Miniprojects and Case Studies.

Police and other agents of criminal justice have a need to know about evidence in action in America's courtrooms and how it does or does not get there. This edition is aimed at achieving that goal.

Paul B. Weston
Marlene Hertoghe

CRIMINAL EVIDENCE FOR POLICE

CHAPTER 1

From Evidence to Proof

CHAPTER OBJECTIVES

- To discuss the refinement of evidence for use in criminal proceedings.
- To show the importance of the admissibility of evidence.
- To show the legal significance of proof in its impact upon the triers of fact (judge or jury).
- To describe the doctrine of presumed innocence and the requirement of proof beyond a reasonable doubt.
- To describe the operation of the two-party system, which distinguishes the American legal system.

In a criminal case, the truth of the accusation against a defendant must be proved beyond all reasonable doubt. The doctrines of presumed innocence and reasonable doubt protect persons accused of crime from injustice. The role of evidence in the trial of criminal cases is to prove guilt or indicate innocence.

Evidence is defined as any matter of fact, the effect, tendency, or design of which is to produce in the mind a persuasion, affirmative or disaffirmative, of the existence of some other matter of fact. To sum up, evidence means testimony, writings, material objects, or other things presented to the senses that are offered to prove the existence or nonexistence of a fact.*

Court procedures limit the exhibits and testimony that may be given in evidence. If there were no rules for the admissibility of evidence, and if any exhibit or testimony with the slightest bearing on the issue before the court could be presented in evidence, it would be impossible to conduct criminal trials within a reasonable span of time. The rules of evidence are designed to enable courts to reach the truth and, in criminal cases, to secure a fair trial for persons accused of crime.

*State and federal rules of evidence have contributed to this text, but readers seeking information on rules of evidence applicable to a specific court should examine whatever published material is applicable.

Guilt Versus Innocence   In a criminal trial the community—"the people"—is represented by a prosecutor and the defendant is represented by a private attorney or a public defender. At trial, exhibits and testimony admitted as evidence are examined from opposite directions to establish the innocence or guilt of the defendant. Evidence is presented in such a manner and of such character that a decision can be made about the defendant's guilt or innocence.

In the apparatus of criminal justice, the process of discovering truth and making decisions is entrusted to a judge or jury. A person accused of crime may waive trial by jury and accept the trial judge as a decision maker, but juries usually function as the "triers of fact" in criminal cases. Most major felony cases in the United States in which defendants claim to be innocent are tried before a jury. The jurors review all the evidence—exhibits and testimony—admitted during the criminal trial to make their decision as to guilt or innocence. The trial judge instructs jurors to avoid any passion, bias, prejudice, or sympathy toward either the victim or the defendant in arriving at their verdict, and he excludes evidence offered exclusively to play on their passions or prejudices. The jurors decide all questions of fact and, under the control of the trial judge, determine the effect and value of the evidence presented to them, including the credibility of witnesses.

It is sometimes difficult to distinguish between evidence and proof. Proof is the effect or result of evidence. Evidence is the medium of proof. More accurately, evidence is the means by which the facts are established, and proof is the effect or the conclusions drawn from such evidence.

Evidence may be either direct or circumstantial. Direct evidence means evidence which in itself, if true, conclusively establishes a fact in issue. Circumstantial evidence, if true, may tend by logical inference to establish a fact in issue.

The weight of the evidence indicating guilt or innocence depends on the impact of the evidence on the trier of fact. Therefore, it is important that evidence be considered in relation to (1) its admissibility and (2) its value as proof of a significant point or element of the prosecution or the defense case. The value of any exhibit or testimony as evidence depends on its nature and on its being recalled and understood by the triers of fact.

The Adversary System

Rational judgments depend on relevant, factual information being brought to the attention of the triers of fact for full assessment. The system of criminal justice in the United States is known as the adversary system, and it is based on fight theory—each party fights to discover and disclose evidence favorable to its side. This system of opposing interest lets us hope to discover facts that will prove or disprove the accusation against the defendant. If there were not two sides, each presenting exhibits and testimony in evidence, there would be no trial. The accusation alone would prove the case against the accused.

Under this system of adversary proceedings, lawyers are necessary for both parties. The assistance of counsel for defendants in criminal prosecutions is a right provided under the Sixth Amendment to the Constitution. In fact, counsel is necessary because of the complexity of modern court procedures. The belief that the presiding judge can see that procedures are fair during a criminal trial without defense counsel has been rejected (but see *People* v. *McKenzie*, 34 Cal. 3rd 616 (1983), which requires the trial court to act if there is unfairness because of incompetent counsel). As early as 1938, the U.S. Supreme Court commented on the necessity of legal counsel for both sides in a criminal prosecution, saying, "The Sixth Amendment stands as a constant admonition that if the constitutional safeguards it provides be lost, justice will not 'still be done.' It embodies a realistic recognition of the obvious truth that the average defendant does not have the professional legal skill to protect himself when brought before a tribunal with power to take his life or liberty, wherein the prosecution is presented by experienced and learned counsel."[1]

The conviction that a person accused of crime cannot be assured a fair trial without legal counsel has become so strong that decisions of the U.S. Supreme Court* require that legal counsel be assigned when accused persons are too poor to hire an attorney, and extend this right to legal representation to juveniles. In *Gideon* v. *Wainwright*[2] the court noted that great emphasis had always been placed on procedural and substantive safeguards designed to assure fair trials before impartial tribunals in which every defendant stands equal before the law. "This noble ideal," the majority opinion states, "cannot be realized if the poor man charged with crime has to face his accusers without a lawyer to assist him." In *Gault* v. *Arizona*[3] a juvenile claimed his basic rights were denied in a juvenile court hearing. In reversing the lower court, the U.S. Supreme Court rejected the parent and probation officer as adequate resources to protect the juvenile's interests saying, "The child requires the guiding hand of counsel at every step in the proceedings against him."

In 1975, despite past opinions declaring the right of the accused to a lawyer and the importance of legal counsel, the U.S. Supreme Court, in *Faretta* v. *California*,[4] held that a competent person accused of a crime has a constitutional right to refuse professional legal assistance and conduct his own defense. Often, though, counsel is appointed to assist a defendant in representing himself so as to avoid unnecessary delay or unfairness to the defendant.[5]

The majority opinion maintains that the Sixth Amendment, in guaranteeing a fair trial, grants to the accused personally the right to make his defense; the

[1]*Johnson* v. *Zerbst*, 304 U.S. 458 (1938).
*See Case Studies for guide to case references.
[2]372 U.S. 335 (1963).
[3]387 U.S. 1 (1967).
[4]422 U.S. 806 (1975).
[5]*McKaskle* v. *Wiggins*, 104 S.Ct. 944 (1984); *United States* v. *Taylor*, 569 F.2d 448 (1978).

right to self-representation, the court claims, is necessarily implied in the Amendment, although it is not stated in so many words. The main thrust of the majority opinion is to remove from the state the power to compel a defendant to accept a lawyer he does not want.

The prosecutor represents the "people" in criminal cases. Defendants who have the necessary funds are represented by legal counsel of their choice, while indigent defendants are assigned counsel by the court. The office of public defender has been playing a role in the administration of justice similar to that of the prosecutor, but serving as defense counsel. The public defender offers indigent defendants a formal organization for defense against accusations of crime or juvenile delinquency.

The concept of a fair trial in an adversary system also requires that the entire criminal proceeding be conducted by an unbiased judge. Kinship, personal bias, or conflict of interest can disqualify a judge. A direct, personal, substantial pecuniary interest in ruling against a defendant certainly disqualifies. Any circumstance that would offer a possible temptation to the average judge to forget the burden of proof required to convict the defendant, or that might lead him not to hold the balance clearly and truly between the state and the accused person, denies the defendant due process of law.[6]

Trial procedure is keyed to the fight theory. Each side, in turn, is given an opportunity to overcome its adversary. Because the people are making the accusation, the prosecutor opens a criminal trial with his side of the case. His goal is to prove the *corpus delicti* of the crime and the "identity" of the criminal agent. *Corpus delicti* is commonly termed the body of the crime or the essential elements of the crime. The essential elements of most criminal cases include the prohibited *act* and the necessary criminal *intent*. After proving these elements, the prosecutor tries to show that the defendant is the person guilty of the crime charged. When the prosecution's case has been completed, the defense has its opportunity. In the closing stages of a trial, both sides are allowed time to repair their cases and answer the opposition's evidence.

Orderly trial procedure consists of presenting evidence in the following order:

1. The people's main case is presented. This is evidence "in chief."
2. The defense presents its evidence and answers the people's "case in chief."
3. "Rebuttal" by the prosecutor is in answer to the defense case and closes the people's case.
4. "Rejoinder" is made by defense to the evidence presented in the prosecutor's rebuttal.

No party to a criminal action is allowed a piecemeal presentation of evidence. The judge is expected to make sure that a party introduces all the

---

[6]*Tumey* v. *Ohio*, 273 U.S. 510 (1927).

evidence he will rely on when he first presents his case. During the rebuttal and surrebuttal or rejoinder, the parties are allowed to amend the evidence structure of their case if they have been surprised by their adversary's evidence.

The proffering of exhibits and witnesses, and specific questions or lines of questioning are also keyed to the adversary system. Proffered evidence and questions may be objected to by opposing counsel. The trial judge examines the substance, purpose, and relevance of the proffered evidence, or the evidence sought by questioning and the form of questions, and scans the grounds of an objection or a motion to exclude or strike evidence.

The prosecution's advantage in being first to present evidence can be negated by defense counsel through effective cross-examination. Capable defense attorneys often seize this opportunity to begin the defense case during the presentation of evidence in chief. Of course, the prosecutor has a similar opportunity to destroy witnesses presented by the defense, but this never seems quite as effective because the people must develop convincing evidence of guilt, and the defense need only produce a reasonable doubt of guilt.

The Burden of Proof

Most criminal trials in the United States result from the police apprehension process. An incident is reported to the police or discovered by them. They respond and investigate the incident. If it constitutes a crime, the search for the criminal is begun. Police continue the investigation until it is closed by arrest, or by administrative action when no arrest is possible. When the police investigator reports to the prosecutor that a crime under investigation has been solved and forwards the investigation report and the collected evidence to the prosecutor, the investigating officer has assumed the burden of proving the accused person guilty.

The prosecutor, after a review of the police case and a pretrial investigation, makes a formal accusation against the individual identified by police as the guilty person. By preparing the accusatory pleading against the defendant and preparing for the trial, it is the prosecutor's burden of proof to show that the defendant is guilty. This burden of proof remains on the prosecution throughout the case. The party claiming that a person is guilty of crime or wrongdoing has the burden of proof on that issue.

Accused persons do not have the burden of proof but rather the burden of overcoming the case made against them by the prosecution. Although the defendant only has to create a reasonable doubt of his guilt, defense counsel attempts the strongest defense and tries to create the highest degree of reasonable doubt so that the defendant will be acquitted.

When the defendant introduces evidence that he was not present when the alleged offense was committed, the burden of proof is not shifted; it remains with the prosecution. The same rule applies when the defendant offers evidence of self-defense or of any of the other common defenses.

At the end of a trial, the presiding judge explains the presumption of innocence and the definition of reasonable doubt to the jury. He does this to orient the members of the jury to the method of weighing the evidence presented by the prosecution to prove the guilt of the defendant, as well as the evidence produced by the defendant to create a reasonable doubt of his guilt. Usually this instruction is worded to highlight the presumption that a defendant in a criminal action is presumed innocent until his guilt is proved, and to emphasize that in case of a reasonable doubt the defendant is entitled to acquittal. This presumption places the burden of proving the defendant guilty beyond a reasonable doubt upon the state, that is, the prosecution. Reasonable doubt is defined as "not a mere possible doubt," because everything relating to human affairs, and depending on moral evidence, is open to some possible imaginary doubt. It is that state of the case that, after the entire comparison and consideration of all the evidence, leaves the minds of the jurors in that condition that they cannot say they feel an abiding conviction to a moral certainty of the truth of the charges.

Burden of Producing Evidence

A party has the burden of producing evidence about a particular fact if a finding against him on that fact would be required in the absence of further evidence. The prosecutor is the first party to produce evidence. If he develops a *prima facie* case, and the defendant does nothing to answer, the defendant fails. The burden of producing evidence is a rule for deciding who must continue presenting evidence.

Even when a negative allegation is made, the party asserting it has the burden of producing evidence despite the inconvenience of proving a negative; but in such instances less evidence will usually shift the burden of producing evidence to the other party. Any evidence that shows the existence of the negative should shift this burden.

During a criminal trial, the burden of producing evidence shifts from one side to the other. When a fact is peculiarly within the knowledge of one of the parties, only slight evidence from the other side is enough to satisfy the initial burden. In determining the amount of evidence necessary to shift this burden, the presiding judge considers the opportunities for either the prosecution or defense to secure exhibits or testimony about the fact to be proved.

If the defendant enters a plea of "Not guilty by reason of insanity," the burden of proving insanity is on the defendant. The legal presumption that the defendant is sane must be overcome by evidence which proves the defendant insane. When the defendant presents evidence of insanity, the burden of producing evidence to the contrary shifts to the prosecution. This is one of the general types of defense called an affirmative defense, one in which the defendant has the burden of proof.

Another affirmative defense is the proof of defendant's age when it is a possible defense to the crime. The burden will be on the defendant to prove, by a preponderance of the evidence, that he is a certain age or under a certain age. If, on the other hand, the victim's age is an essential element of the crime, the prosecution has the burden of proof beyond a reasonable doubt.

Preliminary Determinations on Admissibility

Evidence to which timely objection has been made often requires proof of the existence or nonexistence of a preliminary fact. Usually, the party proffering the evidence has the burden of producing evidence about the preliminary fact. Sometimes, however, the judge decides which party has the burden of producing evidence on the disputed issue. The courtroom procedure varies with the evidence and its nature. The trial judge may invite opposing counsel to approach the bench or he may grant a short recess to permit discussion in his chamber. The jury may be directed to leave the room while evidence about a preliminary fact is produced. It is viable legal strategy for either counsel to request this. The preliminary fact is determined by the judge based upon the relevancy of the proffered evidence and the sufficiency of the preliminary fact. A preliminary fact may be the determination of a privilege, the qualifications of a witness to testify, the existence of unlawful police action, or the authenticity of documents or other preliminary facts determining the relevance of the proffered evidence.

When the admissibility of evidence is questioned, the standards applied in deciding whether to allow it or not depend upon the nature of the objection:

1. If the problem involves *relevancy*, enough evidence must be introduced to warrant a finding of the preliminary fact.
2. If *personal knowledge* is questioned, evidence must justify the court in sustaining a finding of the witness' personal knowledge.
3. If the *authenticity of writings* is in doubt, sufficient evidence must be introduced to sustain a finding by the court of the authenticity of a writing.
4. If *hearsay declarations* are to be admitted, evidence must justify the finding that the hearsay declarant made the statement or acted as specified, and that the circumstances of the statement or act satisfy the minimum standards of trustworthiness required by the applicable exception to the hearsay rule.
5. When a *party's admissions* are questioned, evidence must justify a finding that the party made the statement.
6. When *authorized or adoptive admissions* are questioned, evidence must justify a finding that the admission was made by an authorized agent of the party, or by the party's adoptive conduct.
7. When the *admissions of a co-conspirator* are questioned, evidence must justify finding that there was a conspiracy.
8. When there is doubt whether an *admission or confession* was *freely given*, the court must verify its voluntary nature.

Judicial Notice

Judicial notice is a shortcut used by judges to do away with the necessity for evidence when the proposed testimony concerns a matter of common knowledge. The three requirements for this judicial shortcut are that the matter be (1) common and general knowledge, (2) well established and authoritatively settled, and (3) practically indisputable in the jurisdiction where the case is being tried. It should be noted that what may be common knowledge in one jurisdiction may not be, or is unlikely to be, common knowledge in another.

Courts may often take judicial notice in the following general areas:

1. *Laws*   This category includes federal and state constitutions and statutes, treaties with foreign countries, municipal charters and ordinances, executive orders and proclamations of the president of the United States and the governor of the state, and certain administrative and departmental regulations.
2. *Geographical and Historical Facts*   These include the names of cities, states, counties, and foreign countries, information regarding their historical origins, statistical data regarding their dimensions and borders, and distances computed from a map.
3. *Judicial Proceedings*   The existence, organization, and operation of courts will be judicially noticed. Notice may be taken of well-known conditions such as the fact that the descriptions of witnesses may vary, that memory is not infallible, and that jurors often lack knowledge in the law. The court will also notice its own records of a case.
4. *Public Officials and Records*   This category includes the identity of holders of state and county offices and of local offices within the court's own county, and of the content of journals and records of the state legislature.
5. *Scientific Principles and Procedures*   These include acknowledged laws of nature and observations derived from them, such as the quality of matter, that fruit rots, that eggs develop noxious odors, that glass cuts, and that gasoline burns; the nature of diseases; facts regarding narcotics and alcoholic beverages; and the operation, use, and effect of weapons and poison when commonly known.
6. *Other Matters of General Knowledge*   Judicial notice will be taken of well-known characteristics of human behavior and physiology, such as the average period of gestation, the assumption that a person of good character is less likely to commit a crime than someone of poor character, that persons write their names differently under different circumstances, and that it is difficult to see dark objects at night; the nature of some games such as baseball; the *modus operandi* or patterns of some crimes; the validity of fingerprints; the significance of blood tests; and the habits and instincts of animals.

Rules of Evidence

The rules for presenting evidence are designed to help the court and jury establish truth and administer justice. There is no question that evidence should be previewed in some manner before a jury is allowed to speculate on it.

The rules prescribe the manner of presenting evidence; the qualifications and privileges of witnesses, and the manner of examining them; and which things are logically, by nature, evidential. The rules of evidence appear to be highlighted by negativism. They often exclude exhibits and testimony offered in evidence.

Generally, no evidence is admissible unless it is relevant, and except as provided by state laws, all relevant evidence is admissible. Relevance is the connection between a fact offered in evidence and the issue to be proved. Briefly, "relevant" implies a traceable and significant connection.

The admissibility of evidence and its relevance are not synonymous. An item of evidence may be relevant but not admissible. However, to be admissible, the evidence must be relevant.

To be admitted, evidence must also be material. An item of evidence is material if it is important or substantial, capable of properly influencing the outcome of the trial. Evidence is considered immaterial when it is so unimportant compared to other easily available evidence that the court should not waste its time admitting it.

Another major test of evidence is the competence of the witness in general, or in relation to specific testimonial areas. With certain statutory exceptions, anyone who can perceive and communicate his perceptions can be a witness.

Evidence collected by means that violate the constitution may be excluded on the grounds that its admission would violate the doctrine of due process or the right to a fair trial.

Police investigators should know which evidence is likely to be inadmissible. They must also know about hearsay and opinion evidence, which may be barred if defense counsel objects. Police investigators are not expected to know the legal interrelationships necessary for the conduct of a trial, but they are expected to know the general ground rules for admitting various forms of evidence.

Investigators who have learned the rules of evidence can carry this procedure one step further and preview evidence likely to be offered by the defense to which the prosecutor might object. By doing this, he can use the rules for excluding evidence to support the state's case and its burden of proof.

After thoroughly investigating a case, the investigator should know the facts disclosed and the facts likely to be disputed at trial. Then, in analyzing the evidence collected, the police investigator can project the evidence's admissibility. Like the prosecutor, the investigator should determine disputed facts and answer the following questions:

1. What relevant and material evidence is there about each disputed fact?*

2. Is the witness to any of the disputed facts mentally competent to testify? Is his testimony the result of his own perception or the perception of someone else?

3. What witnesses and testimony may be barred by rules excluding privileged communications, hearsay, or opinion evidence? Can defense objections be overcome?

4. What physical evidence is involved, and is there a sufficient foundation for admitting it? Who can testify to its connection to the crime, its discovery, and that it has been safely kept between discovery and trial?

5. Is the admissibility of any evidence jeopardized by lawless searches and seizures, coerced confessions, or some other violation of the Constitution?

Jurors must make impartial findings based on evidence presented to them during a criminal trial. However, the rules of evidence are designed to keep evidence that would be speculative or confusing from the jury. Therefore, evidence must be fit to pass the tests of admissibility so that it can reach and convince the triers of fact.

Case Studies

Johnson v. *Zerbst*, 304 U.S. 458 (1938).

Faretta v. *California*, 422 U.S. 806 (1975).

Tumey v. *Ohio*, 273 U.S. 510 (1927).

The purpose of these end-of-chapter "case studies" is to indicate where a court decision relevant to the chapter's content may be found and to encourage a close analysis of the court's opinion.

Discussion Questions

1. Is the adversary system the best means for discovering truth in jury trials?

2. What is the legal significance of evidence?

3. What advantages does the prosecution have in being first to present evidence in a criminal trial?

---

*Every essential element of the crime charged is a disputed fact. For instance, in the crime of robbery the following are always matters of dispute: the taking and carrying away of personal property of another, whether the taking was from the person or immediate presence of the victim (possession), whether the means used for the taking was force or fear, and the identity of the robber.

4. How does studying the rules of evidence help a police officer prepare a better case for the prosecutor?

5. Discuss the difference between judicial determination of preliminary facts and judicial notice.

6. What are the major objectives of the rules of evidence? How are the rules designed to achieve these objectives?

Glossary*

Acquittal   Court or jury certification of the innocence of a defendant during or after trial.

Admissibility   Determination of whether evidence, exhibits, or testimony will be allowed in trial; inadmissible evidence cannot be allowed and is therefore not presented in court and is not heard or examined by the triers of fact.

Admission   A statement inconsistent with innocence of a crime; defendant admits a damaging fact.

Bench   The presiding judge (and his position at the front of the courtroom).

Criminal Act   Act or omission prohibited by law.

Criminal Intent   A determination of the mind; an intelligent purpose to commit an act prohibited as criminal by law: *mens rea*.

Confession   A statement acknowledging guilt; defendant's statement that he committed the crime charged.

Cross-examination   Questioning of witness by counsel for opposing party; follows the *direct examination* of a witness by the party calling the witness to court.

Hearsay   Secondhand evidence; testimony of evidence not based on the personal knowledge of a witness, but information someone else has seen or heard and related to a testifying witness.

Identity   Proof of a person's identity as being the individual alleged in the accusatory pleading.

Juveniles   Persons under a specified age (usually eighteen) who may be processed in a special juvenile court on the issues of neglect and delinquency.

Objection   Opposition to the introduction of certain evidence or questions during a criminal proceeding, or to judicial rulings. Linked with a "request to strike," to remove from the record any portion of the opposed evidence or question already before the triers of fact. The objection is granted when the presiding judge *sustains* it; it is *overruled* when denied.

Presumption   The inference of one fact from the existence of a related fact.

Prima Facie   On the fact of; at first view; uncontradicted.

*Terms not defined in the chapter text.

Rebuttal   The answer of the prosecutor to the defense case in chief; an opportunity for the prosecution to repair portions of the prosecution's case damaged by defense evidence.

Rejoinder (Surrebuttal)   The answer of the defense to the prosecutor's rebuttal; an opportunity for the defense to repair portions of the defense case damaged by prosecution evidence during the rebuttal stage of a trial.

CHAPTER 2

Briefing Cases

CHAPTER OBJECTIVES

- To describe case reports/court decisions as primary information stored in the records of America's legal system.
- To indicate access routes to case reports/court decisions.
- To reveal a standard form for briefing court decisions.
- To introduce safeguards designed to assure fair trials before impartial tribunals in which every defendant stands equal before the law.

Court decisions are recorded in all courts of the United States. Courts of appellate jurisdiction usually file a decision and an opinion. This printed report is the holding of the court on the issue/question involved and the judicial reason(s) for the decision. Citations indicate access routes to finding these printed reports. Because these case reports are often lengthy and sometimes tortuous, legal researchers have developed a "shorthand" form for developing an orderly summary of the case being studied:

Access Routes

Case citations listed under Case Studies in the preceding chapter point out where the printed report of a case may be located. These citations give the common or proper name of the case, the volume number, the court concerned, the page number, and the year in which the opinion was delivered. For instance, the *Johnson v. Zerbst* case is cited as 304 U.S. 458 (1938), indicating that the case is reported in Volume 304 of *U.S. Reports* at page 458 and that the decision was made in 1938. Within the cases reported, however, additional citations are given. These are usually to the *United States Supreme Court Reports* of the Lawyers Cooperative Publishing Company, cited as "L. Ed." or "L. Ed. 2nd," and the *Supreme Court Reporter* of West Publishing Company, cited as "Sup. Ct." or "S. Ct." The numerals contained in these references also refer to the volume and page numbers.

All these volumes, *United States Reports; United States Supreme Court Reports, Lawyers Edition;* and the *Supreme Court Reporter* contain the same cases, merely in different volumes and on different pages. For example, *Johnson* v. *Zerbst* can be found at 304 U.S. 458 (1938) or 82 L. Ed. 1461 or 58 S. Ct. 1019. The *United States Reports* is the official citation, while the other citations, called parallel citations, are provided as an additional source to find the cited case.

Cases in which decisions were made in other federal courts, or appellate and district courts, are similarly cited: for example, *Johns* v. *Smyth*, 176 F. Supp. 949 (1959), indicating that the case is reported in Volume 176 of the *Federal Supplement* of West Publishing Co., at page 949, and that the decision is dated in 1959. Within the cases reported, however, additional data are given in such citations to indicate the court involved. For instance, *Johns* v. *Smyth* would be identified as a case from the United States District Court of the Eastern District of Virginia by the additional notation (E.D.Va.).

Cases in which the decisions were made in state courts are identified in similar fashion, with the name of the state included in abbreviated form, and with volume and page numbers of both the state reports and the regional reports: for example, *People* v. *Bob*, 29 Cal. 2nd 321, 175 P. 2nd 12 (1946), indicates that the case will be found in both *California Reports*, 2nd Series, and in the *Pacific Reporter*, 2nd Series. California cases may also be cited to the *California Reporter* (Cal. Rptr.), the complete reporter for all California cases.

The West Publishing Company (St. Paul, Minnesota) publishes the *National Reporter* containing state cases from various regions, indexed by regions. Regions and citation abbreviations are:

Pacific—Western states plus Alaska and Hawaii	P. or P. 2d
Southern—Florida to Mississippi	So. or So. 2d
South Eastern—Georgia to Virginia	S.E. or S.E. 2d
North Western—Nebraska to Michigan	N.W. or N.W. 2d
North Eastern—New York to Ohio	N.E. or N.E. 2d
Atlantic—Maine to Maryland	A. or A. 2d

College and university libraries will have case reports containing opinions of the federal courts and may have state reports. Law school and state or county law libraries will have both federal and state reports.

Reading the Majority Opinion

In preparing to brief a court's decision, the full opinion of the court must be read prior to writing any abstract or summary. Footnotes may be scanned for relevancy, but adequate analysis requires a thoughtful and note-taking reading.

Argersinger v. *Hamlin*, 407 U.S. 25, is a 1972 case focused on the rights of a defendant in less than felony cases who are unable to afford the cost of hiring an attorney. It is an important case as it probes the fair-trial issue.

This is the full text of the majority opinion, minus syllabus and footnotes:

Petitioner, an indigent, was charged in Florida with carrying a concealed weapon, an offense punishable by imprisonment up to six months, a $1,000 fine, or both. The trial was to a judge, and petitioner was unrepresented by counsel. He was sentenced to serve 90 days in jail, and brought this habeas corpus action in the Florida Supreme Court, alleging that, being deprived of his right to counsel, he was unable as an indigent layman properly to raise and present to the trial court good and sufficient defenses to the charge for which he stands convicted. The Florida Supreme Court by a four-to-three decision, in ruling on the right to counsel, followed the line we marked out in *Duncan* v. *Louisiana*, 391 U.S. 145, 159, as respects the right to trial by jury and held that the right to court-appointed counsel extends only to trials "for non-petty offenses punishable by more than six months imprisonment." 236 So. 2d 442, 443.

The case is here on a petition for certiorari, which we granted. 401 U.S. 908. We reverse.

The Sixth Amendment, which in enumerated situations has been made applicable to the States by reason of the Fourteenth Amendment (see *Duncan* v. *Louisiana, supra; Washington* v. *Texas*, 388 U.S. 14; *Klopfer* v. *North Carolina*, 386 U.S. 213; *Pointer* v. *Texas*, 380 U.S. 400; *Gideon* v. *Wainwright*, 372 U.S. 335; and *In re Oliver*, 333 U.S. 257), provides specified standards for "all criminal prosecutions."

One is the requirement of a "public trial." *In re Oliver, supra*, held that the right to a "public trial" was applicable to a state proceeding even though only a 60-day sentence was involved. 333 U.S., at 272.

Another guarantee is the right to be informed of the nature and cause of the accusation. Still another, the right of confrontation. *Pointer* v. *Texas, supra*. And another, compulsory process for obtaining witnesses in one's favor. *Washington* v. *Texas, supra*. We have never limited these rights to felonies or to lesser but serious offenses.

In *Washington* v. *Texas, supra*, we said, "We have held that due process requires that the accused have the assistance of counsel for his defense, that he be confronted with the witnesses against him, and that he have the right to a speedy and public trial." 388 U.S., at 18. Respecting the right to a speedy and public trial, the right to be informed of the nature and cause of the accusation, the right to confront and cross-examine witnesses, the right to compulsory process for obtaining witnesses, it was recently stated, "It is simply not arguable, nor has any court ever held, that the trial of a petty offense may be held in secret, or without notice to the accused of the charges, or that in such cases the defendant has no right to confront his accusers or to compel the attendance of witnesses in his own behalf." Junker, The Right to Counsel in Misdemeanor Cases, 43 Wash. L. Rev. 685, 705 (1968).

District of Columbia v. *Clawans*, 300 U.S. 617, illustrates the point. There, the offense was engaging without a license in the business of dealing in

second-hand property, an offense punishable by a fine of $300 or imprison-
ment for not more than 90 days. The Court held that the offense was a "petty"
one and could be tried without a jury. But the conviction was reversed and a
new trial ordered, because the trial court had prejudicially restricted the right
of cross-examination, a right guaranteed by the Sixth Amendment.

The right to trial by jury, also guaranteed by the Sixth Amendment by
reason of the Fourteenth, was limited by *Duncan* v. *Louisiana, supra*, to trials
where the potential punishment was imprisonment for six months or more.
But, as the various opinions in *Baldwin* v. *New York*, 399 U.S. 66, make plain,
the right to trial by jury has a different genealogy and is brigaded with a
system of trial to a judge alone. As stated in *Duncan:*

> "Providing an accused with the right to be tried by a jury of his
> peers gave him an inestimable safeguard against the corrupt or
> overzealous prosecutor and against the compliant, biased, or eccentric
> judge. If the defendant preferred the common-sense judgment of a
> jury to the more tutored but perhaps less sympathetic reaction of the
> single judge, he was to have it. Beyond this, the jury trial provisions in
> the Federal and State Constitutions reflect a fundamental decision
> about the exercise of official power—a reluctance to entrust plenary
> powers over the life and liberty of the citizen to one judge or to a
> group of judges. Fear of unchecked power, so typical of our State and
> Federal Governments in other respects, found expression in the crimi-
> nal law in this insistence upon community participation in the deter-
> mination of guilt or innocence. The deep commitment of the Nation to
> the right of jury trial in serious criminal cases as a defense against
> arbitrary law enforcement qualifies for protection under the Due
> Process Clause of the Fourteenth Amendment, and must therefore be
> respected by the States." 391 U.S., at 156.

> While there is historical support for limiting the "deep commit-
> ment" to trial by jury to "serious criminal cases," there is no such sup-
> port for a similar limitation on the right to assistance of counsel:

> "Originally, in England, a person charged with treason or felony
> was denied the aid of counsel, except in respect of legal questions
> which the accused himself might suggest. At the same time parties in
> civil cases and persons accused of misdemeanors were entitled to the
> full assistance of counsel....

> "[It] appears that in at least twelve of the thirteen colonies the
> rule of the English common law, in the respect now under considera-
> tion, had been definitely rejected and the right to counsel fully recog-
> nized in all criminal prosecutions, save that in one or two instances
> the right was limited to capital offenses or to the more serious crimes.
> ..." *Powell* v. *Alabama*, 287 U.S. 45, 60, 64–65.

The Sixth Amendment thus extended the right to counsel beyond its
common-law dimensions. But there is nothing in the language of the

Amendment, its history, or in the decisions of this Court, to indicate that it was intended to embody a retraction of the right in petty offenses wherein the common law previously did require that counsel be provided. See *James* v. *Headley*, 410 F. 2d 325, 331–332, n. 9.

We reject, therefore, the premise that since prosecution for crimes punishable by imprisonment for fewer than six months may be tried without a jury, they may also be tried without a lawyer.

The assistance of counsel is often a requisite to the very existence of a fair trial. The Court in *Powell* v. *Alabama, supra*, at 68–69—a capital case—said:

> "The right to be heard would be, in many cases, of little avail if it did not comprehend the right to be heard by counsel. Even the intelligent and educated layman has small and sometimes no skill in the science of law. If charged with crime, he is incapable, generally, of determining for himself whether the indictment is good or bad. He is unfamiliar with the rules of evidence. Left without the aid of counsel he may be put on trial without a proper charge, and convicted upon incompetent evidence, or evidence irrelevant to the issue or otherwise inadmissible. He lacks both the skill and knowledge adequately to prepare his defense, even though he have a perfect one. He requires the guiding hand of counsel at every step in the proceedings against him. Without it, though he be not guilty, he faces the danger of conviction because he does not know how to establish his innocence. If that be true of men of intelligence, how much more true is it of the ignorant and illiterate, or those of feeble intellect."

In *Gideon* v. *Wainwright, supra* (overruling *Betts* v. *Brady*, 316 U.S. 455), we dealt with a felony trial. But we did not so limit the need of the accused for a lawyer. We said:

> "[I]n our adversary system of criminal justice, any person haled into court, who is too poor to hire a lawyer, cannot be assured a fair trial unless counsel is provided for him. This seems to us to be an obvious truth. Governments, both state and federal, quite properly spend vast sums of money to establish machinery to try defendants accused of crime. Lawyers to prosecute are everywhere deemed essential to protect the public's interest in an orderly society. Similarly, there are few defendants charged with crime, few indeed, who fail to hire the best lawyers they can get to prepare and present their defenses. That government hires lawyers to prosecute and defendants who have the money hire lawyers to defend are the strongest indications of the widespread belief that lawyers in criminal courts are necessities, not luxuries. The right of one charged with crime to counsel may not be deemed fundamental and essential to fair trials in some countries, but it is in ours. From the very beginning, our state and national constitutions and laws have laid great

emphasis on procedural and substantive safeguards designed to assure fair trials before impartial tribunals in which every defendant stands equal before the law. This noble ideal cannot be realized if the poor man charged with crime has to face his accusers without a lawyer to assist him." 372 U.S., at 344.

Both *Powell* and *Gideon* involved felonies. But their rationale has relevance to any criminal trial, where an accused is deprived of his liberty. *Powell* and *Gideon* suggest that there are certain fundamental rights applicable to all such criminal prosecutions, even those, such as *In re Oliver, supra,* where the penalty is 60 days' imprisonment:

> "A person's right to reasonable notice of a charge against him, and an opportunity to be heard in his defense—a right to his day in court—are basic in our system of jurisprudence; and these rights include, as a minimum, a right to examine the witnesses against him, to offer testimony, *and to be represented by counsel.*" 333 U.S., at 273 (emphasis supplied).

The requirement of counsel may well be necessary for a fair trial even in a petty-offense prosecution. We are by no means convinced that legal and constitutional questions involved in a case that actually leads to imprisonment even for a brief period are any less complex than when a person can be sent off for six months or more. See, e.g., *Powell* v. *Texas*, 392 U.S. 514; *Thompson* v. *Louisville*, 362 U.S. 199; *Shuttlesworth* v. *Birmingham*, 382 U.S. 87.

The trial of vagrancy cases is illustrative. While only brief sentences of imprisonment may be imposed, the cases often bristle with thorny constitutional questions. See *Papachristou* v. *Jacksonville*, 405 U.S. 156.

In re Gault, 387 U.S. 1, dealt with juvenile delinquency and an offense which, if committed by an adult, would have carried a fine of $5 to $50 or imprisonment in jail for not more than two months (*Id.*, at 29), but which when committed by a juvenile might lead to his detention in a state institution until he reached the age of 21. *Id.*, at 36–37. We said (*Id.*, at 36) that "[t]he juvenile needs the assistance of counsel to cope with problems of law, to make skilled inquiry into the facts, to insist upon regularity of the proceedings, and to ascertain whether he has a defense and to prepare and submit it. The child 'requires the guiding hand of counsel at every step in the proceedings against him,'" citing *Powell* v. *Alabama*, 287 U.S., at 69. The premise of *Gault* is that even in prosecutions for offenses less serious than felonies, a fair trial may require the presence of a lawyer.

Beyond the problem of trials and appeals is that of the guilty plea, a problem which looms large in misdemeanor as well as in felony cases. Counsel is needed so that the accused may know precisely what he is doing, so that he is fully aware of the prospect of going to jail or prison, and so that he is treated fairly by the prosecution.

In addition, the volume of misdemeanor cases, far greater in number than felony prosecutions, may create an obsession for speedy dispositions, regardless of the fairness of the result. The Report by the President's Commission on Law Enforcement and Administration of Justice, The Challenge of Crime in a Free Society 128 (1967), states:

"For example, until legislation last year increased the number of judges, the District of Columbia Court of General Sessions had four judges to process the preliminary stages of more than 1,500 felony cases, 7,500 serious misdemeanor cases, and 38,000 petty offenses and an equal number of traffic offenses per year. An inevitable consequence of volume that large is the almost total preoccupation in such a court with the movement of cases. The calendar is long, speed often is substituted for care, and casually arranged out-of-court compromise too often is substituted for adjudication. Inadequate attention tends to be given to the individual defendant, whether in protecting his rights, sifting the facts at trial, deciding the social risk he presents, or determining how to deal with him after conviction. The frequent result is futility and failure. As Dean Edward Barrett recently observed:

" 'Wherever the visitor looks at the system, he finds great numbers of defendants being processed by harassed and overworked officials. Police have more cases than they can investigate. Prosecutors walk into courtrooms to try simple cases as they take their initial looks at the files. Defense lawyers appear having had no more than time for hasty conversations with their clients. Judges face long calendars with the certain knowledge that their calendars tomorrow and the next day will be, if anything, longer, and so there is no choice but to dispose of the cases.

" 'Suddenly it becomes clear that for most defendants in the criminal process, there is scant regard for them as individuals. They are numbers on dockets, faceless ones to be processed and sent on their way. The gap between the theory and the reality is enormous.

" 'Very little such observation of the administration of criminal justice in operation is required to reach the conclusion that it suffers from basic ills.' "

That picture is seen in almost every report. "The misdemeanor trial is characterized by insufficient and frequently irresponsible preparation on the part of the defense, the prosecution, and the court. Everything is rush, rush." Hellerstein, The Importance of the Misdemeanor Case on Trial and Appeal, 28 The Legal Aid Brief Case 151, 152 (1970).

There is evidence of the prejudice which results to misdemeanor defendants from this "assembly-line justice." Our study concluded that "[m]isdemeanants represented by attorneys are five times as likely to emerge from police court with all charges dismissed as are defendants who face similar charges without counsel." American Civil Liberties Union, Legal Counsel for Misdemeanants, Preliminary Report 1 (1970).

We must conclude, therefore, that the problems associated with misdemeanor and petty offenses often require the presence of counsel to ensure the accused a fair trial. MR. JUSTICE POWELL suggests that these problems are raised even in situations where there is no prospect of imprisonment. *Post*, at 48. We need not consider the requirements of the Sixth Amendment as regards the right to counsel where loss of liberty is not involved, however, for here petitioner was in fact sentenced to jail. And, as we said in *Baldwin* v. *New York*, 399 U.S., at 73, "the prospect of imprisonment for however short a time will seldom be viewed by the accused as a trivial or 'petty' matter and may well result in quite serious repercussions affecting his career and his reputation."

We hold, therefore, that absent a knowing and intelligent waiver, no person may be imprisoned for any offense, whether classified as petty, misdemeanor, or felony, unless he was represented by counsel at his trial.

That is the view of the Supreme Court of Oregon, with which we agree. It said in *Stevenson* v. *Holzman*, 254 Ore. 94,102, 458 P. 2d 414, 418:

> "We hold that no person may be deprived of his liberty who has been denied the assistance of counsel as guaranteed by the Sixth Amendment. This holding is applicable to all criminal prosecutions, including prosecutions for violations of municipal ordinances. The denial of the assistance of counsel will preclude the imposition of a jail sentence."

We do not sit as an ombudsman to direct state courts how to manage their affairs but only to make clear the federal constitutional requirement. How crimes should be classified is largely a state matter. The fact that traffic charges technically fall within the category of "criminal prosecutions" does not necessarily mean that many of them will be brought into the class where imprisonment actually occurs.

The American Bar Association Project on Standards for Criminal Justice states:

> "As a matter of sound judicial administration it is preferable to disregard the characterization of the offense as felony, misdemeanor or traffic offense. Nor is it adequate to require the provision of defense services for all offenses which carry a sentence to jail or prison. Often, as a practical matter, such sentences are rarely if ever imposed for certain types of offenses, so that for all intents and purposes the punishment they carry is at most a fine. Thus, the standard seeks to distinguish those classes of cases in which there is real likelihood that incarceration may follow conviction from those types in which there is no such likelihood. It should be noted that the standard does not recommend a determination of the need for counsel in terms of the facts of each particular case; it draws a categorical line at those *types* of offenses for which incarceration as a punishment is a practical possibility."
> Providing Defense Services 40 (Approved Draft 1968).

Under the rule we announce today, every judge will know when the trial of a misdemeanor starts that no imprisonment may be imposed, even though local law permits it, unless the accused is represented by counsel. He will have a measure of the seriousness and gravity of the offense and therefore know when to name a lawyer to represent the accused before the trial starts.

The run of misdemeanors will not be affected by today's ruling. But in those that end up in the actual deprivation of a person's liberty, the accused will receive the benefit of "the guiding hand of counsel" so necessary when one's liberty is in jeopardy.

Reversed.

Briefing Cases

Briefing a case is to prepare a summary of a court's decision. The full opinion of the court must be read for understanding the key areas of the case: the issue involved and the court's decision and the reason or reasons for this conclusion.

Briefs begin with a full identity of the case, common or proper name, citation, date, and the number of justices voting for the majority opinion. The short analysis of the case is written in four major segments: (1) facts of the case, (2) issue or question that is the core of each case, (3) decision of the court, and (4) reason(s) for the decision.

The facts of a case are presented in a "headnote" at the opening of each case. "Past performances" of a case in court are listed in this section of a full opinion: court, action taken. A good summary can be written by following the court's description of the case as an event; a better summary will reorganize these facts to gain brevity and clarity in fewer words.

The reason for the case being reviewed by the court is usually clearly stated, commonly as a query. It is difficult to summarize what the case is all about so it is best to use the words of the opinion to avoid any misunderstanding. Fortunately, these segments of a majority opinion are usually clearly stated. As a general rule avoid any rewriting.

The decision of the court is another hazardous area in summarizing a court's opinion. Again, avoid any rewriting unless brevity will make the decision easier to understand—conciseness often fosters clarity.

The reason or reasons for the judicial "holding" is usually found linked to the court's decision or segments of it. It is an area with many opportunities for summarizing the judicial views expressed in the majority opinion. In cases citing multiple reasons for a decision, an effective summary may simply list them briefly.

Dissenting and concurring opinions should be noted in margins of a case brief or as postscripts or footnotes. Relationships to other cases may be warranted as cross-indexing and is usually a "See" note at the end of the brief.

A brief of *Argersinger* v. *Hamlin*, 407 U.S. 25 (1972), is developed by reading the foregoing opinion and then summarizing the case as follows:

Facts   In a Florida state court, unrepresented by counsel, this indigent petitioner was convicted (judge, no jury) of a weapons charge and sentenced to 90 days in jail.

Issue   Does the Sixth Amendment right to counsel for indigent defendants apply to criminal trials on petty offenses?

Decision   No person may be imprisoned for any offense—petty, misdemeanor, or felony—unless represented by counsel at trial, unless a knowing and intelligent waiver is made.

Reason   Problems associated with misdemeanors and petty offenses often require legal counsel to ensure a fair trial for the accused.

The advantage of these briefs is that writing them is a learning exercise, the short form lends itself to comparison analysis on related cases, and they are a ready reference for recalling the full opinion of a case.

Case Studies

Gault v. *Arizona*, 387 U.S. 1 (1967).

Pennsylvania v. *Muniz*, 496 U.S. ??? (1990).

Coy v. *Iowa*, 487 U.S. 1012 (1988).

Discussion Questions

1. Comment on the belief that defendants in any criminal trial require the guiding hand of counsel.
2. What are the major segments of a case brief?
3. Why are indigent defendants in criminal trials assigned legal counsel.
4. What segment of a case report (court decision) contains relevant information about the case and a factual summary of the charge, the crime event, and judicial action?
5. Is there a relationship between the three case studies of this chapter?

Glossary

Certiorari   A judicial process calling upon an inferior court to send up a case or proceeding for review.

Indigent   Poor, needy, destitute; unable to afford cost of legal representation.

In Forma Pauperis   As a poor person; a term for a procedure in which a court's permission is sought to submit legal papers without the usual fee or cost.

Syllabus   The headnote of a reported case.

CHAPTER 3

The Roles of Prosecutor and Defense Counsel

CHAPTER OBJECTIVES

- To explain the duties and responsibilities of the prosecutor in preparing accusatory pleadings and in prosecuting persons accused of crime.
- To outline the circumstances under which prosecutors can decline to prosecute, divert selected defendants from the criminal justice system, or engage in plea negotiations for a reduced charge or sentence in return for a guilty plea.
- To examine the client-attorney relationship between defendant and defense counsel, as well as the right of defendants to effective representation by their legal counsel, including complete loyalty and service in good faith to the best of counsel's ability.
- To show the dilemma of an attorney in defending a client when he is convinced of the client's guilt, explaining defense counsel's obligation to disprove charges against an apparently guilty defendant.
- To develop the idea of the adversary system as a structure for the use of evidence to prove guilt or to demonstrate innocence.

The fundamental freedoms of individuals are always threatened by the power of government. Even in the so-called free world the relationship of the state to individual freedom can only be balanced by a government operating under reasonable laws and, in the case of persons accused of crime and threatened with a possible loss of freedom, by an adversary system in which each participant is represented by legal counsel.

The prosecutor represents the people of the jurisdiction in which the trial is held, and defense counsel represents the defendant(s). In acting out these roles, both attorneys serve as advocates for their clients; the prosecutor presents the cause of the state, and the defense counsel presents the defendant's position by witnesses and argument.

Standards relating to the prosecution and the defense in criminal proceedings are fundamental dimensions of conduct acceptable in the role of advocate. Standards developed by the American Bar Association and state bar associations, and through legislative enactment are more than ethical guidelines and rules of decorum or propriety. They present collected data as to the past conduct of the best prosecutors and defense counsel.[1] Although the roles of prosecution and defense counsel differ, each of these advocates is bound, in the interests of justice, to adhere to accepted standards of conduct throughout a criminal proceeding. Their activities range from duties to their clients to the avoidance of unprofessional conduct.[2]

The institution of advocacy and the adversary system seek justice by the production of evidence under fixed rules of procedure whenever there is a confrontation between the community (the people) and an individual accused of crime.

The Prosecutor

The prosecutor ensures that the laws of his state or government are faithfully executed and enforced. He is an administrator of justice and an advocate; and in each capacity he must exercise a sound discretion.

The public prosecutor should be an attorney who is subject to the legal and ethical standards of his profession, and he should avoid any real or apparent conflict of interest with respect to his official duties. He should maintain the reality and appearance of the independence and integrity of his office.

A prosecutor's contact with the courts must be professionally correct. He must not engage in unauthorized *ex parte** discussions with or submission of material to a judge relating to a particular case without affording the defense attorney the opportunity to be present, unless an *in camera*† inspection of evidence is authorized by law.

Decision to Charge

The prosecutor should first determine whether there is evidence that would support a conviction. However, he is not obliged to present all charges which the evidence might support. He may, in some circumstances and for good cause consistent with the public interest, decline to prosecute. Some factors used in exercising his discretion to charge follow:

[1] American Bar Association, *Standards Relating to the Prosecution Function and the Defense Function* (New York: American Bar Association, 1971), pp. 1–15.
[2] Raymond L. Wise, *Legal Ethics*, 2nd ed. (New York: Matthew Bender, 1970), p. 303 *et seq.*
* Outside the presence of the opposing party.
† Evidence viewed only by the court.

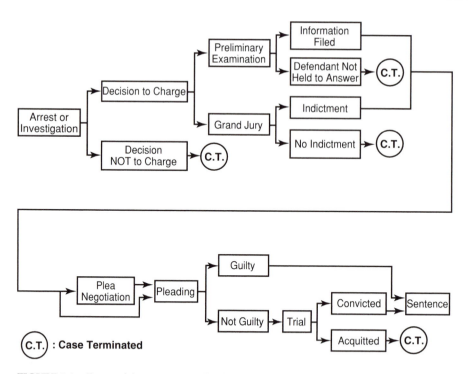

FIGURE 3-1. Route of the accusatory pleading in felony prosecutions.

1. His reasonable doubt that the accused is in fact guilty
2. The extent of the harm caused by the offense
3. The disproportion of the authorized punishment in relation to the particular offense or the offender
4. Possible improper motives of a complainant
5. Prolonged nonenforcement of a statute, with a community acquiescence
6. Reluctance of the victim to testify
7. Cooperation of the accused in the apprehension or conviction of others
8. Availability and likelihood of prosecution by another jurisdiction

In making the decision to prosecute, the prosecutors should give no weight to the personal or political advantages or disadvantages that might be involved, or to a desire to enhance his record of convictions. He should not be deterred from prosecution by the fact that in his jurisdiction juries have tended to acquit persons accused of the particular kind of criminal act in question, particularly when the offense involves a serious threat to the community; and he should not bring charges greater in number or degree than he can reasonably support with evidence at trial.

The Grand Jury's Indictment

The prosecutor is the legal adviser to the grand jury and may explain the law and express his opinion on the legal significance of the evidence. He should not attempt to influence grand jury action in any manner that would be impermissible at trial before a petit jury.

However, because a grand jury is a body of citizens selected from the community without regard to any legal education, for a grand jury indictment the prosecutor must present sufficient available evidence to allow the members of the grand jury to decide whether or not the evidence warrants prosecution. Grand juries require a quorum of their membership to be present and a vote of twelve of those jurors is necessary to return an indictment.

A prosecutor should present to the grand jury only evidence which he believes would be admissible at trial. However, in appropriate cases he may present witnesses to summarize that evidence. He should disclose to the grand jury any evidence which he knows will tend to negate guilt, and he should recommend that the grand jury not indict the accused if he believes the evidence presented does not warrant an indictment under governing law.

If the prosecutor believes that a witness is a potential defendant, he should not seek his testimony before the grand jury without informing him that he may be charged and that he should seek independent legal advice concerning his rights, nor should he compel the appearance of a witness whose activities are the subject of the inquiry if the witness states in advance that, if called, he will exercise his constitutional privilege not to testify.

Preliminary Hearing—Information

In many jurisdictions, prosecutors are given the authority to route a case through court instead of the grand jury and the indictment process. The first step is the preliminary hearing, where the prosecutor assumes an adversary role presenting evidence before the presiding judge in an effort to secure a judicial ruling that there is sufficient evidence to warrant further prosecution. If the decision favors the prosecutor, he then files an information (accusatory pleading) in the trial court. In grand jury sessions, the prosecutor is not confronted by opposing counsel; at a preliminary hearing the defendant and his legal counsel have an opportunity to be heard in response to the accusation.

Defense Counsel

Counsel for the accused is an essential component of the administration of criminal justice. A court properly constituted to hear a criminal case must be viewed as a tripartite entity consisting of the judge (and jury, where appropriate), counsel for the prosecution, and counsel for the accused.

The basic duty of the defense attorney is to serve as the accused's counselor and advocate with courage, devotion, and to the utmost of his learning and ability, and according to law. He has no duty to execute any directive of the accused which does not comport with the law; and it is unprofessional conduct for an attorney intentionally to misrepresent matters of fact or law to the court.[3] Defense counsel must disclose to his client any matter that might involve a conflict of interest or the defendant's choice of attorney.

Except for preliminary matters such as initial hearings or applications for bail, lawyers who are associated in practice should not undertake to defend more than one defendant in the same criminal case if the duty to one of the defendants may conflict with the duty to another.

In accepting payment of fees by one person for the defense of another, a lawyer should be careful to determine that he will not be confronted with a conflict of loyalty because his entire loyalty is due the accused. There must be an explicit understanding that the lawyer's entire loyalty is to the accused who is his client and that the person who pays his fee has no control of the case.

Whether privately engaged, judicially appointed, or serving as part of a legal aid or public defender system, the duties of a lawyer to his client are to represent his legitimate interests, and considerations of personal and professional advantage should not influence his advice or performance.

Defense counsel should seek to establish a relationship of trust and confidence with the accused. The lawyer should explain the necessity of full disclosure of all facts known to the client for an effective defense, and he should explain the obligation of confidentiality which makes privileged the accused's disclosures relating to the case.

As soon as practicable, defense counsel should seek to determine all relevant facts known to the accused. He should probe for all legally relevant information without seeking to influence the direction of the client's responses.

The lawyer may not instruct the client or intimate to him in any way that he should not be candid in revealing facts so as to afford the lawyer free rein to take action which would be precluded by the lawyer's knowing such facts.

The decisions that are to be made by the accused after full consultation with counsel are: what plea to enter, whether to waive jury trial, and whether to testify in his own behalf. The decisions on what witnesses to call, whether and how to conduct cross-examination, what jurors to accept or reject, what trial motions should be made, and all other strategic and tactical decisions are the exclusive province of the lawyer after consultation with his client.

If a disagreement on significant matters of tactics or strategy arises between the lawyer and his client, the lawyer should make a record of the circumstances, his advice and reasons, and the conclusion reached. The record should be made in a manner that protects the confidentiality of the lawyer-client relationship.

[3]Canon 7, Disciplinary Rules 7-101, 7-102, *Code of Professional Responsibility*, American Bar Association.

If the defendant has admitted to his lawyer facts which establish guilt and the lawyer's independent investigation establishes that the admissions are true, but the defendant insists on his right to trial, a lawyer must advise his client against taking the witness stand to testify falsely.

If, before trial, the defendant insists that he will take the stand to testify falsely, the lawyer must withdraw from the case if possible. If withdrawal from the case is not possible, or if the situation arises during the trial and the defendant insists upon testifying falsely in his own behalf, the lawyer may not assist the perjury. Before the defendant takes the stand in these circumstances, the lawyer should make a record of the fact that the defendant is taking the stand against the advice of counsel in some appropriate manner without revealing the confidential communication to the court or prejudicing his or her client. The lawyer must confine his examination to identifying the witness as the defendant and permitting him to make his statement to the trier or triers of the facts; the lawyer should not engage in direct examination of the defendant as a witness in the conventional manner and may not later argue the defendant's known false version of facts to the jury as worthy of belief, and he may not recite or rely upon the false testimony in his closing argument.

It is a lawyer's duty to advise his client to comply with the law, but he may advise concerning the meaning, scope, and validity of a law. However, it is unprofessional conduct for a lawyer to agree in advance of the commission of a crime that he will serve as counsel for the defendant (except as part of a bona fide effort to determine the validity, scope, meaning, or application of the law, or where the defense is incident to a general retainer for legal services to a person or enterprise engaged in legitimate activity). The attorney may not counsel his client or assist his client to engage in conduct which the lawyer believes to be illegal.[4]

Many important rights of the accused can be protected and preserved only by prompt legal action. Defense counsel should immediately inform the accused of his rights and take all necessary action to exercise such rights. He should consider all procedural steps which in good faith may be taken, including, for example, motions seeking pretrial release of the accused, obtaining psychiatric examination of the accused when a need appears, moving for a change of venue or continuance, moving to suppress illegally obtained evidence, moving for severance from jointly charged defendants, or seeking dismissal of the charges.

The duties of defense counsel are the same whether he is privately retained, appointed by the court, or serving in a legal aid or public defender system. He has the continuing duty to keep his client informed of developments in the case and the progress of preparing the defense.

After informing himself fully on the facts and the law, defense counsel should advise his client with complete candor concerning all aspects of the case, including his estimate of the probable outcome. It is unprofessional conduct to

---

[4]*In re De Pamphilis*, 30 N.J. 470 (1959).

intentionally understate or overstate the risks, hazards, or prospects of the case in order to influence the accused's decision as to his plea.

The defense counsel should caution his client to avoid communication about the case with witnesses, except with his approval, to avoid any contact with jurors or prospective jurors, and to avoid either the reality or the appearance of any other improper activity.[5]

Public Statements

Neither the prosecutor nor the defense attorney should exploit the case for his own personal advantage. Neither attorney should utilize the news media for the purpose of influencing public opinion generally, or prospective or serving jurors individually. The attorneys in a case should obey the orders of the court regarding publicity, and when they are of a different opinion than the court order they should seek a legal remedy rather than unilateral disobedience of the court order. There should be no public statements made which could interfere with the defendant's, and the people's, right to a fair trial.[6]

Plea Negotiations

The process of plea negotiations has also been termed plea bargaining. This is consultation between prosecutor and defense counsel for the purpose of entering into an agreement advantageous to the defendant (a reduction in the charges, or a less severe sentence) in return for a plea of guilty. Prosecutors enter these agreements because justice is served by the guilty plea, statistically a conviction is noted in the case, and the local justice system avoids the expenses of a trial. It is a prosecutor's technique to avoid crowding the local courts and at the same time close out cases with convictions.

It is unprofessional conduct for a prosecutor to engage in plea discussions directly with an accused who is represented by counsel, except with counsel's approval. If the accused refuses to be represented by counsel, the prosecutor may properly discuss disposition of the charges directly with the accused. It is unprofessional conduct for a prosecutor knowingly to make false statements or representations in the course of plea discussions with defense counsel or the accused.

The decision to negotiate for a plea is initially a prosecution decision. Although the first mention of negotiation may be from either the defense or prosecution, it is the prosecutor who must decide upon what basis he will

---

[5]*In re Robinson*, 136 N.Y.S. 548 (1912).

[6]American Bar Association Project on Standards for Criminal Justice, *Standards Relating to Fair Trial and Free Press* (New York: American Bar Association, 1968). See also *Sheppard* v. *Maxwell*, 3 U.S. 333 (1966); *Estes* v. *Texas*, 381 U.S. 532 (1965).

negotiate and make the offer to the defendant. It is then for the defendant to react by accepting, rejecting, or making a counter offer.

Whenever a full investigation discloses that a conviction is possible, defense counsel should so advise the accused and seek his consent to engage in plea discussions with the prosecutor, if such appears desirable. In these discussions, it is unprofessional conduct for counsel knowingly to make false statements concerning the evidence in the course of plea discussions with the prosecutor, or to seek or accept concessions favorable to one client by any agreement that is detrimental to the legitimate interests of any other client.

A prosecutor may properly advise the defense what position he, as prosecutor, will take concerning disposition, but he should avoid implying a greater power to influence the disposition of a case than he possesses.

If the prosecutor finds he is unable to fulfill an understanding previously agreed upon in plea discussions, he should give notice to the defendant and cooperate in persuading the court to allow the defendant to withdraw the plea and to restore the defendant to the position he was in before the understanding was reached or the plea made.

Advocates of plea negotiations in the justice system argue that it has been an accepted practice in the past, although not officially recognized; that it is an integral part of the justice system; that it is essential to the expeditious and fair administration of justice; that the great majority (70–90%) of cases are disposed of by guilty pleas and that without these nontrial dispositions the system would collapse under the weight of additional trials; that it allows the court to treat each defendant as an individual, fitting the punishment to the facts and the defendant rather than the crime; that both the defendant and the state benefit, the defendant by a lesser punishment and the state by a savings of trial costs, increased efficiency, and flexibility of the criminal process.

When a sentence does not reflect all of the elements of a plea agreement, the defendant may file a request to withdraw the guilty plea and reschedule his or her arraignment for pleading.

Plea negotiation is a fact of life across the United States despite strong opposition. Arguments against plea negotiations are as follows:

1. A lack of resources should not affect the outcome of the criminal justice process.
2. The number of cases going to trial if plea bargaining were abolished may not increase significantly. Many defendants will still plead guilty to avoid the cost of a trial, in fear of adverse publicity during a trial, or in the nebulous hope that such a plea may result in judicial favor at the time of sentencing.
3. Without plea negotiations, charges filed will more closely correspond to the acts done and to the conviction a prosecutor reasonably thinks can be achieved in court.

4. Where there are reasonably disputable issues, the criminal justice system should not provide an incentive for a defendant to waive a full and fair resolution of those issues in court.[7]

Plea negotiations should be made a part of the official court record, and the prosecutor, defendant, defense counsel, and the court must all agree to the results of the negotiations.[8]

Diversion by the Prosecutor

Defense counsel, whenever the nature and circumstances of the case permits, may explore the possibility of an early diversion of the case from the criminal process through the use of other community agencies. Where diversion is possible it is a prosecutor's decision.

Diversion by prosecutors is the halting or suspending, before conviction, of the formal criminal proceedings against a person on the condition or assumption that the accused will do something in return which will contribute to his or her rehabilitation.

Precharging or postcharging diversion may or may not be available or may take different forms depending upon the particular state statutes. One area of diversion law concerns drug abuse cases. The prosecutor may have a choice or may be directed to initiate the diversion process if a number of circumstances coincide:

1. The defendant has no prior narcotic convictions.
2. The present offense does not involve violence or threat of violence.
3. The present offense is one of those listed for diversion.
4. The defendant has no record of parole or probation violation.

The probation department may be required to submit a prediversion report about the defendant to the court and other necessary parties concerning the following: his age, employment and service records, educational background, community and family ties, prior narcotics or other drug use, history of treatment if any, and factors contributing to the possibility of the educational rehabilitation of the defendant. Before an accused can be diverted there must exist community programs which could benefit him.

When the diversion occurs in the postcharge period, the court holds a hearing to decide whether or not to divert the defendant. Still, the prosecutor may be given, by statute, the power to veto diversion.

---

[7]National Advisory Commission on Criminal Justice Standards and Goals, "The Negotiated Plea," *Report On Courts* (1973), pp. 42–65.
[8]*People* v. *West*, 3 Cal. 3d 595 (1970).

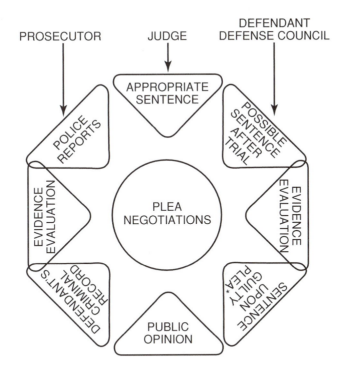

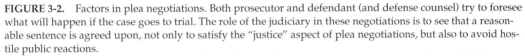

FIGURE 3-2. Factors in plea negotiations. Both prosecutor and defendant (and defense counsel) try to foresee what will happen if the case goes to trial. The role of the judiciary in these negotiations is to see that a reasonable sentence is agreed upon, not only to satisfy the "justice" aspect of plea negotiations, but also to avoid hostile public reactions.

*In addition to other inducements: plea to lesser charge, plea to one or two counts or a multicount indictment, release of spouse codefendant, dismissing other pending charges, and so on.

If the defendant is diverted, his case will be dismissed upon his demonstration, over a given period of time, of successful rehabilitation. This type of diversion was begun as a legislative experiment to determine if it is socially or protectively necessary that all offenders proceed through the justice system. If the case is dismissed, the defendant has no record of a criminal conviction. If the defendant fails to successfully complete the diversion program, the case proceeds through the criminal justice system.

Pretrial Investigation

It is the better course of action for prosecutor or defense personnel, other than the attorney trying the case, to participate in the interviews of prospective witnesses since there is always the possibility the witness may change his or her story, and a participant in the interview will have to testify at trial in the impeachment of the witness. The attorney trying the case should not also become a witness in the trial.

A prosecutor is the chief law enforcement official of his jurisdiction, and ordinarily relies on police and other investigative agencies for the investigation of alleged criminal acts. He also has an affirmative responsibility to investigate suspected illegal activity when this is not adequately done by other agencies.

A prosecutor may not use illegal means to obtain evidence, and he should not obstruct communication between prospective witnesses and defense counsel, or advise any person to decline to give information to the defense.

The prosecutor may not promise a witness immunity from prosecution for some prospective criminal activity, except where such activity is part of an officially supervised investigative and enforcement program.

It is the duty of the defendant's attorney to conduct a prompt investigation of the circumstances of the case and explore all avenues leading to facts relevant to guilt and degree of guilt, or penalty. The investigation should always include efforts to secure information in the possession of the prosecution and law enforcement authorities. The duty to investigate exists regardless of the accused's admissions or statements to his attorney of facts constituting guilt or his stated desire to plead guilty. The defense attorney must not use illegal means to obtain evidence or information or to employ, instruct, or encourage others to do so; or to advise a person (other than a client) to refuse to give information to the prosecutor or counsel for co-defendants.

Both the prosecutor and defense counsel should utilize available discovery procedures to supplement their investigation. An investigation by defense counsel is not completed until he has secured the data in the hands of the prosecutor as to the evidence against his client.

Selection of Jurors

The prosecutor and defense counsel should prepare, prior to trial, the issues and questions appropriate for the jury selection process. Where it appears necessary to conduct a pretrial investigation of the background of jurors, both the prosecutor and defense counsel must restrict inquiries to investigatory methods which will not harass or unnecessarily embarrass potential jurors or invade their privacy and, whenever possible, should restrict this investigation to records and sources of information already in existence. Many jurisdictions have services which make such investigations and provide information on jurors to the attorneys for a fee.

In jurisdictions where both advocates (prosecutor and defense counsel) are permitted personally to question jurors on *voir dire** the opportunity is used to obtain information for the intelligent exercise of challenges. *Voir dire* is not a proper vehicle to present factual matters to jurors.

*Examination under oath as to qualifications.

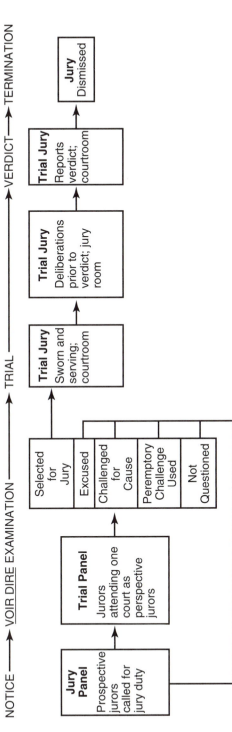

FIGURE 3-3. The jury process in criminal prosecution.

Jurors should be treated with deference and respect. Neither attorney may communicate privately with persons summoned for jury duty, or with those impaneled as jurors, concerning the case prior to or during the trial.

Questions for the purpose of harassing or embarrassing a juror in any way that will tend to influence judgment in the present or future jury service are not permissible.

If a trial attorney has reasonable ground to believe that the verdict may be subject to legal challenge, he may properly, if no statute or rule prohibits such course, communicate with jurors after the trial for that limited purpose, upon notice to opposing counsel and the court.

Defense Counsel for Indigent Defendants

Beginning with *Gideon* v. *Wainwright*,[9] the U.S. Supreme Court has made it clear that states have an obligation to ensure that defendants in criminal cases are provided with defense counsel, regardless of their economic means. A basic question since the *Gideon* mandate is whether the state should leave it up to local communities to provide defense counsel, or whether it should provide the service directly.

The U.S. Advisory Commission on Intergovernmental Relations suggests the following standards:

> Recommendation 31, State Responsibility for Providing Defense Counsel for the Indigent: The Commission recommends that each state establish and finance a statewide system for defense of the indigent, making either a public defender or coordinated assigned counsel service readily available to every area of the state.[10]

A community should adopt the defense counsel system for indigent defendants best suited to its needs, either a full-time public defender office, a contract system, or an assigned counsel system. The following are minimum standards of performance for such legal assistance.

1. Legal representation must be available for every person who is without financial means to secure competent counsel when charged with a felony, misdemeanor, or other charge where there is a possibility of a jail sentence.
2. Standards of eligibility must exist that effectively screen out those with sufficient funds to procure competent private counsel but, at the same time, are not so stringent as to create a class of unrepresented accused.

[9]372 U.S. 335 (1963).
[10]State-Local Relation in the Criminal Justice System (Washington, D.C.: U.S. Government Printing Office, 1971), p. 52.

3. Representation must be available immediately after a person has been taken into custody or arrested, at the first and every subsequent court appearance, and at every stage in the proceeding.[11]

To Remedy Error or Injustice

Representation should be available to persons convicted of crime at appeal or other postconviction proceedings to remedy error or injustice, including parole and probation violation proceedings, extradition proceedings, and proceedings involving possible detention or commitment of minors or alleged mentally ill persons. Probation and parole revocation hearings may involve both disputed issues of fact and difficult questions of judicial or administrative judgment. These hearings lack some of the evidentiary and other technical complexities of trials, but where the facts are disputed the same process of investigating, marshaling, and exhibiting facts is often demanded as at trial. A lawyer for the defense is needed in these proceedings because of the range of facts which will support revocation, the breadth of discretion in the court or agency to refuse revocation even though a violation of the conditions of release is found, and the absence of other procedural safeguards which surround the trial of guilt.

Client-Attorney Relationship: Fair Trial

Counsel for the defense is bound, by all fair and honorable means, to present every defense that the law of the land permits, to the end that no person may be deprived of life or liberty except by due process of law. One of the cardinal principles confronting every attorney in the representation of a client is the requirement of complete loyalty and service in good faith to the best of his or her ability.

The right to an attorney embraces effective representation throughout all stages of a trial. Where the representation is of such low caliber as to amount to no representation, the guarantee of due process has been violated. In a criminal case, the defendant is entitled to a fair trial, but not a perfect one.[12]

Case Studies

Johns v. *Smyth*, 176 F. Supp. 949 (1959).

Gideon v. *Wainwright*, 372 U.S. 335 (1963).

Powell v. *Alabama*, 287 U.S. 45 (1932).

---

[11]Ibid., pp. 52–53.
[12]*Johns* v. *Smyth*, 176 F. Supp. 949 (1959).

Discussion Questions

1. List five factors likely to support a prosecutor's decision not to prosecute.
2. What decisions regarding the conduct of his defense should be made by an accused after full consultation with his legal counsel? What decisions are the exclusive province of defense counsel after consultation with his client?
3. What kind of evidence should a prosecutor present to a grand jury in seeking a criminal indictment?
4. Discuss the implications of this situation: A defendant admits to his lawyer facts that establish guilt, but insists on his right to trial.
5. Outline the pretrial investigation a defense attorney pursues as a duty to his client.
6. What provisions exist to provide indigent defendants with legal counsel?
7. Discuss the statement "In a criminal case the client is entitled to a fair trial, but not a perfect one."

Glossary

Advocacy   Defending, assisting, or pleading for another; to defend by argument.

Advocate   One who renders legal advice and pleads the cause of another before a court or tribunal; a counselor; one who speaks in favor of another.

Appeal   Judicial review; a postconviction step in judicial proceedings. After the decision of a trial court, the removal of the case (cause) to a higher court with authority to review the decision of the lower court for the purpose of obtaining a retrial.

Bail   Release of a defendant upon his or her written agreement to appear in court as required. Cash or other security may be required.

Discovery   Disclosure by the prosecution of certain evidence regarding a defendant in a pending trial. There is limited disclosure by the defense. Term is generally identified with defense pretrial request to prosecutor to disclose facts of the police case against defendant.

Expert Witness   An individual, with reference to a particular subject, who possesses knowledge not acquired by ordinary persons; a man of science or a person possessing special or peculiar knowledge acquired from practice and experience.

Grand Jury   A certain number of persons selected according to law and sworn to the duty of receiving complaints and accusations of crime in criminal cases, to hear evidence presented by the "state," and to return indictments when they are satisfied a trial is warranted. The term "grand" developed because, at common law, the number of persons on this jury was set at not fewer than twelve nor more than twenty-three, while the ordinary *trial jury* (petit jury, as distinguished from grand jury) was a body of twelve persons.

Guilty The result of a guilty verdict in a criminal prosecution (jury or judge); the result of judicial acceptance of a guilty plea; the opposite of innocence.

Motion Application to court for a legal remedy.

Preliminary Hearing A judicial hearing or examination of witnesses to determine whether or not a crime has been committed, and if the evidence presented by the prosecutor is sufficient to warrant the commitment, or bailing, of the accused pending trial.

Presentence Report A report by a probation officer of an investigation conducted at court direction into the social and criminal history and resources of a convicted defendant, and containing a recommendation to the sentencing judge concerning the best program of corrections for the offender.

CHAPTER 4

Testimony

CHAPTER OBJECTIVES

- To discuss testimony as distinguished from other evidence.
- To reveal the procedures for securing the attendance of witnesses in court, including explanations of subpoenas and writs of *habeas corpus*.
- To examine the foundation that must be established to qualify witnesses and outline the circumstances of privileged communications.
- To disclose the primary attack areas of cross-examination and the manner of impeaching witnesses.

Most evidence in criminal trials is testimonial. Testimony is a method for establishing disputed facts through the questioning of witnesses in open court. The witness's attendance in court allows personal scrutiny by the trier of fact. Testimony is the oral transmission of information from witness to jury.

Testimony has a trilogy of weaknesses: half-truths, lies, and silence. A witness can convince himself that he clearly observed a very nebulous or confused event or one that never happened. He may stretch his imagination to conform his testimony to any necessary story line. Sometimes, a lying witness may be really convinced he is telling the truth. The witness may be in the marginal area of consciousness, unwilling either to tell the truth or to deliberately lie. A silent witness may conceal true facts within his personal knowledge.[1] Another weakness of testimonial proof may be exploited by cross-examination showing friendship, dislike, indebtedness, or animosity.

Perception, recall, and verbalization all militate against a witness' describing an observed event exactly as it happened. Generally, an observer sees the things he expects to see. The process of distortion also carries over into memory. The observer only remembers what he perceived minus what has been stamped out or obliterated by the decaying function of time—from the event to the statement or testimony of a witness. Putting memory into words in a courtroom lessens relia-

---

[1] Harry P. Kerr, *Opinion and Evidence: Cases for Argument and Discussion* (New York: Harcourt Brace Jovanovich, 1962), pp. 41–44.

bility because of the effect of the audience (jury, questioner, and spectators) on a witness. Fear, anger, and annoyance distort recall and verbalization. This effect is often heightened by the questioner's planned words and actions.[2]

Memory loss is probably the primary reason for the legal conclusion that affirmative testimony is stronger than negative testimony. The story of a credible witness about some observed happening is stronger than the story of an equally credible witness that nothing happened. The latter witness may have forgotten the event, but it is unlikely that any person would recall an event that did not happen.

In general, parties in a criminal case are allowed to call as many witnesses as necessary to establish their accusation or defense. Each side chooses the order in which it summons witnesses to give testimony.

In the interest of justice, any competent witness who appears to have personal knowledge of some relevant and material fact should be called to testify. The court, on its own motion or on the motion of any party, may call witnesses and question them as if they had been produced by a party to the action. The parties may object to the questions asked by the judge and the evidence offered as if such witnesses were called and examined by an adverse party. Such witnesses may be cross-examined by all parties.

Witnesses who are not parties to the action may be barred from hearing the testimony of other witnesses. They usually wait in the hallway or a nearby room until called to testify. Witnesses who are neither parties to the action nor serving as legal counsel are excluded from the courtroom. This practice makes certain that no witness' testimony is influenced by the answers of other witnesses, or by the queries of an attorney or the court. This may not prevent collusion between witnesses, but it does make it less hazardous. This procedure makes witnesses acting in concert about untrue facts more vulnerable to cross-examination.

Attendance of Witnesses

Citizens have a duty to appear and testify to such facts within their knowledge as may be necessary for the administration of justice. A criminal defendant has the right to be confronted with the witnesses against him at trial under the Sixth and Fourteenth Amendments. The right of confrontation prevents the use of depositions or *ex parte* affidavits against a defendant in place of personal examination and cross-examination of the witness.

The process used to compel appearance as a witness is the subpoena *ad testificandum*. A subpoena *duces tecum* compels the witness to bring specified books, documents, and records to court.

[2]L. R. C. Howard, "Some Psychological Aspects of Oral Evidence," *The British Journal of Criminology*, 3, no. 4 (April 1963), 342–60.

A properly served subpoena is a court order compelling the person named therein to be in court on a certain day. Fees and expenses are usually offered to persons residing a substantial distance away from the trial court. Special arrangements are made to secure the attendance of expert witnesses. Subpoenas are issued by the trial court, but either the prosecutor or defense counsel may secure subpoenas as necessary.

Witnesses who fail to respond to a subpoena may be cited and punished for contempt of court. Continued refusal to appear as a witness may result in the issuance of a body attachment or arrest warrant, ordering an appropriate court or peace officer to bring the reluctant witness to court. Out-of-state witnesses can be compelled to appear and testify.[3] Flight to avoid testifying as a witness in a felony trial is punishable as a federal offense.[4] The fugitive witness will be returned, when apprehended, to the federal judicial district in which the original crime was committed or is being tried. He may be prosecuted in federal court, and he may be served with a subpoena ordering him to appear and testify at the original trial.

It is usually improper to call a witness at trial when it is known the witness will exercise a valid privilege not to testify.

When the testimony of a person in the custody of a law enforcement or correctional agency is material, his attendance at trial is obtained by a court order or writ: *habeas corpus ad testificandum*. The party calling the witness applies to the trial judge in writing saying that (1) the testimony to be given is material and (2) the witness is detained in custody. If the trial judge concludes the application is in good order and good faith, he directs the person having custody of the prisoner-witness to bring him to court on a specific date to testify.

A witness is not considered "unavailable" for confrontation and cross-examination by the defendant unless the prosecutor has made a good faith and timely effort to obtain his presence at trial.[5]

Once in court, a witness who refuses to swear or affirm to tell the truth or to testify may be punished for contempt. When a witness refuses to answer a question, the court may rule that the question is both material and relevant and order the witness to answer. If the witness still refuses, he may be charged with contempt of court.

Competence

The competence of a witness and his or her credibility are closely related, but should not be confused. A witness's testimony must be based on his observation

---

[3]The Uniform Act to Serve the Attendance of Witnesses from Without the State in Criminal Cases (9 Uniform Laws Annotated 86) adopted by most states. (See Section 1334 *et seq.*, California Penal Code, for an example of the text of this act.)
[4]Title 18, United States Code, Section 1073.
[5]*Barber* v. *Page*, 390 U.S. 719 (1968).

of the subject matter he is testifying about. In the proper case, a nonexpert may give opinion evidence, but during cross-examination opposing counsel can determine whether the witness's opportunity for observation was sufficient to afford a reasonable basis for the conclusion or opinion he expresses. A witness who has had a chance to observe should be considered competent to testify about what he observed unless he is otherwise disqualified. The court rules upon a witness's competence; the credibility of a witness's testimony is evaluated by the jurors—or by the court in a trial without a jury. Competence is determined before evidence is given; credibility is evaluated after evidence is given. Briefly, a witness is competent if he is legally qualified to testify. He must have all the required characteristics and none of the disabilities.

At common law, a potential witness who lacked religious belief was incompetent. Most states, by constitution or statute, no longer require a potential witness to believe in a supreme being or divine punishment. Instead of taking the oath, such witnesses affirm that they will tell the truth.

Infamy was also a common law disqualification. Treason and felonies were designated many years ago as infamous crimes. After conviction for treason or felony a citizen lost the right to vote, to hold office, to serve on a jury, and to testify as a witness. Today, however, prior convictions of crime may reduce credibility but not competence.

Persons interested in the outcome of a case before the court were also excluded from the role of witness at common law. This exclusion even disqualified the defendant as a witness. Today, bias or interest may be shown to attack the credibility of a witness but not to prevent his testimony.

Mental incapacity can bar the testimony of a witness. A witness is ordinarily presumed to have the mental capacity to testify. However, his capacity may be challenged. The challenge may be based on the fact that the proffered witness is an infant, or insane, or intoxicated. The trial judge determines the competence of a child to testify. His decision is based on the child's comprehension of the obligation to tell the truth and his intellectual or physical capacity to observe and recall. The same general tests apply to the competence of an insane person. Intoxication may relate to the witness's condition at the time of the event he intends to testify about, or his condition at the time he is offered to testify. If the witness is intoxicated in court, his condition is pertinent to his competence as a witness. Intoxication at the time of the event has a bearing only on his credibility, unless the witness was too intoxicated to observe or recollect the event.

Policemen, attorneys in the case, jurors, and trial judges may all be competent to give evidence. If the evidence may be obtained through other witnesses, however, it is considered poor practice to call an attorney, juror, or judge in the case as a witness, and it raises dangerous questions of due process. The Federal Rules of Evidence prevent the judge presiding at the trial, or a juror sitting in the trial, from testifying to evidence relevant to the issues of the trial.

Parties to a crime and accomplices are competent to testify, although their participation in the offense or the advantages they might gain by giving testimony may affect their credibility. Although an accomplice is a competent witness, his testimony may be legally insufficient to convict the defendant unless it is corroborated by other admissible evidence.

A witness may be considered incompetent because of the confidentiality of privileged relationships such as husband and wife, or attorney and client.

Privileged Communications

A witness may have a privilege not to testify, or one of the parties involved in the trial may have a privilege not to have the witness testify, when the matter sought to be disclosed is a communication made in confidence in the course of a husband and wife, lawyer and client, clergyman and penitent, or physician or psychotherapist and patient relationship.

The concept of privileged communications in Anglo-American criminal justice is based on the confidentiality of communications between husband and wife, attorney and client, priest and penitent, and physician and patient. Originally, privileged communications may have been based on the honor of a spouse, an attorney, a priest, or a physician. More recently, privileged communications have been protected for their inherent confidentiality. The privilege is based on the need to free a person from apprehension about matters he might communicate in the close relationship of marriage, while consulting a legal advisor, in the role of penitent, or as a patient receiving treatment. The success of the relationship requires that the communication be treated in confidence and not be disclosed. Confidentiality is an essential element of these relationships. Disclosure of any communication within these relationships is believed to threaten the foundations of community life and is likely to do more harm to community life than the benefit that could be gained from dispensing with the confidential relationship.

Spouses, by common law and most statutes, are either partially or entirely incompetent to testify against each other. The basic reason for this rule is to promote the unity or confidential and close relationship between the husband and wife, because a different rule would tend to disrupt the home life of married couples. There is usually an exception to this rule when a crime is committed by one spouse against the other or against their children.

There is one jurisdiction which distinguishes a "marital privilege" and a "confidential marital communication." The marital privilege gives only the testifying spouse the privilege of not testifying against a spouse who is a party to the action, as well as not being called as a witness. The spouse who is a party to the action does not hold the privilege under this part of the statute. When the communication between spouses has been made in confidence while they were husband and wife, both spouses have the privilege against disclosure and also of preventing the disclosure by the other. In addition, neither spouse need be a party to the action in order to claim this privilege. This "confidential marital communication privilege" is sufficiently broad to prevent the testimony of an eavesdropper or the testimony of a third party to whom one of the spouses has revealed the confidential communication. The usual exceptions apply, such as to actions between spouses or to communications made to enable anyone to commit a crime.

A client would be unwilling to communicate or cooperate with his own attorney without attorney-client privilege. In criminal cases, this lack of confidentiality would destroy the adversary system of justice. The privilege is basically with the client, and though the attorney may claim the privilege, it is only on behalf of the client. If the client waives the privilege, the attorney loses his right to claim the privilege.

However, there may be no attorney-client privilege when the service of the attorney is sought to enable anyone to commit a crime or a fraud, when the communication is relevant to a breach of duty by the attorney to his client or the client to his attorney, or when the attorney has attested to a document relevant to the issues of the case. In addition, there is authority that the attorney-client relationship does not apply to physical evidence in the possession of the attorney.[6]

In connection with penitents and patients, the penitent would be unable to fulfill his commitments to his God or his religion. Full disclosure by patients is essential to proper care and treatments; and such care and treatment would be impossible if disclosures were not confidential but could be the basis of, or used to aid, a criminal prosecution against a patient.

All too often, under common law, the privileged claimant was required to show the confidentiality of the communication. While this issue would be heard out of the presence of jurors, often in chambers, it did compel many claimants to reveal the subject matter of the communication. These presumptions or statements avoid the need for such disclosure.

The privilege of not revealing the content of a privileged communication is waived when any holder of the privilege, without coercion, discloses a significant part of the communication or has consented to such disclosure by others, or fails to claim the privilege when he has the standing and opportunity to claim it. However, one spouse's waiver of the privilege does not affect the right of the other spouse to institute a claim of privilege, and this is true of other joint holders of a privilege (two or more). The waiver of this right by any one joint holder of the privilege does not affect the right of another joint holder to claim the privilege.

The Personal Knowledge Requirement

Although each witness must affirm or swear to his willingness to testify truthfully and can be heard only in the presence and subject to the examination of all parties to an action, the major test for admitting testimony is personal

---

[6]*People* v. *Meredith*, 29 Cal. 3d 682 (1981).

knowledge. The testimony of a witness about a particular matter is inadmissible unless he has personal knowledge of the matter. When a party objects, such personal knowledge must be shown before the witness may testify. A witness who gives second-hand testimony under an exception to the hearsay rule must have personal knowledge about the hearsay conduct or words. To a limited extent, expert witnesses are allowed to offer their opinion on fact situations which are not based on personal knowledge. However, the general requirement for both expert and nonexpert witnesses is personal knowledge. Did the witness perceive the event or incident about which he is willing to testify? Did he receive this knowledge through his senses (seeing, hearing, touching, smelling, or tasting)? If he did (and that may be shown by otherwise admissible evidence including the witness's own testimony), then his testimony satisfies this basic requirement of personal knowledge.

A witness with personal knowledge of an event or happening is generally assumed to recall it. A witness's faulty recollection may impair his recall of a perceived event or incident but is more of a trade-off of problems than a part of the personal knowledge requirement. A witness may only claim that a certain item of testimony is true to his best recollection, but he implies he has knowledge about the matter. A witness often prefaces his recollection of a perceived event or incident with the words, "I think." Rulings over many years of courtroom use of this prefatory term make it synonymous with the words, "I believe." The testimony then given is viewed from this frame of reference: The witness is telling what he remembers.

The memory of a witness may be refreshed by questioning. Unfortunately, this is most often done by a hostile cross-examiner, but it may be done by the counsel who called the witness or by the trial judge. Sometimes, the testimony of one witness casts doubt about the recollection of another witness.

Any kind of reminder by association is a device which stimulates recollection. Police investigators often use open-ended questions when interviewing witnesses to aid total recall: "And then what happened?" "What gave you that impression?" During pretrial conferences in the office of the prosecutor or defense counsel, witnesses are interviewed as a necessary step in preparing a case for trial. The memory of a witness may need refreshing at this time. A witness is often given the opportunity, in these pretrial conferences, to view a previous statement he made to police, or to review prior testimony or other data which may assist in total recall.

Record of Past Recollection When recall of an observed event is less than perfect, counsel questioning a witness in court may hand a memorandum over to the witness for inspection to refresh the witness's memory. If the memorandum, upon inspection by the witness, does improve his recollection, he may testify from this revived recall of the fact involved.

Because such memorandum is not evidence but only aids in eliciting testimony, it may not be proffered as tangible evidence by the party calling the witness. Counsel for the opposition, however, is entitled to inspect the memorandum handed to an in-court witness to search for grounds for objecting to its use. He may request it be made available for his reference during cross-examination. In some circumstances, he may ask that the memorandum be submitted to judge or jury for examination.

When recollection of the witness is not refreshed, the memorandum may be proffered as tangible evidence if the witness testifies that he has no present recollection of the event described but does recognize the writing as made by him when the facts were still fresh in his mind. In effect, he testifies that the memorandum is a factual account of his past recollection. For a record of past recollection to be admissible, the witness must testify he knew the facts from personal knowledge and correctly recorded them when the facts were fresh in his memory.

When a writing is handed to a witness to revive present recollection, all parties to the action must be given an opportunity to inspect it before any questions concerning it may be asked of the witness. Production at the trial of any writing used to refresh the memory of a witness is required at the request of the adverse party—whether the witness used the writing to revive his recollection when testifying or before appearing in court. It does not matter when the writing was used to revive the witness's recollection. If the writing is not produced, the witness's testimony on the matter involved will be stricken from the court record. However, production may be excused and the testimony allowed to remain in the record if the writing is not in the possession or control of the witness or the party calling him, and cannot be procured by the witness or the party involved through the use of legal process or other means available to them. California discovery procedures (see Chapter 12) permit discovery of all written statements by a witness on the subject of his testimony so that the witness may be thoroughly cross-examined.

Reasonable Opportunity for Observation

A witness can testify to an observable fact when he appears to have had a reasonable opportunity to observe it. If no reasonable opportunity existed within the scope of the witness's five senses, then he lacks personal knowledge, and his testimony is inadmissible. The invalidation of proffered evidence for lack of personal knowledge is often confused with hearsay. This is understandable. Many witnesses seek to testify by claiming personal knowledge when they only know the fact involved from the reports of others. Although there are exceptions which permit this retelling of another's story, there is no exception to the doctrine of personal knowledge—no one can testify to a fact he did not observe.

There is a line of questioning which establishes the opportunity of a witness for observation.

Q: Where were you at approximately 11:00 P.M. on the 28th of July?

A: Home. 62 Cathcart Street.

Q: Did anything unusual occur at or about that time?

A: Yes.

Q: What?

A: I heard a lot of noise out front.

Q: What did you do?

A: I went to the window and I looked out.

Q: What did you see?

This line of questioning places the witness in relation to the place of occurrence, orients his recall to the date and time of the event involved, and indicates he was attentive and had an opportunity to observe. It establishes a foundation of place, time, and circumstances for further questioning. Also, the noisy event which is the subject of the above series of questions must be within the scope of at least two senses, hearing and sight. Is it reasonable to assume that an average person would hear the noise of the event from his inside location? Is it possible for a person of average eyesight looking out of the same window to observe the location of the event?

Examination of Witnesses

The examination of all witnesses during a trial should be conducted fairly, objectively, and with due regard for the dignity and legitimate privacy of the witness, and without seeking to intimidate or humiliate the witness unnecessarily. An advocate's belief that the witness is telling the truth does not necessarily preclude appropriate cross-examination in all circumstances but may affect the method and scope of cross-examination. In examining witnesses, a questioner will not be allowed to use questions assuming facts not proved, double (compound) questions, queries that are argumentative or indefinitive and uncertain. Cross-examination is the form of inquiry used to attack adverse witnesses. Trial judges will not permit witnesses to be abused beyond the reasonable techniques of cross-examination. Most courts permit some excesses in this area because it is often the role of the cross-examiner to discredit the witness if possible, to help the triers of fact determine the truth from conflicting testimony.

The questioning of a witness is controlled by the trial judge. He must see that questioning is effective for ascertaining the truth, that a witness is protected from undue harassment or embarrassment, and that a witness gives responsive answers to questions. The witness is expected to be responsive to a question. Unless he is restricted by the question's form, he may give more than a simple yes or no. Answers that are not responsive are stricken from the record on the motion of any party.

The examination of a witness generally proceeds along the following lines:

1. There is direct examination, cross-examination, redirect examination, recross-examination, and continuing thereafter, redirect and recross-examination.
2. Each phase of the examination of a witness is usually concluded before the succeeding phase begins.
3. After direct and cross-examination, the court may allow additional testimony on new subject matter by the witness under examination if the interests of justice will be served by the new testimony. The adverse party may cross-examine upon this new subject.
4. The defendant in a criminal action may not, without his consent, be subject to direct examination by another party to the action.

Evidence on Direct Examination

The first questioning of a witness about a matter that is not within the scope of any previous examination of the witness is direct examination. This is a fundamental method of producing testimonial proof. It is the means by which a composite story is heard from the mouths of witnesses. It is the opportunity for the prosecutor or the defense counsel to ask questions designed to establish the existence or nonexistence of facts, favorable or unfavorable to the party represented by the questioner.

The party calling the witness conducts the direct examination. The questioner is friendly, anxious to help the witness repeat the story he told during a pretrial interview or interviews. Of course, the witness is expected to tell his story in his own words as he best recalls it, but the questioner guides him to keep him from straying too far from facts relevant to the case at trial.

Questioners conducting a direct examination may use direct questions or the narrative form of inquiry. The direct question, in its most simple form, calls for a direct one-sentence answer. The narrative query offers the witness a chance to tell what happened at a certain time and place. The type of questions used will depend on the questioner's evaluation of the witness and his potential coherence in answering narrative questions. Direct questions are safe. Responses are not likely to deviate from the basic line of questioning.

Leading questions—phrased to suggest an answer—are not permitted. However, this type of question is permitted concerning noncontroversial data necessary as a prelude to the witness's testimony, or when necessary because of the witness's youth, age, lost memory, or lack of intellectual capacity to elicit the desired information.

The following illustrates an acceptable use of leading questions when the facts are not in controversy:

Q: Mrs. R _____, were you home on the evening of July 28?

A: Yes I was.

Q: At 10:30 or 11:00 o'clock that evening, did you have occasion to receive a phone call?

A: Yes, I did.

A prosecutor must be particularly adept at direct examination. He must create a clear visual picture of the crime and culprit through questions he asks witnesses and the answers he receives. The picture (or theory) of the crime must be sufficiently clear to convince each juror beyond a reasonable doubt that the crime was committed and the defendant committed it.

Direct examination is directive, but it is not suggestive of the desired or expected answer. Foundations of time, place, and circumstances are a necessary prelude to the essential testimony. The best basis for asking clear questions and receiving relevant answers is a pretrial conference with the witness. This is not an attempt to coach the witness, and there should be no feeling on the part of the attorney or witness that a discussion of the witness's testimony before the trial is a questionable practice. The purpose of the pretrial conference and discussion is to make certain that the attorney knows all the information this witness can testify to, and to advise the witness of the type of questions he should expect so the witness understands what information the attorney desires to obtain by the particular question asked.

Pretrial preparation by attorney and witness is the key to a well-presented case in chief, and if this part of the pretrial preparation is ignored or forgotten, some of the information available from a witness will be lost to the jury because the attorney does not know that the witness has it, or because the witness is unable to understand what information is sought by direct-examination questions.

An example of direct examination is the following extract of a prosecutor's examination of a police officer who had investigated a double killing and searched the rooms of the suspect. The testimony is on a motion to suppress the physical evidence seized at the suspect's rooms:

Q: (By the prosecutor.) Lieutenant W., would you state your occupation, please?

A: I'm a detective lieutenant in the police department.

Q: And which detail do you work in that department?

A: In the homicide detail?

Q: And how long have you worked in that detail?

A: Approximately four years.

Q: Who is the head of that unit?

A: I am.

Q: I'd like to direct your attention to February 4th of this year and ask you if you were the officer in charge of the investigation of the shooting murder incident which occurred at the Torch Club that morning?

A: Yes, I was.

Q: How many homicides in your career have you investigated?

A: Oh, between one hundred and twenty-five, one hundred fifty.

Q: And the morning of February 4th, did you come in contact with a suspect in the Torch Club homicide case?

A: Yes, I did.

Q: And who was that?

A: Mr. B.

Q: Do you see Mr. B. in the courtroom today?

A: Yes, sir.

Q: Could you point him out, please?

A: He is the gentleman in the red shirt there on the end.

Q: Lieutenant, what time did you come in contact with Mr. B.?

A: It was about five minutes after 5:00 in the morning.

Q: And where was that contact made?

A: In my office.

Q: And at the time of the contact, was Mr. B. handcuffed or in any way restrained?

A: No, sir.

Q: And you did have a conversation with him, is that correct?

A: Yes, sir.

Q: Who was present during that conversation?

A: Sergeant G. was in and out of the office. He was present during most of it.

Q: At the time you made contact with Mr. B. that morning, what did you know of his background?

A: Sergeant G. told me that he was on parole.

Q: Did you know at that time for what crime he was on parole?

A: No, sir.

Q: At the time contact was made with Mr. B., what knowledge did you have of the Torch Club case? How many people had been involved?

A: We had information that there were two male Negroes involved in the double homicide at the Torch Club.

Q: And how many were in custody at the time you made contact with Mr. B?

A: Just one.

Q: That would be Mr. B.?

A: Yes.

Q: And the other person's whereabouts; did you have any idea where that person was at the time?

A: No, sir.

Q: What type of a homicide had it been at the Torch Club?

A: There had been a homicide by means of a shooting. Best information we could gather, it was a rifle of some type. The witness described some type of rifle and some type of hand revolver, handgun.

Q: At the time you contacted Mr. B., had those weapons been recovered?

A: No, sir.

Q: What about clothing?

A: We had a clothing description, it consisted of red pants and a red and white, or red plaid shirt.

Q: And when you contacted Mr. B., was he wearing that clothing?

A: No, sir.

Q: And what did you know about Mr. B. being at or around the scene of this homicide?

A: We had developed information from a taxicab driver that he had taken Mr. B. out of the area from the bus station immediately after the shooting.

Q: The bus station is near the Torch Club?

A: One block away, yes.

Q: Now, when you first met Mr. B. that morning, could you explain to us what happened and the nature of your conversation?

A: Sergeant G. brought him into my office and introduced us. And we had the Miranda advisement form there. And we asked him, told him we had to advise him of his rights and asked him to read the Miranda advisement form out loud, which he did.

Q: Did he read the entire Miranda form aloud?

A: Yes, sir.

Q: And when he got through reading it, what did he indicate to you regarding his Miranda rights?

A: He stated that he knew his rights, that he had been advised of his rights before and he wasn't going to sign anything as he was not involved in anything. He followed up this statement of facts that he wasn't involved in anything by relating his activities for the night. He related that he had been home watching television, that he had gone to a bar, 21st and L., I think it was the Redwood Lounge. We then asked him if he had been down to the bus station at all that night, and he said he hadn't been in that area or at the bus station. Asked if he had taken a cab that night, he said that he had not.

Q: Now, did your conversation, after he laid out where he had been that day, or—pardon me, laid out where he indicated where he had been that evening, get around to a search of his residence?

A: Yes, it did.

Q: And how did you approach that question with Mr. B.?

A: I told him that it was necessary that we search his apartment.

Q: And what did you indicate, as far as the search itself was concerned?

A: Well, I indicated that there was three different—three alternatives that were available for searching his apartment.

Q: And what did you tell him the alternatives were?

A: I told him that we could get a search warrant. Number two, we could contact his parole officer, as he was on parole, and go along with the parole officer to conduct a search of his apartment. Or number three, he could give his consent and we have a consent form in the police department, which Sergeant G. gave to him. I asked him to read it; he didn't read it out loud. He did read it, and at that point he reached in his pocket, took out his keys, laid them on the desk and signed the consent form.

Q: Now, after you explained the three ways, what did Mr. B. do?

A: There was some conversation. He asked did his parole officer have a right to search his apartment.

Q: Who was that question directed to?

A: To me.

Q: And what did you tell Mr. B.?

A: I explained to him that yes, in fact that he was on parole, that his parole officer did have a right to search his apartment when there was evidence that—reasonable cause or evidence to believe that he might be involved in a felony, which is part of his parole. That would not violate any laws.

Q: And did you explain anything more to him about the parole officer's power of search?

A: The reasons why the parole officer would search?

Q: Yes.

A: No, that's about basically what I told him.

Q: After you told him that, did he have any further questions about the power of a parole officer to search?

A: No, sir.

Q: Did Mr. B. question you at all regarding the possible use of a search warrant to gain access to his residence?

A: No, sir.

Q: How long did your conversation last with Mr. B.?

A: Between fifteen and twenty minutes, best I recall. Then Sergeant G. brought the form in, consent-to-search form, and he read it, or appeared to be reading it. And like I testified, took his keys out, signed it, and we told him that we would be back in a little while. And we placed him back in the interrogation room and left.

Cross-Examination and Attack Techniques

Cross-examination is the method by which a party to an action probes the knowledge, recollection, bias, and credibility of an adverse witness. Cross-examination is an absolute right and not merely a privilege. It is part of the constitutional mandate that an accused must be confronted by the witnesses against him. Testimony is not allowed to remain as evidence if the accused has not had the opportunity to fully cross-examine the witness giving the testimony.[7]

Ordinarily, a party may not cross-examine his own witness. However, the court may allow an exception if the witness is recalcitrant, unwilling, reluctant, uncandid, unfriendly and evasive, adverse, or hostile, or if the witness's testimony surprises the party who called him and is inconsistent with prior statements. The exception is not lightly granted by the court.

Cross-examination of a witness will be and should be thorough and probing and will not be unduly restricted by the court. It should be allowed to extend to anything that is relevant to show the improbability of the direct evidence and the credibility of the witness testifying.

A witness may be cross-examined about anything on which he has been directly examined. Cross-examination must be broadly related to the scope of the direct examination but is not confined to a mere repetition of the testimony given on direct examination.

If a witness testifies about a portion of a transaction or conversation, the cross-examination may probe the entire transaction or conversation. All matters connected with the crime are within the scope of the cross-examination, and such searching questions may produce evidence which conflicts with other testimony produced by the opposing party.

Questions and subjects which are impeaching in nature, though not part of the direct examination, are within the province of cross-examiners if they are relevant to credibility and not merely attempts to degrade the witness. The court will generally allow a wide latitude in this area of cross-examination.

More jurisdictions are allowing impeachment of any witness by any party, even the party calling the witness. The basis for this new direction is the premise that a party has no choice or selection of witnesses and thus should not be required to hold out any witness as worthy of belief.[8]

Inconsistent statements are important areas of attack by the cross-examiner. However, the inconsistent statements must concern relevant or material issues. Knowledge, accuracy, and recollection are also open subjects for inquiry on cross-examination. Knowing about sincerity, motive, bias, friendship,

---

[7]*Barber* v. *Page*, 390 U.S. 719 (1968).

[8]*United States* v. *Freeman*, 302 F. 2d 347 (1962); 3 Wigmore Sec. 905. The statutes of Illinois, Massachusetts, New Mexico, and Vermont allow impeachment by any party under varying circumstances; the same result is reached in California, Kansas, and New Jersey—Rule 607, Federal Rules of Evidence.

interest, and relation to parties helps the jurors evaluate the worth of the testimony given. Religious beliefs are not generally considered proper areas for cross-examination unless, of course, the religion is an issue in the case.

A prior conviction for a felony is also considered to be relevant to the credibility of any witness. In some jurisdictions this method of impeachment is limited by statute or court discretion to crimes which involve honesty or to recent, rather than remote, crimes. All require, at a minimum, that the prior crime be a felony. One jurisdiction admonishes the court to weigh the probability of the prior crime on the issue of credibility against the collateral prejudice which may be suffered by the defendant.[9]

When a witness is examined about a statement or other conduct inconsistent with any part of his testimony at the hearing, he need not usually be given any information about the statement or other conduct. Nor is it necessary in examining a witness concerning a writing to show, read, or disclose to him any part of the writing.

A witness may be led—and to a certain degree—pushed, nudged, persuaded, and cajoled into positions contradicting his previous testimony or out-of-court statements. The techniques used by cross-examiners to obtain this desirable result are many and varied, but certain basic concepts govern most good cross-examinations. According to expert cross-examiners, there are three primary areas of attack: perception, memory, and candor. Each area has its special problems, but there is one universal technique used by conscientious cross-examiners and this is "fencing." The witness is led into the area of attack and surrounded with his own answers until he has no opening through which to escape when the critical question is finally asked. if this is done thoroughly, and if the witness is vulnerable, the question will call for an answer which clearly shows the witness's lack of perception, or recollection, or that his previous testimony was somewhat less than the truth. And, if the questioner is extremely fortunate, it may show two or all three of the above. This type of questioning may even force the witness to make a statement directly inconsistent with other evidence or testimony.[10]

The ability of the cross-examiner to accomplish this result is directly related to the completeness of his previous investigation and pretrial preparation. This inquiry and diligence must provide him not only with the critical question but also with a knowledge of the horizons he must maintain to prevent the witness from explaining away a possible conflict or inconsistency. Unfortunately, many witnesses fail to realize that the cross-examiner will know about their expected testimony and the surrounding evidence. If a witness is lazy or lying and does not prepare himself to recall and testify to the facts he knows, or attempts to lie about them, he will find himself inside a "fence" and in danger of jeopardizing the case for the party who called him to testify.

---

[9]*People* v. *Beagle*, 6 Cal. 3d 441 (1972); Rule 609, Federal Rules of Evidence.
[10]Paul B. Weston and Kenneth M. Wells, *The Administration of Justice*, 2nd ed. (Englewood Cliffs, N.J.: Prentice-Hall, Inc., 1973), Chapter 9.

It is just as important to know what questions *not* to ask and when to stop cross-examination, as it is to know the questions to ask that will assist in destroying the effect of a witness's testimony.

It is rarely productive, and in fact may be damaging, for the cross-examiner to ask questions of a witness if he does not know the answers that must be given. Cases are lost by the cross-examiner who, by his own questions, allows the witness to give answers or explanations that injure his client's position in the case, and that the proponent failed to develop during his direct examination of the witness.

An example of cross-examination is found in the following extract from a transcript of the questioning of Lieutenant W. by defense counsel on a motion to suppress evidence seized as a result of an alleged consent to search:

Q: Lieutenant W., this conversation that you had with Mr. B. was in your office?

A: Yes, sir.

Q: And where is your office, in relation to what you call the interrogation room?

A: Well, it's down a hallway, around a couple corners, I'd say probably sixty feet away or so.

Q: Did you have someone bring Mr. B. to your office, sir?

A: Yes, sir. Sergeant G.

Q: Mr. B., was he at that time in an interrogation room?

A: Yes, sir.

Q: When you say Mr. B. wasn't under restraint, you mean that he wasn't in irons or wasn't handcuffed?

A: Yes, sir.

Q: He was under arrest, wasn't he?

A: Yes, sir.

Q: He was in your custody?

A: Yes, sir.

Q: He wasn't free to come and go as he wanted to do?

A: No, sir.

Q: And why was it that you had Mr. B. brought to your office rather than going to the interrogation room?

A: Because the interrogation rooms are quite small, and it is awfully crowded in there. There is only one chair usually in an interrogation room.

Q: Did you tape your conversation with Mr. B.?

A: No, sir.

Q: However, you do have the facilities to do that?

A: Yes, sir.

Q: Had you been told about any weapons being discovered at that time?

A: No, sir.

Q: When were you told about weapons being discovered?

A: Seems to me it was after daylight.

Q: Was it before you searched his apartment?

A: No, sir.

Q: Now, when you talked to Mr. B., you indicated that, and I think your words were, it was necessary for you to search his apartment?

A: Yes, sir.

Q: Those were your words to him?

A: Yes, the best I recall.

Q: And by the way, up to that point no one had made any identification of Mr. B. as being a person in the Torch Club when the crime had been committed, had they?

A: No, sir.

Q: When you were talking to Mr. B. after you indicated to him that it was necessary that you search his apartment, you immediately went into an explanation of the various ways that you wanted him to understand you could search his apartment; is that right?

A: Yes, sir.

Q: And the three ways that you wanted him to understand you could search his apartment, is that you could get a search warrant or you could have his parole officer search his apartment or you could get his consent. Are those the three ways?

A: Yes, sir.

Q: The search that you made was not based upon a search warrant, was it?

A: No, sir.

Q: You had no search warrant?

A: That's correct.

Q: It was based only and solely upon the consent that has been shown to you, is that right?

A: Yes, sir.

Q: And the conversation that you had with Mr. B.?

A: Yes, sir.

Q: By the way, on this consent form, now shows Sergeant G.'s signature. When was that put on that piece of paper?

PROSECUTOR: Objection, your Honor, it's irrelevant.

DEFENSE ATTORNEY: This is one of your exhibits, sir.

THE COURT: Excuse me, the objection is overruled.

A: I don't know when that was placed on there.

Q: (Defense Attorney) Weren't you present when that was placed on there?

A: No, sir.

Q: Weren't you present when Sergeant G. placed that signature on it in Mr. Sears' (prosecutor) office the day of the preliminary hearing?

PROSECUTOR: Objection, your Honor; question assumes facts not in evidence.

THE COURT: Sustained.

Q: Was Sergeant G. present when the defendant signed the document?

A: Yes, sir.

Q: Is that when you signed the document?

A: Yes, sir.

Q: But Sergeant G. did not?

A: That's correct.

Q: When you told Mr. B. that the—the three ways that you were going to, that you could search his apartment, then he indicated to you some problem in his own mind about his parole officer searching his apartment without a search warrant, did he not?

A: Yes, sir.

Q: And he asked you specifically whether or not his parole officer could search his apartment without a search warrant?

A: Yes, sir.

Q: That's before he signed the consent form?

A: Yes, sir.

Q: And before he gave you any verbal consent, is that right?

A: Yes, sir.

Q: And before he gave you any keys?

A: Yes, sir.

Q: And you told him at that time that yes, you could have a parole officer search his apartment; didn't you tell him that?

A: Yes, sir.

Q: And that under those circumstances, the parole officer did not need, or neither did you need a search warrant?

PROSECUTOR: Objection, your Honor.

Q: (Defense Attorney) Did you tell him that?

PROSECUTOR: I'm going to object to the nature of the question. It is compound as to who needed a search warrant.

THE COURT: It is compound. Sustained.

Q: (Defense Attorney) Did you tell him that, in response to his question about a search warrant, as to whether or not you could search without a search warrant or whether or not the parole officer, his parole officer, could search without a search warrant; you told him that the parole officer could search without a search warrant, is that right?

A: Yes, sir.

Q: And you indicated to him that you could be there and would be there and search without a search warrant if his parole officer was there, didn't you?

A: No, sir, I don't think I said that.

Q: Did you indicate to him that you were going to be with the parole officer?

A: Yes, sir.

Q: When he searched?

A: Yes, sir.

Q: All right. And did you indicate to him that you could contact the parole officer for the purposes of that search?

A: Yes, sir.

Q: And it was only after all of this discussion, wasn't it, that he then said, "Okay, I'll sign," and signed?

A: It was after the discussion that he was presented the form, yes.

Q: That we have just been talking about that he signed, the form?

A: Yes, sir.

Q: And gave you the keys?

A: Yes, sir

Q: I don't have any other questions, your Honor.

Case Studies

Barber v. *Page*, 390 U.S. 719 (1968).

Pointer v. *Texas*, 380 U.S. 400 (1965).

Griffen v. *California*, 380 U.S. 609 (1965).

Discussion Questions

1. What is testimonial evidence.
2. What are the strengths and weaknesses of testimonial evidence?
3. Why are witnesses excluded from court unless they are testifying?
4. What methods may be used to obtain the presence of witnesses from inside or outside the state?

5. What factors bar a witness from testifying?

6. What matters may a witness testify to?

7. Explain the order of, and various methods of, examining witnesses.

8. How are witnesses attacked by the opposing attorney?

Glossary

Foundation (of Testimony)   Establishing the fact that the opportunity of a witness to observe was sufficient to afford a reasonable basis for the proposed testimony.

Habeas Corpus   A name for writs seeking to bring a party in custody before a court or judge to examine into the lawfulness of imprisonment. Its sole function is to release from unlawful imprisonment. Technically habeas corpus *ad subjiendum*.

Habeas Corpus *ad testificandum*   Directed to a person having legal custody of a prisoner in a jail or prison and ordering him to bring a prisoner to court to testify. ("You have the body to testify.")

Impeachment (of Witness)   Attacking the credibility of a witness.

Infamy   Status of person convicted of crime such as treason and other major felonies. Infamous crimes are those that are scandalous or heinous; usually linked with severe punishment upon conviction.

Subpoena   A process commanding the person named therein to appear before a court to testify as a witness.

Subpoena *duces tecum*   A process commanding a witness to bring to court a document or other record in his possession or control which is pertinent to trial issues.

CHAPTER 5

Witnesses

CHAPTER OBJECTIVES

- To divide into groups the universe of witnesses in a criminal action.
- To categorize the groups broadly according to the type of witness and the nature of the witness's testimony.
- To describe the broad dimensions of the role of the witnesses in each group and to discuss the legal baselines for the admission of the testimony of each type of witness.
- To discuss the dilemma of protecting a defendant in a child sexual abuse case from false accusations and shielding the victim-witness from the trauma of courtroom testimony.

A rigid categorizing of witnesses is unnecessary to an understanding of testimony as evidence, but a generalized grouping of witnesses is helpful to a better understanding of testimonial evidence.

Lay witnesses may be called by either the prosecutor or defense counsel. They are the casual witnesses to a crime but may have an interest in one side or the other—depending upon the circumstances of the case.

Police witnesses do have an interest in the prosecution of the defendant, as do accomplice witnesses and an informer called upon to be a witness at trial. The police witness may have prepared the case initially, the accomplice usually testifies to gain some benefit from the prosecutor, and informers are often paid for their services.

A defendant may become a witness in his or her defense, supplementing the testimony of any lay witnesses on their behalf, and defense counsel may call for character witnesses to show the reputation of the defendant.

Last, both sides may employ as a witness any person who can qualify as an expert in the scientific area of their testimony.

Lay Witnesses

Lay witnesses may be found in three overlapping classifications: the identification witness, the public-spirited witness, and the interested witness.

The casual witness to a crime is honest though often mistaken in portions of his perception or in his memory of his perceptions. He does not keep notes of what he sees or what he does. A trial, several or many months later, may find him with a defective memory of the event and susceptible to suggestion by police, prosecutor, or defense attorney. If a report has been made of the witness's observations at or near the time of the event, it may be used to refresh his recollection or to impeach him if he testifies differently than shown on the original report. As with all witnesses, the attorney who calls the witness should determine prior to his testimony that the witness still recalls the event, and that his testimony will conform with any previous testimony.

In addition to events, the lay witness may testify to the identity of the criminal. It is identification testimony that is subject to the most critical error. Incidents of wrongful conviction are due, almost entirely, to incorrect identification. Incorrect identification may be due to an honest mistake, exaggeration caused by a desire to be spotlighted, or by the overeagerness of the investigator. In any case, identification evidence should be treated with caution by both the prosecutor and defense attorney. Although not legally necessary, it is important for the prosecutor to find and present other consistent evidence to strengthen his eyewitness case. The combination of direct (eyewitness) evidence and indirect (circumstantial) evidence is rarely overcome by the defense. A prosecution which relies on only one or the other is dangerously weak.

The lay witness may be a public-spirited witness or an interested witness. He is public spirited when he feels it his duty to testify to the things within his knowledge which are relevant to the charge against the defendant. Public-spirited witnesses testify to what they believe, whether or not it is helpful or harmful to prosecution or defense. They testify though they may suffer enormous hardship, loss of friendships, or even be subject to physical danger. The opposing cross-examiner is well advised to treat him cautiously.

The interested witness has a reason to testify for the side that calls him. The reason may be economic, friendship to a party to the action, or ego desire to be the key witness in a real-life drama. Interest may result in exaggeration or deceit, either by testimony or by silence. It may be directed to any form of testimony but is most common with eyewitnesses (identification) and alibi witnesses. Interested witnesses can also include police, experts, and family of one of the parties. Little weight is given family members or close friends who testify. A case relying upon such witnesses is weak and vulnerable. Interest on the part of a witness is admissible evidence to show bias, a motive, or an intent to deceive.

The Police Witness

Police officers, no matter how objective at the investigative stage of a criminal proceeding, are usually considered biased witnesses during the period after a defendant has been charged. This is a natural and obvious human reaction.

Police officers have spent their time and expertise in the investigation, they have gathered the evidence, and they have "solved" the crime. The reports prepared by the officers and the evidence they have collected have persuaded the prosecuting attorney to charge the defendant. A subsequent guilty verdict or plea will indicate a job well done. A not-guilty verdict will be a failure and ego bruising. Few persons take well to failure, and the police are no exception.

The prosecutor must take care that police witnesses are fully prepared; that they have refreshed their memories from their own reports; that their expected testimony is consistent with their reports and that if there are inconsistencies, they are aware of them and can explain them; and that they do not feel the need to exaggerate or lie if their investigation or investigative procedures have been less than perfect.

Police officer witnesses often not only accept, but look forward to the challenge of defeating the defense attorney at trial. The defense attorney cannot expect officers to testify favorably to the defendant unless the officers are not aware they are doing so or have stated the information on their reports. The cross-examination must be cautious and must be directed only to those areas the defense attorney can verify and that are helpful to the defense case.

It is a risky adventure to call a police officer as a defense witness at trial. It is advisable only when the area of examination is limited and the attorney *knows* what the answers must be and can produce impeaching evidence if the police witness deviates from the expected testimony.

It is sometimes to the advantage of the defense to call a police officer as a defense witness at a preliminary hearing to gain discovery of the police investigation if no other avenue of discovery is available. The evidence produced at a preliminary hearing is not binding, at trial, upon either side. It can be and is used as grounds for impeachment, however, when a witness deviates at trial from his testimony at the preliminary hearing, or when he is legally unavailable to testify at trial.

The Accomplice Witness

An accomplice witness is one who is liable to prosecution for the identical offense charged against the defendant on trial. As a witness for the prosecution, he or she has been offered and accepted some benefit for giving testimony against his former crime partner. The benefit which the prosecutor may offer an accomplice for this testimony can be as complete as immunity from prosecution on the instant crime (and perhaps others) or as minor as a plea to a lesser offense or a lesser punishment for a plea to the instant offense. Because of this arrangement between an offender and the prosecutor, the law looks with suspicion on the accomplice's testimony. This suspicion is translated into the legal concept that there may be no conviction of the defendant based upon the testimony of an accomplice alone. Accomplice testimony must be corroborated by other independent evidence which tends to connect the defendant on trial with the crime itself. The corroboration must be evidence which does more than cast a suspicion.[1]

Courts have consistently held that it is within the prosecutor's discretion to use accomplice witnesses. Failure to prosecute law violators who have agreed to become informers does not constitute unlawful administration of the law or evidence of discrimination in prosecution; nor will the fact that others equally guilty of a crime are not prosecuted preclude punishment of another, also guilty. The extension of immunity to a crime partner of the accused who has turned state's evidence has existed from the beginnings of the justice system.[2]

The prosecutor should, however, divulge at trial any promises made to an accomplice witness pursuant to any understanding or agreement as to a future prosecution. This is relevant to the credibility of the accomplice witness, and the jury is entitled to know of it.[3] Common sense suggests that accomplices to a crime, in testifying against a crime partner, often have a greater interest in lying in favor of the prosecution than against it, especially if the accomplice is still awaiting his own trial or sentencing. While one accomplice may lie to save a crime partner, there is little doubt that others will lie to obtain favors from the prosecution for themselves.

The Informer Witness

The informer witness is closely aligned with accomplice witnesses. A convicted prisoner awaiting sentence may offer his or her testimony in another pending case; persons against whom criminal charges are pending may offer their services in securing evidence against a suspect in another case; or an individual with entree into the local underworld may offer investigators for the prosecutor knowledgeable assistance in "making a case."

A common informer witness is the "special employee" used by police and federal agents to make the purchases of drugs that will support application for a search and/or an arrest warrant. In making these buys, this special employee acts as a go-between, using his or her contacts in the local drug scene to introduce undercover police and federal agents to drug sellers.

While accomplice witnesses are known to one or more defendants in a case, informers may not be known to a defendant or to defense counsel. For this reason, disclosure of an informer's identity may be demanded by defense counsel. (See Chapter 13.)

[1]*People* v. *Robinson*, 392 P. 2d 970 (Ca. 1964).
[2]*State* v. *Jourdain*, 225 La. 1030, 74 So. 2d 203 (1954); *Saunders* v. *Lowry*, 58 F. 2d 158 (5th Cir. 1932).
[3]*Giglio* v. *U.S.*, 405 U.S. 150 (1972).

The Defendant Witness

Whether the defendant testifies in his own case is a decision he must make. The defense attorney must counsel and advise the defendant in this decision. The decision is a major one and is often critical to the case.

Neither the prosecutor nor the judge should comment on a defendant's failure to testify.[4] However, even without comment, there can be a negative juror reaction to the defendant's failure to deny the charge or explain the evidence against him under oath to the jury. In addition prosecutors are often allowed comment in their argument at the end of a trial that the testimony of various witnesses adverse to the defendant has not been rebutted or denied. While this is comment common to the prosecutor's argument in any case, it often has special significance for jurors in cases in which the defendant does not testify.

An equally serious consequence may follow if the defendant chooses to testify. A major consideration in this decision must be the effect of cross-examination upon the defendant and the defense case. Thorough investigation of the defendant's story is a necessary prerequisite to this decision. The attorney must be able to advise the defendant on the strengths and weaknesses of his testimony, the conflicts with other evidence, and the effect of prior convictions on the jury.

Proof of a defendant's prior record and evidence of unrelated crimes are inadmissible to show that the defendant is an evil or vicious person, thereby inferring guilt of the crime charged at trial.[5] However, defendants with a prior criminal record expose themselves to the type of cross-examination aimed at showing them as such persons and, therefore, inferring guilt on the present charge.

The defendant's demeanor and personality are factors to be weighed in this decision, as is the availability of other witnesses or evidence which will set out the defense case and the strength of the prosecutor's case. If the defendant as a person is unlikely to appear favorably as a witness to the jury, it is unwise to use him as a witness, unless other witnesses are not available to spell out the defense, and/or the prosecution's case is strong and apparently has impressed the jurors with its theory of the case.

The prosecutor's cross-examination of the defendant can be as extensive as allowed with any other witness. The prosecution has a right to show by cross-examination or rebuttal evidence, that the defendant's testimony is false. The cross-examination need not be confined to a mere categorical review of the matters, dates, or times mentioned in the direct examination. The prosecutor may ask questions directed to overcoming or qualifying the effect of the testimony given by the defendant on direct examination. When a defendant testifies to a denial, or qualified denial, of the crime charged, the scope of cross-examination may be very broad.[6]

[4]*Griffin* v. *California*, 380 U.S. 609 (1965).
[5]*United States* v. *Beno*, 324 F. 2d 582 (2d Cir. 1963); *Michelson* v. *United States*, 335 U.S. 469 (1948).
[6]*People* v. *Zerillo*, 223 P. 2d 223 (Ca. 1950).

All the factors that may be detrimental to the defense are weighted against the positive effect of the defendant's denial of the charge or explanation of the evidence against him under oath. The analysis of all the factors involved in a particular case may suggest the defendant testify or that he remain silent.

Defense counsel can request judicial instructions to the jury when the decision is that the defendant will not testify—that the defendant has the right not to testify and that no adverse inference can be drawn from the defendant's failure to take the stand.

The decision as to the defendant as a witness for the defense, wise or unwise, often becomes the basis for the jury's final decision on guilt or innocence.

Character Witness

A character witness testifies about the reputation of a defendant or another witness.

The character traits of a witness or a defendant which are in issue at the trial may be proved, when admissible, by evidence of the reputation of the witness or defendant. The reputation of a witness or defendant is shown by what a witness knows or has heard about the individual whose character trait is in question.

The common law rule allows only questions directed to the general reputation of the individual and not the character witness's own personal knowledge or opinion of him or his reputation.[7] Individual state statutes may broaden the rule and allow both opinion and evidence of specific acts as character evidence.

The character of a witness for truth and veracity is relevant and admissible for the purpose of impeaching that witness. Questioning a witness's truthfulness is always a proper cross-examination or rebuttal technique. The limits for production and cross-examination of character evidence are the same as those for the introduction and cross-examination of such evidence on behalf of a defendant.

If the proponent presents a witness, the opponent may, in rebuttal, offer evidence of that witness's reputation for truth, honesty, and integrity; the opponent's character witness may be cross-examined as to his basis for his knowledge of the reputation; and the proponent may meet evidence of bad reputation with evidence of good reputation, subject to the cross-examination of the opponent.

The proponent of a witness may not produce evidence of the good character of the witness for truth and veracity unless the witness has been impeached by evidence of his bad character for that trait.

Evidence of the defendant's evil character to establish guilt is inadmissible in the prosecutor's case in chief. There is no presumption of good character, but the law closes the whole matter of character, disposition, specific criminal acts, or reputation as proper evidence in the prosecutor's case in chief.

---

[7]*Michelson v. United States,* 335 U.S. 469 (1948).

The evidence of character may be relevant and probative but it also may cause undue prejudice, unfair surprise, and a confusion of the issue.

Although the evidence of character of the defendant on the issue of guilt or innocence is prohibited to the prosecution, it is available to the defense if relevant to resolve probabilities of guilt or innocence in the defendant's favor:

Q: Do you know the defendant?

A: Yes.

Q: How long have you known him?

A: About fifteen years.

Q: Do you know other people who know him?

A: Yes.

Q: Have you talked to others and heard others discuss his reputation for peace and quietude?

A: Yes.

Q: What is the defendant's reputation in the community for peace and quietude?

A: Very good.

The witness who testifies to another's character trait is subject to a cross-examination which explores his basis for the reputation testified to:

Q: You have discussed the defendant's reputation for peace and quietude with a number of other persons in the community?

A: Yes, many times.

Q: And these discussions were had over a long period of time?

A: Yes, periodically for many years.

Q: Did you ever hear discussed in the community that the defendant was arrested for assault and battery upon his wife?

Just as the character trait offered in evidence must be relevant to the issue in the case, so must the cross-examination be relevant to that character trait.

Where self-defense is an issue, reputation of the complainant as violent, or a person with a bad reputation for peace and quietude, may be admissible to raise the probability that he was the aggressor rather than the defendant.

Any reputation evidence, to be admissible, must not be too remote in time from the date of the offense charged or of the trial.

The Expert Witness

The expert witness is a person who has the education, training, and experience to testify to matters which cannot be determined, without clarification, by the ordinary lay juror.

An expert witness is usually paid by one side or the other. These experts may be employees of the prosecutor, the county, the state, or even a large public defender's office, or the defense counsel's legal firm. Many are self-employed, in that they will contract on a case basis with whichever side contacts them first.

Autopsy surgeons are usually county employed; criminalists either state or county employed; chemists county or state employed. Psychiatrists are generally employed by contract for individual cases.

There are private organizations of experts willing to testify and available for contract, usually to the small prosecutor's office or defense attorney. This is a growth business, many of these groups have a wide range of experts and extensive laboratory facilities.

The expert witness testifies in an area of evidence in which there is a potential for differing but honest opinions. The attorney will not call an expert unless he is helpful to that "side." It is a rare occasion that an expert paid by one side will testify to an opinion which is hostile to that side. There are occasions, however, where the expert will report an opinion to his employer which is hostile to that attorney's position. If the expert's report is discoverable by the opposition, he can be called by the opposition to testify to opinions or evidence harmful to the employer. If such an expert is called by the employer, he may be compelled to give favorable testimony to the cross-examiner.

Expert testimony is generally termed opinion evidence, but there is opinion evidence which can be testified to by nonexperts. Intoxication, age, distance, time, speed, and other matters which are common and widely known can be the subject of opinions by lay witnesses. (See Chapter 7.)

Child Sexual Abuse: Victim/Witness

A child victim of sexual abuse is both a complaining and material witness. He or she offers testimony likely to be compelling on the issue of guilt or innocence. There is no minimum age, but the ordinary requirement of personal knowledge is inherent in the role of victim in a sexual abuse case. Prior to testifying, the child is expected to demonstrate a capacity to observe and the ability to communicate, adequate intelligence and memory (recall), an awareness of truth as opposed to lies and half-truths, and the obligation of a witness to tell the truth.[8]

This witness most likely spells out the essential elements of the crime or crimes charged and, in identifying acts done, adds time and place and an identification of the defendant as his or her abuser.

In America's adversary system of seeking truth in courtrooms this kind of testimony is devastating to the case for the defense. The child victim-witness becomes a target of opportunity for destruction on the witness stand. An

---

[8]Nancy Walker Perry and Lawrence S. Wrightsman, *The Child Witness—Legal Issues and Dilemmas* (Newbury Park, Calif.: Sage, 1991), p. 49.

acquittal cannot be expected unless defense counsel discourages the child from taking the witness role at all or discredits him or her if they do testify.

The vehicle for destroying or discrediting a child victim-witness is the right of a defendant to a public trial in which an accuser must confront the accused and submit to cross-examination by counsel for the defense.

This Sixth Amendment constitutional right protects innocent persons falsely accused of criminal behavior, but it also exposes the child victim-witness to emotional trauma resulting from the courtroom confrontation. Of course, trauma varies with each case, but the impact of the cast and scenario can be severe. Just consider the frightened child facing his or her abuser while an aggressive adult asks very intimate questions and demands that the child respond in front of a roomful of people.

Judges in trial courts have known of this likelihood of traumatizing the victim-witness in these cases, in *in camera*, closed-circuit television or screened testimony have had legal hassles over this protection of the child. In *Coy* v. *Iowa*, 487 U.S. 1012 (1988), the U.S. Supreme Court held that a courtroom screen between witness and defendant violated the defendant's right to a face-to-face confrontation. However, Justice O'Connor in her concurring opinion (joined by Justice White) writes:

> I agree with the Court that appellant's rights under the Confrontation Clause were violated in this case. I write separately only to note my view that those rights are not absolute but rather may give way in an appropriate case to other competing interests so as to permit the use of certain procedural devices designed to shield a child witness from the trauma of courtroom testimony.[9]

Two years later in *Maryland* v. *Craig* (1990), 497 U.S. 836, the U.S. Supreme Court picked up with O'Connor's language in *Coy* and found that the right to face-to-face confrontation could be disposed of where the denial of such confrontation is necessary to further an important public policy and where the reliability of the witness is otherwise ensured. In *Craig*, trial procedures allowed the use of one-way closed-circuit television testimony of a child-victim witness. The defendant was able to communicate with his attorney during the testimony, and his attorney could cross-examine the witness.

The reasoning of the high court was that the purpose of the confrontation clause was to ensure the reliability of the evidence against the defendant by the witness being under oath, subject to cross-examination, confronting the defendant face to face while the jury was able to observe the witness's demeanor. In a case such as this, the state has a strong interest in the well-being of child-victims and that reliability was assured because of the existence of the witness's testimony under oath, being subject to cross-examination and the jury's ability to observe the witness's demeanor.

[9]*Coy* v. *Iowa.*

The court also held that to dispense with the confrontation requirement, there must be a finding that it is the defendant and not the courtroom that will traumatize the witness and that the emotional distress must be more than *de minimis*.

Shortly after *Craig*, Congress codified the Court's holding in 18 U.S.C. Section 3509. Under this section, a court may order the testimony of a child-victim witness be taken by closed-circuit television if the court finds that the child is unable to testify in open court in the presence of the defendant for any of the following reasons:

1. The child is unable to testify because of fear.
2. There is a substantial likelihood, established by expert testimony, that the child would suffer emotional trauma from testifying.
3. The child suffers a mental or other infirmity.
4. Conduct by the defendant or defense counsel causes the child to be unable to continue testifying.

This code section was recently tested and upheld by the Ninth Circuit Court of Appeals in *United States* v. *Garcia* (1993), 93 Daily Journal D.A.R. 13275. The court clarified that Section 3509 codified the *Craig* requirement that the child be unable to testify in open court because of the presence of the defendant.

Case Studies

United States v. *Wade*, 388 U.S. 218 (1967).

Michelson v. *United States*, 335 U.S. 469 (1948).

Giglio v. *United States*, 405 U.S. 150 (1972).

Miniproject

Brief the *Wade* case. Add a "See" comment on *United States* v. *Ash*, 413 U.S. 300 (1973), summarizing the relationship between the two cases.

Discussion Questions

1. What matters may a lay witness testify to?
2. Are police witnesses considered persons with an interest in the outcome of the case? Why?
3. What characteristics of the role of accomplice witness are likely to lower their credibility?

4. What is the difference between an accomplice witness and an informer called to testify in a criminal trial?

5. What are the hazards of a defendant testifying in his or her own behalf?

6. What are the differences and similarities between character witnesses and persons testifying as experts in various scientific fields?

7. Do child victim-witnesses in sexual abuse cases suffer trauma from exposure to the harsh atmosphere of the typical courtroom?

Glossary

Accomplice   A principal in a crime.

Common Law   Principles and rules of action derived from ancient usages and customs, or from judgments and decrees of courts enforcing such usages and customs.

De Minimis   Insignificant, minute, frivolous.

CHAPTER 6

Hearsay Evidence

CHAPTER OBJECTIVES

- To define the concept of hearsay evidence, stressing the fact that hearsay evidence is normally excluded because triers of fact have an inadequate opportunity to evaluate the truthfulness of hearsay declarants.
- To identify those types of hearsay evidence that, because of their inherent trustworthiness, are admissible as evidence, explaining the justification for these exceptions.
- To call attention to the exceptions to the hearsay rule listed under the Federal Rules of Evidence for purpose of comparison.

Hearsay evidence is evidence of a statement that was made by someone other than the witness testifying at the hearing, and that is offered to prove the truth of the matter stated. Except as provided by law, hearsay evidence is inadmissible. This definition of hearsay evidence and the rule barring its admission are generally known and cited as "the hearsay rule."

For purposes of the hearsay rule, a "statement" is usually defined as an oral or written verbal expression or nonverbal conduct intended as a substitute for oral or written expression. Testimony describing assertive conduct, clearly meant as a communications medium, is hearsay; nonassertive conduct is not hearsay.

Hearsay evidence is testimony about someone else's "story," or a story out of another's mouth. The out-of-court originator of the story (known as the declarant) cannot be observed by the trier of fact for clues as to his willingness or capacity to tell the truth, which might be apparent if he were an in-court witness, nor can his veracity be tested by cross-examination. Observation and cross-examination are basic devices for evaluating the credibility of a witness.

The accuracy of any evidence once removed from the in-court witness's personal knowledge is less than perfect. Written statements can be tested for validity and genuineness. Oral statements are notorious for poor reporting. Memory and perception of meaning frustrate accurate reporting of oral statements: Is the statement related in the words of the declarant or is it what the witness interpreted those words to mean?

The controlling reason for rejecting hearsay when a party objects is that the objecting party has the right to prevent the trier of fact (juror or judge) from being improperly influenced by evidence which appears fair but which carries hazards that could be exposed or eliminated if the declarant were present to be cross-examined.

To be admitted, hearsay evidence must meet the conditions of the exceptions established by law. Exceptions to the hearsay rule may be found in statutes or in decisional law. Exceptions which permit hearsay evidence are operable only if the proffered evidence meets the other requirements of evidence generally, otherwise admissible hearsay might be excluded by some other rule of evidence such as the "privileged communications" or "best evidence" rule, or because the court decides its probative value is less than its prejudicial nature, or that it might confuse the issues or mislead the triers of fact.

The exceptions to the hearsay rule permit this type of evidence to be received in court only when it is necessary to diligent inquiry and the circumstances under which the evidence is developed will provide some guarantee of basic or inherent trustworthiness to substitute for the oath, cross-examination, and other tests of a witness's credibility. Usually the need for hearsay evidence is based on inability to locate and produce a witness, but the normal procedure for producing evidence may be stymied in some other fashion. Exceptions to the hearsay rule are justified by circumstances pointing to trustworthiness; the statement itself, or the circumstances under which it was made, indicates the probability of its truth.

The exceptions to the hearsay rule are both a maze and a jungle for legal scholars. However, some simplification can be achieved by isolating the exceptions likely to be encountered in police investigations. These exceptions range from dying declarations through entries made in the regular course of business, and spontaneous utterances, and statements showing mental or physical conditions, to extrajudicial admissions.

Dying Declarations

Evidence of a statement made by a dying person about the cause and circumstances of her death is admissible if the statement has been made upon her personal knowledge and under a sense and belief of immediately impending death. It is thought that when a person knows she is going to die she will tell the truth because there is no longer a need or reason to lie and there is, perhaps, a religious reason to tell the truth.

In most states, dying declarations are admissible only when the crime charged is the homicide of the hearsay-declarant—who is thus unable to appear in court and testify.

The declarant who is the real witness must have possessed the required qualifications to be accepted in court as a competent witness if he were alive.

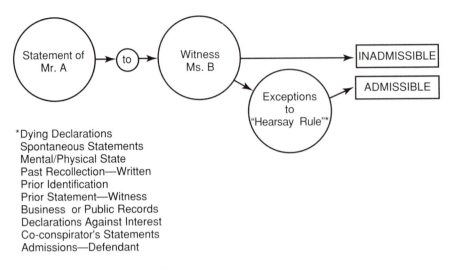

*Dying Declarations
Spontaneous Statements
Mental/Physical State
Past Recollection—Written
Prior Identification
Prior Statement—Witness
Business or Public Records
Declarations Against Interest
Co-conspirator's Statements
Admissions—Defendant

FIGURE 6-1.   The "Hearsay Rule."
Note: Evidence of a statement made by someone other than the witness testifying is generally inadmissible but may be admissible when vital to the in-court search for truth and when the statement and its circumstances are inherently trustworthy.

Investigators should be alert for negative evidence about a dying declarant, just as they would for a live witness. Evidence tending to impeach the declarant might well be admissible under the same rules of evidence that would have applied to the declarant if he had testified in person. This is particularly true of prior statements by the declarant contradicting his dying declaration.

There are two key elements of a dying declaration: the victim's personal knowledge of the circumstances under which he received the likely-to-be-fatal injury and his belief that death from the injury is imminent.

The personal knowledge of a dying declarant must be more than suspicion or conjecture. It should be shown that he knew, or had an opportunity to know, the circumstances of his injury.

The declarant must have had a settled, hopeless belief that his death was about to occur without loss of time. Although the declarant must have had this settled and hopeless belief in a swift and certain death, his credibility is not impaired if he did not die shortly after his statement. The time lapse between statement and actual death may cause the court to question the admissibility of a dying declaration because a lengthy time span will have a bearing on the issue of the victim's realization of impending death, but there is no requirement that the facts of life or death support the victim's expectation of a swift death.

The person taking a dying declaration statement must make sure the requirements of competence, personal knowledge, and settled and hopeless belief in impending death are satisfied by the form and content of the statement, or by some act or circumstances which show the victim's belief in impending death. An affirmative response to the following questions should be sufficient to allow admission of the declaration: Do you remember what happened to you? Do you think you are going to die now?

The actual development of a dying declaration within the evidence structure of a criminal trial is probably the best illustration of the needs to be satisfied in the statement taking. First, the preliminary facts are shown. Then the statement taker is introduced and qualified as a witness. Finally, the statement itself is introduced.

Spontaneous and Contemporaneous Statements

Closely aligned with the rationale for including dying declarations among the exceptions to the hearsay rule are the exceptions for spontaneous and contemporaneous statements. The inherent trustworthiness of a spontaneous statement is based on the declarant's lack of opportunity for reflection and deliberate fabrication. A contemporary statement clarifies the conduct of a declarant when the action and statement are linked and the action alone is equivocal or ambiguous. For instance, a prisoner staggered bleeding into the arms of a correctional officer. He pointed to another inmate and said, "He cut me." Then he died. Testimony describing both the act and the statement was admissible against the accused.

These statements narrate, describe, or explain an act, condition, or event perceived by the declarant. They are made spontaneously while the declarant is under the stress of excitement brought on by these perceptions, or while the declarant is engaged in some act, and they help to explain, qualify, or make understandable the conduct of the declarant.

Statements of Mental and Physical State

Testimony about a declarant's statement of intent, plan, motive, design, mental feeling, pain, or bodily health may be admitted if it is offered to (1) prove the declarant's state of mind, emotion, or physical sensation at the time of the statement or at any other time when it is itself an issue in the action or (2) prove or explain the declarant's acts or conduct.

In most states such evidence is admitted only when the previously existing mental or physical state is itself an issue in the criminal action, and the evidence may not be used to prove any other fact. However, such statements are often circumstantial evidence of other facts important to the prosecution or defense of a criminal case. A mental state may be proved to have existed at the time of a crime which will serve to excuse the crime. The classic example is the claim of self-defense in homicide cases.

The record of the trial of Norman St. Martin for the murder of a fellow state prison inmate, Glen Howard Mason, contains testimony admitted under this exception. In this case, death was caused by stab or puncture wounds. The crime took place at a state prison. The "people" claimed that the defendant, Norman St. Martin, inflicted the death wounds on the deceased (Mason) maliciously, intentionally, and knowingly; the defense said it was a case of self-defense: yes, there had been a killing; the circumstances were substantially as detailed by the state's presentation of the evidence; but the defendant had been threatened by the victim and feared for his life when the victim approached in an apparent assault attempt, and the fatal blow was struck in fear and self-defense. The pertinent testimony on the declarant's (St. Martin) state of mind follows:

Prosecutor (Direct Examination of Witness)

Q: Can you tell us then, the best you can recall, what that conversation was between you and Mr. St. Martin?

A: Mr. St. Martin stated that these cats around the California institution were nothing, that they were just a bunch of jerks. Some of the people that he has done time with in institutions in the East were real cool cats; that in a place back East they did their own number. They didn't fool with another guy. They didn't stab some guy over nothing; that it meant something when they knocked a guy off. That they had the—they had the guts to do it face to face. They didn't do it in the back. At that time I asked him if that was how Mason had been stabbed, if he had done it face to face? His reply was that, "Mason saw who stabbed him." I asked him if he had stabbed with an upward swing, a jab, or a downward swing. He said, "Man, I don't know. I just did it. That's all."

Q: Recall any other conversation?

A: He asked—or I asked him—if he had got any hit or anything. He stated that Mason had made a motion towards his face and just got his eyelid, and that's why it happened.

Q: Did he say anything about Mr. Mason?

A: No, other than, "He scratches like a woman."

Q: Did he say anything else about Mr. Mason or what his role was there in the prison?

A: That he was a loudmouth, that he wouldn't let a man do his own number.

Defense Counsel (Cross-examination of Witness)

Q: Now, as to this conversation that you stated you had with Mr. St. Martin. During this conversation, Mr. St. Martin seemed to be obsessed with the thought that persons were being stabbed in the back, isn't that correct?

A: I don't get your general—

Q: He made numerous references, didn't he to being stabbed in the back, isn't that so? Persons being stabbed in the back?

A: In regard to how the general run of stabbings is done in institutions in California, yes.

Q: That's right. He seemed quite concerned about that, didn't he?

A: Yes.

Q: All right. Did he seem concerned about doing his own number, his own time?

A: Yes.

Q: What does that mean?

A: It means being left alone. Just completely left alone by their terminology where nobody bothers them.

Q: All right. And he further stated in this conversation to you, did he not, that somebody had been bothering him?

A: Yes.

Q: And did he say—did he make any mention as to how Mr. Mason had been bothering him?

A: Badmouthing him, I believe, is the way he put it.

Q: And what does that mean to you, badmouthing him?

A: I could mean a number of things.

Q: All right. By badmouthing, do you take that to mean saying things derogatory toward Mason—I mean toward Mr. St. Martin?

A: Could be. Yes.

Q: Could—? What else could badmouthing mean?

A: In some places, it could be a big noise, punk, anything of that type.

Q: Calling him things, is that right?

A: Could be. Correct. Yes.

Q: All right. As a matter of fact, didn't Mr. St. Martin state that Mr. Mason called him a punk?

A: He did, previously.

Q: What else did he say Mr. Mason had said about him, Mr. St. Martin?

A: I believe the only thing he said that he called—direct quote—would be that he called him a big noise, called him a punk. I believe that was all.

Q: And also perhaps that Mr. St. Martin didn't have the guts to do anything about anything?

A: I believe so, sir.

Although the direct examination of this witness did little more than suggest St. Martin's state of mind at the time of the attack, the contents of the cross-examination revealed the defendant's fearful state of mind.

Written Statements of Past Recollection

A written statement made when the fact recorded actually occurred, or within a short enough time thereafter to ensure that the fact was fresh in the writer's memory, qualifies under an exception to the hearsay rule for the same reason that spontaneous and contemporary statements are admissible.

Recorded past recollections can usually be read into evidence by the recorder if they concern matters the witness cannot then recall fully and accurately, and if the statement is in a writing which meets the following criteria:

1. It was made when the recorded fact actually occurred or was fresh in the witness's memory.
2. It was made by the witness, or under his or her direction, or by some other person to record the witness's statement at the time.
3. It is offered after the witness testifies that the statement he or she made was true.
4. It is offered after the writing is authenticated as an accurate record of the statement.

Prior Identification

Prior identification of a suspect as the perpetrator of a crime, made by a witness while the crime or a related occurrence was fresh in his memory, is also considered contemporaneous with the crime. Evidence of prior identification is admissible under an exception to the hearsay rule, whether the witness admits or denies the prior identification.

The prior identification statement must identify a person who participated in a crime or other occurrence, and must be offered as evidence after the witness's testimony about the identification. If the identifying witness contradicts a prior identification statement, the prior statement may be used to discredit his testimony at the trial. If the witness reaffirms the prior statement, it may be used as an earlier identification for its probative and rehabilitative value during the trial.[1]

Business Records

In the United States today the definition of a business includes every kind of business, governmental activity, profession, occupation, calling, or operation of institutions, whether carried on for profit or not. A business record may be

---

[1]*Judy* v. *State*, 218 Md. 168 (1958); *State* v. *Simmons*, 63 Wash. 2d 17 (1963).

admissible in criminal trials under an exception to the hearsay rule if it is in writing and meets the following requirements:

1. It was made in the regular course of business.
2. It was made at or near the time of the act, condition, or event recorded.
3. The custodian or some other qualified witness testifies to its identity and the mode of its preparation.
4. The sources of its information, and the method and time of preparation indicate trustworthiness.

The indicia of trustworthiness are important to investigators. The special reliability of business records is that they are based on the firsthand observation of someone whose job it is to know the facts and record them. The recorder's business role must involve observing and recording the event, circumstances, occurrence, or incident reported, and the record must be based on his personal knowledge or come from someone with a business duty to report to the recorder. For instance, police accident reports are not admissible under this rule because they are based on the personal knowledge of participants and witnesses who have no business duty to report to the police. They are admitted into evidence to show the event happened, not how it happened.

Evidence concerning the absence of an entry in business records is acceptable under an exception to the hearsay rule to prove the nonoccurrence of an act or event, or the nonexistence of a condition, when (1) in the normal course of that business all such acts, events, or conditions are recorded at or near the time they occur or exist; (2) such records are preserved; and (3) the sources of information and the method and time of preparation of the records of that business are such that the absence of a record is a trustworthy indication that the act or event did not occur or that the condition did not exist. Similarly, evidence concerning the absence of a public record or writing may be admissible under an exception to the hearsay rule when a public official, on demand, provides an authenticated certificate or its equivalent stating that he did not find a designated public record or writing after a diligent search.

Public Records

Official public records and writings made as a record of an act, event, or condition may be admissible under an exception to the hearsay rule when offered to prove the act, event, or condition. The records must be as follows:

1. They were made by a public employee acting within the scope of his duty.
2. They were made at or near the time of the act, event, or condition.
3. They were prepared by sources of information and at a time that indicates trustworthiness.

In certain public records there are also specific indicia of trustworthiness because of the nature of the public records involved. These are such records as the written finding of presumed death made by a federal employee authorized to make such findings pursuant to the Federal Missing Persons Act; official reports concerning birth, death, and marriage; and reports by a federal employee that a person is missing, captured, or the like.

Declarations against Interest

A declaration against interest is believed to have inherent trustworthiness because a reasonable person in the same position as the declarant would not have made the statement unless he believed it to be true. Every attempt must be made to bring the declarant into court to testify and allow the functioning of oath, observation, and cross-examination to test the statement for credibility and accuracy. However, a declaration against interest is usually admissible under an exception to the hearsay rule when the declarant has knowledge of the subject in issue, is not available as an in-court witness, and the statement—when made— was (1) so far contrary to the declarant's pecuniary or proprietary interest; or (2) so far subjected him to the risk of civil or criminal liability; or (3) so far tended to render invalid a claim by him against another; or (4) so far tended to create social disgrace, hatred, or ridicule for the declarant in the community that a reasonable man in his position would not have made the statement unless he believed it to be true.

Declarations against interest are considered more reliable than hearsay evidence admissible under the various other exceptions on the assumption that a reasonable person does not state facts in conflict with his or her own interests. Many states limit this exception. However, the basic assumption in most states is that declarations are not made against interests described as pecuniary or financial, or proprietary or property.

Statements of Co-Conspirators

An essential element of the crime of conspiracy is joint action by two or more persons. Therefore, all the participants in a criminal conspiracy are responsible for all the acts done during the conspiracy. Because of this concept of joint responsibility, the testimony of one conspirator about statements made by another conspirator may be admissible as an exception to the hearsay rule. A conspirator who admits his guilt prior to trial often agrees to cooperate with the prosecutor and testify against his fellow conspirators at their trial. This witness may testify about a statement made by a specified defendant during the conspiracy in which he and this defendant participated and for which this defendant is now on trial. Such testimony is admitted solely on the issue of guilt or innocence of the specified defendant, and the prosecution must establish a foundation of sufficient evidence to sustain a judicial conclusion that the conspiracy existed and that this defendant participated in it. When a person involved in a criminal conspiracy makes a written statement of guilt and implicates other conspirators but refuses to testify against them at their trial, the written statement may be admissible in place of the testimony of the reluctant witness.

Admissions and Confessions

Testimony concerning an admission by a person accused of crime may qualify under an exception to the hearsay rule if the admission is not prohibited on constitutional grounds. An authorized or adoptive admission, authorized by the party against whom it will be used or endorsed by his conduct, may also be admissible.

Under the Federal Rules of Evidence, an admission by a party opponent is not hearsay when the statement is offered against a party and is as follows:

1. It is his own statement, in either his individual or a representative capacity.
2. It is a statement of which he has manifested his adoption or belief in its truth.
3. It is a statement by a person authorized by him to make a statement concerning the subject.
4. It is a statement by his agent or servant concerning a matter within the scope of his agency or employment made during the existence of the relationship.
5. It is a statement by a co-conspirator of a party during the course and in furtherance of the conspiracy.[2]

These admissions are excluded from the category of hearsay evidence because their admissibility is more the result of the adversary system than of the satisfaction of the condition of hearsay rule. No guarantee of trustworthiness is necessary in the case of an admission.

Prior Statements—Witnesses

Witnesses who have not been unconditionally excused, and who have had a chance to explain or deny a contradictory statement, may be confronted with prior inconsistent statements to discredit testimony given at trial. When the credibility of a witness is attacked, such prior statements may be acceptable to show that their content is consistent with the trial testimony of the witness.

[2]Rule 801(d)(2), Federal Rules of Evidence.

Although the prior statements of witnesses are generally admissible under "exceptions to the hearsay rule," a problem comes up when the accused is the witness concerned. A defendant cannot be compelled to testify about his own guilt or innocence. A prior inconsistent statement may be admissible under an exception to the hearsay rule to impeach the defendant-witness, but only when the prior statement contradicts something he said under oath.

The Federal Rules of Evidence take a different direction concerning prior statements of witnesses.[3]

A statement is not hearsay if the declarant testifies at the trial or hearing and is subject to cross-examination concerning the statement and the statement is (a) inconsistent with his testimony, or (b) consistent with his testimony and is offered to rebut an express or implied charge against him of recent fabrication or improper influence or motive, or (c) one of identification of a person made after perceiving him.

The effect of this evidentiary change is to give such statements the status of substantive evidence, upon which a conviction may be based. In the U.S. Supreme Court case of *California* v. *Green,*[4] the California statute[5] which allowed such statements as substantive evidence was ruled constitutional and not a violation of the confrontation clause. In that case, the only witness to the crime (furnishing marijuana to a minor) made changes in his testimony from that given at a preliminary hearing and in a prior oral statement given to a police officer. The trial court, on the authority of the California statute, allowed the prosecution to introduce evidence of both the witness's testimony at the preliminary hearing and his oral (unsworn) statement to the police officer, both of which were inconsistent with his trial testimony. The witness's testimony at trial exculpated the defendant, and the evidence of his prior statements (preliminary hearing and oral statement to the officer) incriminated the defendant. The trial court instructed the jury members that they could base a conviction on the evidence of the witness's prior statements if they believed them rather than his trial testimony. The key to the court's ruling was that the witness was on the witness stand at trial and subject to examination by both parties and to personal observation by the jury.

Exceptions—Federal Rules

The Federal Rules of Evidence also set out new language for old exceptions and new concepts concerning hearsay evidence in an extensive list of exceptions to the hearsay rule. Exceptions to the hearsay rule in this listing are divided into

---

[3]Rule 801(d)(1), Federal Rules of Evidence.
[4]399 U.S. 149 (1970).
[5]California Evidence Code, Section 1235.

two categories (1) those in which the availability of the declarant is immaterial and (2) those in which the declarant is not available.

The following are exceptions which do not require the declarant to be available:

1. *Present Sense Impression*   This is a statement describing or explaining an event or condition made while the declarant was perceiving the event or condition, or immediately thereafter.

2. *Excited Utterance*   This is a statement relating to a startling event or condition made while the declarant was under the stress of excitement caused by the event or condition.

3. *Then Existing Mental, Emotional, or Physical Condition*   This is a statement of the declarant's then existing state of mind, emotion, sensation, or physical condition (such as intent, plan, motive, design, mental feeling, pain, and bodily health), but not including a statement of memory or belief to prove the fact remembered or believed unless it relates to the execution, revocation, identification, or terms of the declarant's will.

4. *Statements for Purposes of Medical Diagnosis or Treatment*   These are statements made for purposes of medical diagnosis or treatment and describing medical history, past or present symptoms, pain, or sensations, or the inception or general character of the cause or external source thereof insofar as reasonably pertinent to diagnosis or treatment.

5. *Recorded Recollection*   This is a memorandum or record concerning a matter about which a witness once had knowledge but now has insufficient recollection to enable him to testify fully and accurately, which is shown to have been made when the matter was fresh in his memory and to reflect that knowledge correctly. If admitted, the memorandum or record may be read into evidence but may not itself be received as an exhibit unless offered by an adverse party.

6. *Records of Regularly Conducted Activity*   These include a memorandum, report, record, or data compilation, in any form, of acts, events, conditions, opinions, or diagnoses made at or near the time by, or from, information transmitted by a person with knowledge, all in the course of a regularly conducted activity, as shown by the testimony of the custodian or other qualified witness, unless the sources of information or other circumstances indicate lack of trustworthiness.

7. *Absence of Entry in Records of Regularly Conducted Activity*   This takes into account evidence that a matter is not included in the memoranda, reports, records, or data compilations, in any form, of a regularly conducted activity, to prove the nonoccurrence or nonexistence of the matter if the matter was of a kind of which a memorandum, report, record, or data compilation was regularly made and preserved, unless the sources of information or other circumstances indicate lack of trustworthiness.

8. *Public Records and Reports*   These include records, reports, statements, or data compilations, in any form, of public offices or agencies that set forth (a) the activities of the office or agency; or (b) matters observed pursuant to a duty imposed by law; or (c) in civil cases and against the government in criminal cases, factual findings resulting from an investigation made pursuant to authority granted by law, unless the sources of information or other circumstances indicate lack of trustworthiness.

9. *Records of Vital Statistics*   These are records or data compilations, in any form, of births, fetal deaths, death, or marriages, if the report thereof was made to a public office pursuant to requirements of law.

10. *Absence of Public Record or Entry*   To prove the absence of a record, report, statement, or data compilation, in any form, or the nonoccurrence or nonexistence of a matter of which a record, report, statement, or data compilation, in any form, was regularly made and preserved by a public office or agency, evidence is needed in the form of a certification in accordance with Rule 902, or testimony is required that diligent search failed to disclose the record, report, statement, or data compilation, or entry.

11. *Records of Religious Organizations*   These include statements of births, marriages, divorces, deaths, legitimacy, ancestry, relationship by blood or marriage, or other similar facts of personal or family history, contained in a regularly kept record of a religious organizations.

12. *Marriage, Baptismal, and Similar Certificates*   These are statements of fact contained in a certificate that the maker performed a marriage or other ceremony or administered a sacrament, made by a clergyman, public official, or other person authorized by the rules or practices of a religious organization, or by law, to perform the act certified, and purporting to have been issued at the time of the act or within a reasonable time thereafter.

13. *Family Records*   These are statements of fact concerning personal or family history contained in family Bibles, genealogies, charts, engravings on rings, inscriptions on family portraits, engravings on urns, crypts, or tombstones, or the like.

14. *Records of Documents Affecting an Interest in Property*   These are records of documents purporting to establish or affect an interest in property, as proof of the content of the original recorded documents and their execution and delivery by each person by whom they purport to have been executed if the records are records of a public office and an applicable statute authorized the recording of documents of that kind in that office.

15. *Statements in Documents Affecting an Interest in Property*   These are statements contained in documents purporting to establish or affect an interest in property if the matter stated was relevant to the purpose of the documents, unless dealings with the property since the documents were made have been inconsistent with the truth of the statements or the purport of the documents.

16. *Statements in Ancient Documents*   These are statements in documents which have been in existence for twenty years or more and whose authenticity has been established.

17. *Market Reports, Commercial Publications*   These include market quotations, tabulations, lists, directories, or other published compilations, generally used and relied upon by the public or by persons in particular occupations.

18. *Learned Treatises*   Such treatises may be included to the extent that they are called to the attention of an expert witness upon cross-examination or relied upon by him in direct examination. Also included are pamphlets on a subject of history, medicine, or other science or art, established as a reliable authority by the testimony or admission of the witness or by other expert testimony or by judicial notice. If admitted, the statements may be read into evidence but may not be received as exhibits.

19. *Reputation Concerning Personal or Family History*   This refers to one's reputation among members of a family by blood, adoption, or marriage, or among one's associates, or in the community, concerning that person's birth, adoption, marriage, divorce, death, legitimacy, relationship by blood, adoption or marriage, ancestry, or other similar fact of personal or family history.

20. *Reputation Concerning Boundaries of General History*   This pertains to reputation in a community, arising before the controversy, as to boundaries of or customs affecting lands in the community, and reputation as to events of general history important to the community, or state, or nation in which located.

21. *Reputation as to Character*   This pertains to reputation of a person's character among his associates or in the community.

22. *Judgment of Previous Conviction*   This is evidence of a final judgment, entered after a trial or upon a plea of guilty (but not upon a plea of *nolo contendere*), adjudging a person guilty of a crime punishable by death or imprisonment in excess of one year, to prove any fact essential to sustain the judgment, but not including, when offered by the government in a criminal prosecution for purposes other than impeachment, judgments against persons other than the accused. The pendency of an appeal may be shown but does not affect admissibility.

23. *Judgment as to Personal, Family, or General History, or Boundaries*   These are judgments offered as proof of matters of personal, family, or general history, or boundaries, essential to the judgment if the same would be provable by evidence or reputation.

24. *Other Exceptions*   Into this category fall statements not specifically covered by any of the foregoing exceptions but having comparable circumstantial guarantees of trustworthiness.[6]

---

[6]Rule 803, Federal Rules of Evidence.

The exceptions to the hearsay rule that require the declarant to be unavailable are situations in which the declarant

1. Is exempted by ruling of the judge on the ground of privilege from testifying concerning the subject matter of his statement.
2. Persists in refusing to testify concerning the subject matter of his statement despite an order of the judge to do so.
3. Testifies to a lack of memory of the subject of his statement.
4. Is unable to be present or to testify at the hearing because of death or then existing physical or mental illness or infirmity.
5. Is absent from the hearing and the proponent of his statement has been unable to procure his attendance by process or other reasonable means.

A declarant is not unavailable as a witness if his exemption, refusal, claim of lack of memory, inability, or absence is due to the procurement or wrongdoing of the proponent of his statement for the purpose of preventing the witness from attending or testifying.[7]

The following are not excluded by the hearsay rule if the declarant is unavailable as a witness:

1. *Former Testimony* This is testimony given as a witness at another hearing of the same or a different proceeding, or in a deposition taken in compliance with law in the course of another proceeding, at the instance of or against a party with an opportunity to develop the testimony by direct, cross, or redirect examination, with motive and interest similar to those of the party against whom it is now offered.
2. *Statement of Recent Perception* This is a statement, not in response to the instigation of a person engaged in investigating, litigating, or settling a claim, which narrates, describes, or explains an event or condition recently perceived by the declarant, made in good faith, not in contemplation of pending or anticipated litigation in which he was interested, and while his recollection was clear.
3. *Statement Under Belief of Impending Death* This is a statement made by a declarant while believing that his death was imminent, concerning the cause or circumstances of what he believed to be his impending death.
4. *Statement Against Interest* This is a statement which was at the time of its making so far contrary to the declarant's pecuniary or proprietary interest, or so far tended to subject him to civil or criminal liability or to render invalid a claim by him against another or to make him an object of hatred, ridicule, or social disgrace, that a reasonable man in his position would not have made the statement unless he believed it to be true. A statement

---

[7]Rule 804(a), Federal Rules of Evidence.

tending to expose the declarant to criminal liability and offered to exculpate the accused is not admissible unless corroborated.

5. *Statement of Personal or Family History* This is either (a) a statement concerning the declarant's own birth, adoption, marriage, divorce, legitimacy, relationship by blood, adoption, or marriage, ancestry, or other similar fact of personal or family history, even though declarant had no means of acquiring personal knowledge of the matter stated or (b) a statement concerning the foregoing matters, and death also, of another person, if the declarant was related to the other by blood, adoption, or marriage or was so intimately associated with the other's family as to be likely to have accurate information concerning the matter declared.

6. *Other Exceptions* These include statements not specifically covered by any of the foregoing exceptions but having comparable circumstantial guarantees of trustworthiness.[8]

Hearsay Within Hearsay

There are other problems which arise in connection with hearsay. In the situation in which the hearsay declaration itself includes a further hearsay statement (hearsay within hearsay), the further hearsay should be admissible if it also conforms to the requirements of a hearsay exception. A hospital record that contains an entry of a patient's age based upon information furnished by his wife should be admissible as a regular hospital entry and the wife's statement qualifies as a statement of pedigree (if she is available), or as a statement made for the purpose of diagnosis or treatment. A dying declaration may incorporate a declaration against interest by another declarant.[9]

The opposing party may attack the credibility of the declarant just as if the declarant were a testifying witness.[10] Thus, character and conduct of declarant will be in issue as well as his prior conviction of crime when applicable. Inconsistent statements may also be introduced as impeachment even though there is no opportunity for the declarant to explain.[11]

Where the declarant is a witness, only prior inconsistent statements may be offered to impeach him. Where the declarant's statement is admitted, though hearsay, there is strong authority to allow both statements prior to and subsequent to the statement that was the subject of hearsay.[12]

---

[8]Rule 804(b), Federal Rules of Evidence.
[9]McCormack, Section 290, p. 611; Rule 805, Federal Rules of Evidence.
[10]Rule 806, Federal Rules of Evidence.
[11]Rule 613(b), Federal Rules of Evidence.
[12]McCormack 37, p. 69; 3 Wigmore, p. 1033; *People* v. *Rosoto* 58 Cal. 2d 304 (1962); *Carver* v. *U.S.* 164 U.S. 694 (1897); *People* v. *Hines* 287 N.Y. 93 (1940); California Evidence Code, Section 1202.

Case Studies

People v. *Bob,* 29 Cal. 321, 175 P. 2d 12 (1946).

Moore v. *Helm,* 562 F. Supp. 216 (1983).

United States v. *Pizarro,* 717 F. 2d 336 (1983).

Discussion Questions

1. How valid is the assumption that jurors have an inadequate opportunity to discover the truthfulness of a hearsay-declarant?
2. How would you define hearsay evidence?
3. Under what circumstances will the admission of hearsay evidence increase the chances of discovering truth in a criminal trial?
4. Proffered evidence, to be admissible under an exception to the hearsay rule, must meet the conditions of reliability and necessity. Explain.
5. Which are more reliable, declarations against interest or spontaneous and contemporaneous utterances? Why?
6. Why are prior statements of witnesses admissible as exceptions to the hearsay rule?
7. Define "unavailability of a witness" under the Federal Rules of Evidence.

Glossary

Best Evidence Rule   The best evidence of the content of writing is the writing itself.

Conspiracy (Criminal)   A combination of two or more persons for the purpose of committing by joint effort an unlawful act or using unlawful means for the commission of a lawful act.

Declarant   A person who makes a declaration (statement).

Nolo Contendere   No contest; designation of a plea in a criminal action having the legal effect of a guilty plea but which cannot be used elsewhere as an admission.

Privileged Communication   A communication between persons in a confidential relationship who are under a special obligation of fidelity and secrecy, and which the law will not allow to be divulged (or inquired into) for the sake of public policy: husband and wife, attorney and client, and so on.

CHAPTER 7

Opinion Evidence

CHAPTER OBJECTIVES

- To describe and define opinion evidence, with its relationship to testimony given by a witness from personal observation or under an exception to the hearsay rule, and to the introduction into evidence of articles and exhibits.
- To develop the expertise factor as comparable to the personal knowledge requirement of lay witnesses.
- To explore the in-court methodology of qualifying expert witnesses.

The ultimate issue in a criminal trial is the defendant's guilt or innocence. The trier of fact, juror or judge in nonjury trials, must reach a conclusion about this ultimate issue from the evidence produced in court. Witnesses are usually asked to confine their testimony to facts within their knowledge and are not allowed to express their opinions or conclusions because this would usurp the role of juror or judge. There is a logical problem in distinguishing an observed and reported "fact" from an opinion or conclusion. The process of perceiving, recalling, and reporting involves a person's belief in what he observed and this is akin to an opinion or conclusion. Whether testimony is "fact" or opinion is a decision for the trial judge, subject to postconviction review by appellate courts.

When a witness's opinion or conclusion is necessary to provide the triers of fact with data useful in their decision making, such testimony may be admitted under an exception to the general rule.[1] Exceptions to the rule barring opinion evidence are broadly classified under four major headings. They are as follows:

1. Any witness—when necessary to summarize a total or collective event.
2. Any witness—when questioned about a matter not amenable to the report-of-an-observer technique.
3. Witnesses who possess a special knowledge through experience—when non-expert testimony is necessary in an area of special knowledge related to the defendant, such as a particular business or occupation, or some point in issue.

[1]Rule 701, Federal Rules of Evidence

4. Witnesses qualified by education and experience as experts, when such expertise is necessary.

Subject matter that is nonprofessional or is commonly known may not be the subject of expert opinion. An expert may state his opinion only on matters within his expertise. It would be improper for an expert to render an opinion as to whether a train stopped long enough to discharge passengers at a station. An "expert" could not express an opinion as to whether a suspect can be recognized by the flash of his pistol.

Neither a lay witness nor an expert will be allowed to testify to matters which call for a conclusion of law.

Nonexperts

Lay witnesses are divided into two general categories—the real nonexpert and the person with some special knowledge or qualification.

The nonexpert lay witness can express an opinion about areas of common knowledge, such as

1. Drunkenness or sobriety
2. Emotional aspects of appearance and conduct
3. Age
4. Speed, distance, and size (from observation)
5. Identity based on physical characteristics and voice

A nonexpert witness, however, is not permitted to guess or speculate about what another person thought or intended. He may not give a supposed reason for another's action or observable attitude.

The lay witness with limited expertise may, after he is shown to have the qualifications or opportunity necessary for forming a valid opinion, be asked for his opinion in the area of his special knowledge or qualifications. These areas usually include (1) value of the witness's services and property, (2) handwriting the witness can recognize, (3) sanity of an intimate acquaintance, and (4) character.

The scope of lay witness opinions permitted by law varies from one jurisdiction to another, but the words of California's Evidence Code sum up the general requirements for admitting this type of testimony: "If a witness is not testifying as an expert, his testimony in the form of an opinion is limited to such an opinion as is permitted by law, including but not limited to an opinion that is (a) rationally based on the perception of the witness, (b) helpful to a clear understanding of his testimony."[2]

---

[2]California Evidence Code, Section 800.

Basis for Nonexpert Testimony   Of course, cross-examination about details of the observations that form the basis for an opinion is proper. Even on direct examination, the witness may be asked to give the reasons for his opinion and the data on which his opinion is based. Before allowing a witness to offer an opinion, the trial judge may require an examination concerning the matter used as a basis for the opinion, to determine whether some provision of law forbids the use of such a basis for the proffered opinion.

The court may, and upon objection must, exclude opinion testimony that is based, in whole or in significant part, on matter that is not a proper basis for such an opinion. In such cases, the witness may, if there remains a proper basis for his opinion, then state his opinion after excluding from consideration the matter determined to be improper.

Experts—Qualifications

An expert may give an opinion within his area of expertise as a means of enriching the triers of fact with his special knowledge. The expert helps the triers of fact to understand areas not within the common knowledge of nonexperts. The basic test of the need for an expert is whether his special expertise will be helpful to the jury in understanding the evidence or determining a fact in issue.[3] The experts' opinion is advisory, no more.

The jury must decide how much credibility to award an expert witness and how much weight to give his testimony in reaching a verdict, just as it is expected to evaluate all the evidence it receives. An expert witness may be asked about the compensation and expenses paid (or to be paid) to him, and whether he was appointed by the court or called by a party. This may help the jury evaluate the witness' credibility and decide how much weight to give to his testimony.

If the triers of fact believe expert testimony is incorrect, they may disregard it. In California, the trial judge is required to instruct jurors about experts and their testimony. Such instruction must be made part of the judge's charge to the jury in any criminal proceeding during which an expert is allowed to express his opinion while testifying. These instructions are generally given as follows:

> A person is qualified to testify as an expert if he has special knowledge, skill, experience, training or education sufficient to qualify him as an expert on the subject to which his testimony relates. Duly qualified experts may give their opinions on questions in controversy at a trial. To assist you in deciding such questions, you may consider the opinion with the reasons cited, if any, by the expert who gives the opinion. You should give an expert opinion the weight to which you find it to be entitled, but you are not bound to accept it as conclusive. If you find any such opinion to be unreasonable, you may disregard it.

[3] Rule 702, Federal Rules of Evidence.

Experts must be qualified in court. That is, they must be questioned under oath so that the trial judge may rule on their competence as experts. Knowledge qualifies an expert. His knowledge is usually shown to be based on both experience and study, but the study need not be formal training or be marked by any significant achievement. However, in scientific areas related to an academic discipline, it is desirable that the expert have at least a basic degree in his chosen field. Advanced degrees, teaching assignments, and publications support an expert's claim of special knowledge. The basic qualification required of an expert witness is that he satisfy the trial judge that he is an expert. He should be shown to have skill, experience, training, and education in the area of expertise he will testify about. If one of the parties objects that an expert is not qualified, his special knowledge must be shown before the witness may testify as an expert, but a witness's special knowledge may be shown by any admissible evidence, including his own testimony.

Recently, the Supreme Court appeared to lower the threshold for admissibility of scientific evidence. In reviewing the appropriate standard for the admission of scientific evidence, the Court held that only the Federal Rules of Evidence should be used to determine whether scientific evidence was admissible. In so doing, the Court cast aside the prior standard enunciated in *Frye* v. *United States*, 293 F. 1013 (1923), which required a showing that the expert opinion was based on scientific evidence generally accepted in the relevant scientific community.[4]

The Federal Rules of Evidence allow the use of scientific, technical, or other specialized knowledge if it will assist the trier of fact to understand the evidence.[5]

This is not to say that all experts can now claim to testify on the basis of scientific knowledge, for the Court cautioned that the trial judge will still have to make the preliminary assessment of whether the expert is relying on "scientific knowledge." In making that assessment, though, the trial judge need only find the scientific theory or technique is reliable and relevant to the issue at hand.

The practical effect of *Daubert* will likely result in forensic evidence developed by emerging technologies, such as DNA, facing a less rigid standard for admissibility at criminal trials.

Objections to the qualifications of an expert may be based on the credibility of his claims of expertise, as well as on the application of the proffered witness's special knowledge to his expected testimony. The objecting party may claim he is not an expert, or that he does not have the expert qualifications for the particular subject matter in issue at the trial.

Questions to develop the qualifications of an expert witness may proceed along the following lines:

Q: Your occupation, sir?

A: Physician and surgeon.

[4]Daubert v. *Merril Dow Pharmaceutical, Inc*, 113 S. Ct., 2786 (1993)
[5]Rule 702, Federal Rules of Evidence.

Q: Are you licensed to practice in this state?

A: I am.

Q: And when were you licensed, Doctor?

A: 1937, I believe.

Q: At the present time do you occupy any official position in this county?

A: I am one of the autopsy surgeons for the county coroner.

Q: How long have you held that position?

A: Over ten years.

Q: What are your educational qualifications, doctor?

A: I have a B.S. and an M.D. degree. The B.S. is from the University of California, and the M.D. is from St. Louis University.

Q: Now, doctor, what duties does your position as autopsy surgeon entail?

A: My duties are investigating causes of death of deceased persons that are brought to the coroner's office.

Q: And you develop, conduct autopsies and postmortem examinations, do you?

A: I do.

Q: Now, doctor, on the 22nd of June of this year, did you have occasion to perform an autopsy examination on the body of _____?

A: I did.

A more involved direct examination and aggressive cross-examination is likely when the expert is to testify in an uncommon area. The following transcript of a successful effort to qualify a psychologist as an interpreter of lie detection tapes on the issue of the mental condition of a subject-defendant in a murder trial illustrates this.

Direct Examination

(By _____, counsel appearing in behalf of the defendant.)

Q: Your name is Hudson Jost?

A: Right.

Q: Where do you live, Mr. Jost?

A: Tempe, Arizona.

Q: And you are temporarily, or at least you came today, or came yesterday from Chicago?

A: Yes, that's right.

Q: Now, Mr. Jost, would you relate what your educational background is, sir?

A: My training was all at the University of Chicago. I had two years in a small college in the Midwest, went to the University of Chicago in 1933, received my Ph.D. there in 1940.

Q: What was your Ph.D. in, sir?

A: My Ph.D is in the biological sciences with a major in psychology.

Q: And was your other educational background, was there anything in your other educational background concerning psychology?

A: Yes, my undergraduate major was psychology.

Q: And what has been your professional experience since 1940?

A: After 1940 I worked a year or so at the Institute for Juvenile Research. Then I was an instructor at the Gary Junior College. I then went to Antioch College, Yellow Spring, Ohio, as an assistant professor in psychology, also working at the Phells Research Institute. Then I went back to Chicago for a year as a research associate.

Q: Was that in the field of psychology?

A: That was in the field of psychology. Then I was associate professor in the Department of Psychiatry, University of Tennessee College of Medicine from 1945 to 1952. From 1952 to 1959 I was professor of psychology at the University of Georgia and head of the psychology department. In 1959 I went to Arizona State University as professor of psychology and chairman of the department.

Q: All right. Now, Dr. Jost, do you have any membership in any professional associations?

A: I'm a Fellow in Division Three of the American Psychological Association— this is a division of experimental psychology; in Division Six of the American Psychological Association, which is the division of physiological psychology. Fellow in the American Association for the Advancement of Science; member of the Arizona Psychological Association; and some others which I don't think are important at this time.

Q: And during the course of your professional career in psychology, have you had occasion to publish any works or studies in that field?

A: I have published between twenty-five and thirty articles in the area of psychology, primarily in the area of physiological psychology.

Q: And have you on any occasion prior to today testified in the courts of any state in the United States in the field of psychology?

A: Yes, I have testified in the courts of Georgia and Tennessee, in the area of electroencephalography, which is a branch of my work, and in Massachusetts in the area of the polygraph.

Q: You have previously then testified in courts concerning the polygraph?

A: Yes, that's true.

Q: Now, during the course of your professional career, have you made any special studies which would relate physical reactions to mental illness or disorder?

A: Yes, this has been one of the primary areas of all of my research. The area of physiological psychology is one. This is an attempt to understand the relationship between physiological reactivity and what we might call mental states or intelligence, or behavior would probably be a better word. And these studies have indicated that the physiological reactivity of an organism is related to the behavior of the organism. There is no question about this.

Q: In what specific fields in physiological psychology have you made special studies, Dr. Jost?

A: My area of interest has primarily been in the autonomic nervous system. This is the nervous system which is primarily related to emotional reactivity.

Q: When did you begin your studies in the field of physiological psychology?

A: This began around 1936 or 1937, when I was searching for a problem for my dissertation. I was working at the University of Chicago. There were no commercial polygraphs available at that time. They weren't being manufactured. So it was necessary for us, Dr. Mandel Sherman and myself, to build our own polygraph similar to the ones that are available now except we used a photographic recording device rather than pens that are now being used.

THE COURT: Rather than what, Doctor?

THE WITNESS: The ink recordings now being used.

Q: And you began that work in that field in the, approximately, the late '30s?

A: In the late '30s.

Q: Now, I think you say that you have made special studies in the field relating to reaction on the polygraph to mental illnesses or disorders?

After several questions probing this expert's publications and research in this area, the counsel for the defense relinquished the witness for *voir dire* examination by the prosecutor—a necessary preliminary to any further questioning.

VOIR DIRE EXAMINATION

(By _____, counsel appearing in behalf of the prosecution.)

Q: Doctor, have you ever taken any formal courses in polygraph work of any kind?

A: No. I got into the field before there were any schools available for this.

Q: But since that, I understand that's true, you started out with your own homemade machine.

A: Yes.

Q: But have you taken this work in polygraph?

A: No, I haven't, I have taught at the schools, however. I taught at the Keeler School from 1952 to 1954, I believe I taught the psychology section at the Keeler School.

Q: How many tests have you run on polygraphs, approximately, would you have any idea?

A: Hundreds.

Q: And those would be for different purposes, would they not?

A: Oh, yes, they were all experimental runs.

Q: Did you do any tests for purposes of determining deception?

A: Only very indirectly. I don't consider myself qualified in this particular area.

Q: You don't feel that you are qualified to read polygrams—

A: Oh, yes.

Q: Just a minute. And determine therefrom whether or not there is a pattern of deception?

A: Oh, yes, I am able to do that, but I don't consider that my main responsibility.

Q: You say that most of your testing in the area of the polygraph has been done in the area of research?

A: Right.

Q: Or in conjunction with your research?

A: Right.

Q: When you state that you tested—Well, I believe I will save that for cross-examination. That's all I have.

Experts—Opinion Testimony

Even after a witness has been qualified as an expert, his opinion testimony is limited. Expert opinion testimony is usually accepted if it meets the following tests:

1. The testimony is related to a subject that is sufficiently beyond common experience that the opinion of an expert would assist the trier of fact.

2. The testimony is based on matter (including the expert's special knowledge, skill, experience, training, and education) perceived by, or personally known to, the witness, or made known to him at or before the hearing. The matter does not have to be admissible, but it must be of a type that may reasonably be relied on by an expert in forming an opinion on the subject to which his testimony relates and not matter an expert is precluded by law from using as a basis for his opinion.

The many areas of expertise, and the wide range of subjects on which an expert's opinion may be sought, may force the expert to rely on reports, statements, and other data which might not be admissible at trial. This is proper if he bases his opinion on data that would be relied on by other experts in forming an opinion in the subject area involved.

In criminal trials, expert testimony may embrace all the arts and sciences but is usually given in the general areas of criminalistics, the medicolegal field, traffic accident reconstruction, engineering, finance, mathematics, and the behavioral sciences.

Older theory, case law, and statutes contained rules against allowing witnesses to express opinions on the ultimate issues. The reasoning behind this prohibition was to prevent the witness from usurping the province of the jury. Contemporary law and court decision tend to abandon this restrictive rule and allow an otherwise properly admitted opinion to embrace an ultimate issue to be decided by the trier of fact. In an abortion case an opinion on the issue of whether the abortion was performed for the preservation of life was admissible: "there was no other practicable way of framing the questions if they were to serve the purpose of obtaining the benefit of the witnesses' expert knowledge as to matters on which enlightenment of the jury by the expert was proper."[6]

In criminalistics, the expert witness is expected to offer his opinion about the identifying characteristics of some item of physical evidence. His opinion must necessarily be based on his examination of the evidence and various physical and chemical tests he may have made. As a general rule, the criminalist must testify about the basis for his opinion before stating his beliefs or conclusions.

Criminalistics is synonymous with forensic science. The British criminalist H. J. Walls summarizes the growth and identifies the origin of forensic science in a few well-chosen though unusual words: "The pedigree of forensic science, as it is practiced today, is by forensic medicine out of police work."[7] Criminalistics has a related field of on-the-scene evidence technology. Evidence technicians or scenes-of-crime officers now process crime scenes for physical evidence such as weapons, fingerprints, and other traces. They often help to connect the evidence examined by criminalists with the crime scene and to offer testimony about the integrity of the scientific means used to collect the evidence.

Medicolegal experts also testify about the basis for their opinions. This area of forensic medicine covers opinions about injuries, wounds, suspected weapons, and death. Medicolegal opinions must be prefaced by testimony about the medicolegal examinations they are based on.

An expert in the area of traffic accident reconstruction may give his opinion after he is shown to have examined the accident scene and usually one or more of the vehicles involved.

---

[6]*People* v. *Wilson*, 25 Cal. 2d 343 (1944); *Clifford-Jacobs* v. *Industrial Comm.* 19 Ill. 2d 236 (1960); *Dowling* v. *Shattuck, Inc.* 91 N.H. 234 (1941); *Schwieger* v. *Solbeck* 191 Ore. 454 (1951).
[7]H. J. Walls, *Forensic Science* (New York: Praeger, 1968), p. 1.

Other experts may have no personal knowledge on which to base a specific opinion. They may gain such knowledge by sitting in court and listening to the testimony of witnesses. They may take the witness stand and answer a hypothetical question based on facts which have become part of the court record through the testimony of previous witnesses.

In the first instance, on direct examination, the expert witness is asked whether he was in court and heard all of certain testimony given by a specific witness or specified witnesses. The expert's "yes" answer "places" the exact portion of previous in-court testimony which he will use as a basis for his opinion. This gives the court and the triers of fact a means of evaluating the expert's opinion for scope and credibility.

The hypothetical question sets out the exact limits of previous evidence on which the expert may base his opinion. In phrasing this question, the direct examiner uses only facts which are part of the trial record. However, he need not use all of them. The hypothetical question spells out or summarizes the facts forming the basis for the expert's opinion.

An example of the testimony of an expert witness who has listened to in-court evidence is contained in the testimony of Dr. Jost, qualified as an expert in the field of polygraph tests and psychology.

Q: Now, Dr. Jost, did you receive from me a month or so ago a reproduction of three polygraph charts?

A: Right, I did.

Q: I want to show you—And did those polygraph charts purport to be charts on a person named Barry Sigal?

A: Right.

Q: I want to show you Defendant's Exhibits D-1, which is a Peak of Tension test, D-2 and D-3, which are Relevant-Irrelevant tests. This is D-1, and D-2, and D-3.

A: Yes.

Q: And ask you if those appear to be the originals of the reproductions which I sent you?

A: I'm sure they are, yes.

Q: Now, did I also send you, Dr. Jost—By the way, you were here during my reading of the testimony of Sergeant K. E. Campbell?

A: Right.

Q: Did I send you, also, the material generally that I read here in front of this jury?

A: Yes.

Q: The questions and answers and the critical questions as testified to by Mr. Campbell?

A: Yes, I saw those.

Q: Did you make a study of these charts?

A: Yes, I did.

Q: Were you able to form any opinion—from the charts and the material that I submitted to you based upon Sergeant Campbell's testimony from the charts that you saw, of which those are the originals, and the material that I gave to you based on Sergeant Campbell's testimony—relative to the mental condition of the individual whose reactions were recorded on that chart, on those charts?

In his response to this question, the witness gave his expert opinion that the defendant had a mental disorder, and then answered questions which justified his use of the polygraph charts to ascertain the characteristic physical reactions of the defendant (while being tested for deception by Sergeant Campbell) which led to his conclusion.

A: Yes, I spent quite a bit of time going over these in comparing them with charts which I had obtained on populations before, and these charts are very similar to those which were obtained on psychotic individuals.

An illustration of the hypothetical question is taken from a case, *People* v. *McCaughan*,[8] where the cause of death was in question, and the determination of whether death was a result of the defendant's act was a crucial issue. The prosecuting attorney, after the usual questions qualifying the witness as a physician-expert, asked the following hypothetical question:

Q: If a person is sitting on a chair, and her head is held back by the hair of her head so that her face is looking up towards the ceiling—also, her arms are being held, and another person is sitting on her lap—and then an amount of food is placed into the person's mouth, and she is resisting the—and then a towel is placed over her mouth and her nose is also being held for a period of time, and then the person slumps over and thereafter expires, and approximately four heaping tablespoons of food is found lodged in the trachea; now, Doctor, based upon this hypothetical question, what would be the case of death, Doctor?

A: The cause of death would be due to asphyxia, caused by obstruction of the trachea with food.

When a hypothetical question is used in a trial, the trial judge, in his charge, will usually instruct the jury as follows:

In examining an expert witness, counsel may use a type of question known as a hypothetical question. The witness is asked to assume to be true a

---

[8] 49 Cal. 2d 409 (1957).

hypothetical state of facts, and to give an opinion based on that assumption. In accepting such a question, the court does not rule or necessarily find that all the assumed facts in this question have been proved. The court only determines that those assumed facts are within the probable or possible range of the evidence. It is for you, the jury, to ascertain from all the evidence whether or not the assumed facts in a hypothetical question have been proved. If you should find that any assumption in such a question has not been proved, you are to determine the effect of that failure of proof on the value and weight of the expert opinion.

Experts—Cross-Examination

Specific Attack Areas   Opposing counsel can probe the scientific principle and methodology involved in the experts' opinion during cross-examination. An expert witness may be cross-examined as any other witness is. He may also be fully cross-examined as to (1) his qualifications, (2) the subject of his expert testimony, and (3) the matter his opinion is based on and the reasons for his opinion.

A witness usually may not be cross-examined about the content or tenor of any scientific, technical, or professional text, treatise, journal, or similar publication that he has not referred to, considered, or relied on in forming his opinion, unless the publication has been admitted in evidence.

A science book may be admitted as evidence during cross-examination to prove an opinion contained in the book, or to contradict the opinion of the witness, but only when the witness refers to it as an authority in his testimony. A standard cross-examination question is whether the witness considers a certain book to be a recognized and standard, authoritative text on the subject of his opinion or on any portion of it. When the witness admits a text is a standard work in the field, the cross-examiner directs the attention of the witness to an opinion in the text which contradicts the opinion of the expert. The trial judge will not allow this line of questioning to prove the textual opinion but will allow it as bearing on the weight the triers of fact should give to the expert's testimony.

If an expert witness is allowed to give an opinion based, in whole or in part, on the opinion or statement of another person, the other person may be called and cross-examined about the opinion or statement relied on by the first witness.

General Attack Area: Bias or Interest   Experts may also be attacked on the basis of interest or bias. A cross-examiner can often destroy an expert witness by a line of questioning which will identify him as a paid witness. The state's criminalistics experts are vulnerable to questions designed to show that the criminalist is a salaried witness. Although a salary scheme seems to have more integrity than the fees of nonsalaried experts, the scheme has weaknesses when a cross-examiner probes whether the criminalist has ever testified for the defense, or against the police. This line of questioning puts the witness in a difficult situation. He works for the police or the prosecutor. He is an employee of a law enforcement agency.

He is paid a salary, and he hardly ever testifies for a defendant. Some defense experts are vulnerable to the same type of attack. That is, that they have always testified for and been paid by the defense.

Case Studies

Ramsey v. *Virginia*, 200 Va. 245, 105 SE 2d 155 (1958).

Wetherill v. *University of Chicago*, 565 F. Supp. 1553 (1983).

Ernst v. *Ace Motor Sales, Inc.*, 550 F. Supp. 1220 (1982).

Discussion Questions

1. What is the difference between a "fact" and an "opinion"?
2. Who may give opinion evidence? When?
3. To what opinions may experts testify?
4. To what opinions may nonexperts testify?
5. How are experts "qualified" to testify?
6. What are the limits on expert testimony in your jurisdiction?
7. How may experts be attacked by opposing counsel?
8. Why are answers to hypothetical questions a weak type of evidence?

Glossary

Criminalistics The application of science to the examination of physical evidence; linked to forensic science, the general application of science to the solution of crimes. Evidence technicians represent a subclassification of this field.

DNA "Fingerprinting" Every human being possesses a unique genetic code. Forty-six chromosomes are used to hold the code and these are made of the chemical DNA (Deoxyribonucleic acid). Scientists can examine evidential material (bloodstains, hair roots, semen, vaginal fluid) and read the genetic code of an individual. With the exception of identical twins, DNA "fingerprinting" (profiling) can be used for the elimination or association of suspects with a crime victim or a crime scene.

Experts Capable of being qualified in court as expert witnesses: men and women of science educated in art or science, or persons possessing special or unusual knowledge acquired from practical experience.

Forensic Related to courts of justice.

Judicial Instructions A charge to the jury by trial judge; instructions as to the principles of law in a case and their application to the circumstances of the case being tried.

Voir Dire In-court preliminary examination of juror or witness when competency, interest, etcetera, is in dispute.

CHAPTER 8

Articles and Exhibits of Evidence

CHAPTER OBJECTIVES

- To discuss issues surrounding articles and exhibits of evidence.
- To define real evidence with a focus on physical evidence and its utility in court. Associative evidence is also explored, as is the concept of the transfer of things and traces from or to a crime scene or suspect.
- To examine the role of nontestimonial evidence in the identification of persons.
- To examine the nature of documentary evidence, and to explore the best evidence and parol evidence rules.
- To show how mute articles or exhibits of evidence can communicate when they are viewed in court and are linked to testimonial evidence.
- To define videotaping as a most promising means of producing compelling evidence at trial.

Real, demonstrative, objective, or autopsic evidence consists of tangible items submitted as exhibits or articles for inspection which can be personally scrutinized by the judge or jury. Submission of tangible evidence by either party to a criminal proceeding calls for a belief or conclusion, but the fact-finder is not asked to believe that certain facts are true on the sole basis of any witness's testimony. The triers of fact can use their own sense of observation and perception in evaluating the exhibits and articles of evidence submitted to them. Testimonial evidence is necessary, however, to introduce and identify the exhibit or article, and to relate its connection with the issue.

Exhibits and articles of evidence may be either persons or things that can be produced in court and seen. They are exhibitive or demonstrative. Decisions about admitting this type of evidence are made by the trial judge. Persons or articles shown to the triers of fact should be connected with the crime in issue. Their admissibility depends on the circumstances under which they are proffered.

Tangible evidence may be admitted to illustrate the crime or the transaction on which the charge of crime is based. Tangible evidence includes (1) the fruits of crime, such as the stolen property in theft cases; (2) the instrumentalities or agencies of crime, such as burglar's tools or an assailant's weapons; (3) contraband, such as drugs and illegal weapons; and (4) other articles of evidential value.

Physical Evidence

Physical evidence is a term developed by police investigators and criminalists to describe a tangible "thing"—in solid, liquid or gaseous form—or a "trace" which can be scientifically examined in a laboratory. In the application of scientific techniques to the problems of crime and criminals, the term "physical evidence" is used to describe articles of evidence which can be the subject of scientific inspection.

The main purpose of a police search of a crime scene is to look for clues and evidence as to what happened at the time of the crime and who committed the crime. It is a selective searching for objects, materials, things, and traces. The police may locate and collect various items of evidence at the crime scene which may reveal a suspect's opportunity to commit a crime, identity, and possible motive. Police procedures in this portion of the investigation require a continuing chain of searching for and possessing evidence all the way from finding to introduction in court. Such evidence is usually associated with reports (and expected testimony) of expert criminalists who have processed the physical evidence by applying various scientific tests.

One of the major thrusts of discovery procedures by the defense counsel is to secure information about the physical evidence in a case—where it was found and any reports made of an examination. Defense attorneys may supplement the information about physical evidence by discussing the item or items of evidence with their client. The frequent discussions with the defendant about the case may develop evidence which will indicate some inadequacy of the police search, or offer a reasonable explanation which is not connected with the crime for the damaging implications of the item or items of evidence.

In criminal homicide cases, the autopsy report of the postmortem examination of the victim is aligned more with the area of physical evidence than it is with testimonial evidence despite the fact that the surgeon doing the examination testifies at trial to the details of the autopsy. The findings of these medicolegal experts are available to defense counsel prior to trial upon appropriate discovery procedures, and they usually contain sufficient detail to afford an opportunity to examine the circumstances of death. While any part of this report is of interest to the defense, the cause of death and the nature of wounds are of prime importance.

The mute testimony of the objects, materials, things, and traces that comprise physical evidence, plus the testimony of the officer discovering such evidence, and the testimony of an expert criminalist who processes it, can have a tremendous impact on the triers of fact, even though the legal significance of the evidence may be no more than supportive or corroborative of other evidence. This may be particularly true of the testimony of the autopsy surgeon in criminal homicides.

Traditionally, attacks by the defense on the introduction of physical evidence have been concentrated upon the circumstances of its finding, its nature, the chain of possession, and the qualifications of the expert witness involved. Defense attorneys also closely examine the circumstances for indications of blatant perjury and distortion of facts. Defense counsel have pursued inquiry into whether the appropriate scientific examinations were made and whether these tests were properly carried out.

Associative Evidence

Associative evidence is a nonlegal term for physical evidence which has been examined by an expert criminalist and which may be used for evidence through comparison. The theory of association is inherent in the concept of transfer evidence: Some thing or trace is both left at the crime scene and carried away from it by the criminal. Associative evidence is developed when expert examination reveals a relationship between (1) physical evidence found at the crime scene, and (2) apparently similar evidence located on the person of the suspect, his clothing, home, or automobile. A bullet recovered from a homicide victim is found to match a bullet fired from a weapon found on an arrestee at the time of arrest. A unique shoeprint found at a crime scene, adequately identified as the footprint of the crime's perpetrator, is shown to match the prints of shoes owned by the defendant. A strangely shaped bludgeon is suspected of causing the multiple wounds in a murder case, and a hammer with a strangely shaped head is found in the trunk of a suspect's car upon arrest. Autopsy surgeons say this weapon caused the victim's wounds.

A major objective of the science of criminalistics is the identification of physical evidence. An item of evidence is placed in a certain class or "set" and then its uniqueness is developed. The goal is to identify qualities that set the item apart from other items within the class or set—to "individualize" it within reasonable limits of probability. Once physical evidence is thus individualized, other suspect materials can be tested for the traditional "match"—identification. This aspect of criminalistics has contributed to the growing use of associative evidence in criminal trials.

Quite frequently, the associative items of evidence are sufficiently similar to give the result of the comparison analysis sound probative force—particularly when it is the expressed opinion of the expert that a "match" has been discovered.

Associative evidence, when properly demonstrated as an exhibit (alone or supplemented by the opinion of an expert), is beyond the realm of opinion evidence and emerges as a new concept in the truly physical demonstrative field.

Body Examination Evidence

Nontestimonial evidence related to the person of a suspect or accused person can be classified in two broad groups: identifying and incriminating.

There is a unique quality of identification in body evidence. Any eyewitness who views suspects in a police lineup is examining real evidence—the person and appearance of the individuals in the lineup. A suspect or prisoner may be asked to speak for identification, and the resulting sounds can also be categorized as real evidence. The physiological process of speaking is an observable, physical, and quite distinctive characteristic. Handwriting samples can be compared with suspect handwriting for the purpose of identification. Blood may serve to identify a body abnormality such as alcohol in the blood. Hair, nail scrapings, the residue of firearms use, and similar physical evidence may also help in identification after processing by criminalists in police laboratories.

The main problems in searching for and retrieving body evidence involve discovering the evidence and preventing its destruction. Body evidence is frequently concealed in the human body. Such evidence has been recovered from the mouths of suspects, from the rectums of prisoners, and an attempt has been made to retrieve contraband from the stomach of an arrested person.[1]

It might appear that a suspect or prisoner would be protected from these intrusions by the Fifth Amendment's guarantee against self-incrimination, but body evidence has been defined as nontestimonial.[2] The privilege against self-incrimination does not protect the suspect or defendant from being compelled, in appropriate circumstances, (1) to submit to fingerprinting, photography or measurements; (2) to write or speak for identification; (3) to appear in court; or (4) to stand, to assume a stance, or walk, or to make a particular gesture.[3]

Eyewitness Evidence of Identification

Identification by eyewitnesses to a crime involves using the body of the person viewed as an item of evidence. This is real evidence in use, and it is direct evidence of prime importance when it places the defendant at the crime scene.

Every precaution should be taken by investigators not to ruin the legal significance of eyewitness identification by substandard pretrial investigative techniques. Among these precautions are (1) recognizing that the post-indictment police lineup is a "critical stage" of the pretrial procedure against a person accused of crime, and (2) not letting eyewitnesses view photographs of suspects that a reviewing court might consider "suggestive."

[1]*Rochin* v. *California*, 342 U.S. 165 (1952).
[2]*Schmerber* v. *California*, 384 U.S. 757 (1966).
[3]*United States* v. *Wade*, 388 U.S. 218 (1967).

The cases that developed these guidelines for police were *United States* v. *Wade*, and *Kirby* v. *Illinois*.[4] The *Kirby* case limited the requirements in *Wade* to lineups after the indictment against the defendant has been filed in court. Thus, a preindictment lineup was not deemed by the supreme court in *Kirby* as a critical stage of the proceedings. In a later case, *United States* v. *Ash*,[5] the court redefined the term *critical stage of the proceedings* by saying that it pertains "when there is a physical confrontation with the accused at which he requires aid in coping with legal problems or helping in meeting his adversaries." Using this definition, the court in *Ash* approved the viewing of photographs of the defendant and others for the purpose of identification by witnesses after the indictment was filed in court against the defendant.

After the *Wade* decision, police procedures provided for defense counsel at lineups so that attorneys could observe the lineup and identification procedures in each case in which the defendant refused to waive such attendance. During the period between *Wade, Kirby*, and *Ash*, defense attorneys, by their presence, comments, suggestions, and protests of prejudicial lineup procedures, served to update and improve those procedures to the point that a court attack based upon the "unfair" lineup was virtually precluded. If the effect of *Kirby* and *Ash* is to again keep defense attorneys out of the lineup procedure, police and prosecutors should expect in-court attacks on "unfair" lineup proceedings to increase significantly. The California Supreme Court has apparently placed the restriction of silence and observation on attorneys at a police lineup.[6]

Unless the right to an attorney in a post-indictment lineup is intelligently waived, the prisoner and his counsel must be present at the lineup. When the attorney is present he can effectively reconstruct or prevent any unfairness that may occur at the lineup and use any unfairness as a basis for attacking the credibility of the eyewitness identification.

As in the visual scanning of five to seven "suspects," witnesses attempting to make auditory identifications must scan the voice samples of all participants in the lineup and select the voice they believe they heard at the time of the crime.

The court said in the *Wade* decision that during a proper lineup, the prisoner could be required to exhibit his physical characteristics and wear a selected article of clothing. In these procedures, the court found no compulsion to disclose any knowledge the prisoner possessed. This was no different from the taking of a blood sample[7] or wearing a blouse.[8]

Similarly, compelling Wade to speak within earshot of the eyewitnesses as they viewed the lineup, even requiring him to speak the words the witnesses said they had heard spoken during the robbery by the robber, was not considered compulsion to testify. Wade was not asked to speak about his guilt or

[4]388 U.S. 218 (1967); 406 U.S. 682 (1972).
[5]413 U.S., 300 (1973).
[6]*People* v. *Bustamonte*, 30 Cal. 3d 88, 99 footnote 7 (1981); *People* v. *Williams*, 3 Cal. 3d 853 (1971).
[7]*Schmerber* v. *California*, U.S., 757 (1966).
[8]*Holt* v. *U.S.*, 218 U.S. 245 (1910).

innocence, but simply to speak, because the human voice is an identifiable physical characteristic. This constitutes nontestimonial identification evidence.

Therefore, real evidence such as articles of clothing, the defendant's physical characteristics, and the human voice may be used as evidence of identity when coupled with testimonial evidence.

The body of the defendant in court is the best source for eyewitness identification. The in-court identification is not a suggestive process. It is similar to the examination of any article of evidence for identification. It is also a "matching" from memory, a comparison of the defendant's general appearance, or other means of ready identification, with a recollected image.

Identification: Blood, Handwriting, and Fingerprints

Blood samples, handwriting, and fingerprints are major items of body evidence. Court decisions about body intrusions in these evidence areas have established guidelines for collecting this type of evidence, and for comparing and analyzing body fluids and characteristics for the purpose of identification. In 1957, blood taken from an unconscious person injured in a traffic accident blazed the path for court approval of minor and reasonable intrusions on the body.[9] The rule categorizing body characteristics as nontestimonial followed in 1966.[10] In 1967, handwriting samples, as distinguished from the content of writings, were defined as identifying physical characteristics.[11]

Blood Samples

The U.S. Supreme Court decision in *Breithaupt* v. *Abram*[12] demonstrates judicial willingness to permit reasonable body intrusions to develop evidence that a person has ingested a certain amount of alcohol. Breithaupt was injured when the car he was driving collided with another vehicle. The occupants of the other car in the accident were killed. Breithaupt survived. While he was unconscious from his injuries and receiving emergency medical care in a nearby hospital, at the request of police investigating the accident, the attending physician took a blood sample and turned it over to the police for analysis to determine whether Breithaupt was intoxicated. Laboratory tests revealed 0.17% alcohol in Breithaupt's blood. He was convicted of manslaughter at a trial in which evidence about the blood sample was admitted over defense objection. It was argued on appeal that Breithaupt's constitutional rights had been violated because an unconscious man could not give consent and waive his privilege against self-incrimination, and that the actual taking of a blood sample was a

[9]*Breithaupt* v. *Abram*, 352 U.S. 432 (1957).
[10]*Schmerber* v. *California*, 384 U.S. 757 (1966).
[11]*Gilbert* v. *California*, 388 U.S. 263 (1967).
[12]352 U.S. 432 (1957).

brutal and offensive procedure that violated the defendant's rights to due process. The court said blood was a nontestimonial body substance and not within the Fifth Amendment's protection against self-incrimination. The court also held there was nothing brutal or offensive in the taking of blood sample by a physician or medical technician, noting that many persons willingly submitted to such tests with proper medical precautions, as a matter of course, and said that the taking of the blood without consent while Breithaupt was unconscious did not violate his constitutional rights.

The court's acceptance of blood samples to show that someone is likely to have been intoxicated, and its willingness to permit the body intrusion involved, was firmly established in *Schmerber* v. *California*.[13] Schmerber was arrested for driving a vehicle while under the influence of intoxicating liquor. He was asked to cooperate in testing his possible blood-alcohol content. He refused on advice of his attorney, and a blood sample was extracted by a physician at a hospital. He was convicted and appealed. The appeal argued a trilogy of constitutional violations: (1) self-incrimination, (2) right to counsel, and (3) search and seizure.

The court's decision rejected Schmerber's claim of protection under the Fifth Amendment. The privilege against self-incrimination concerns the communications of an accused person, according to the court. The extraction of a body fluid for chemical analysis or the body fluid itself were neither compelled testimony nor enforced communication by Schmerber. In studying the requirements of the Sixth Amendment under these circumstances, the court concluded that because the privilege against self-incrimination did not exist, there was little point in providing legal counsel to advise Schmerber at this time. The court's opinion said Schmerber was entitled to the protection of the Fourth Amendment proviso against unreasonable searches but held that there was no violation, that the search was reasonable on these grounds:

1. There was probable cause for arresting Schmerber and charging him with driving a vehicle while under the influence of intoxicating liquor. (There was testimony at trial about the smell of alcohol on Schmerber's breath and the condition of his eyes—bloodshot, watery, glassy.)
2. The bodily intrusion could not be delayed while application was made to court for a search warrant because of the oxidation of alcohol in the human body with the passage of time.
3. There was no objection to the test on the grounds of fear, health, or religion.
4. The search was performed in a reasonable manner.

Handwriting Exemplars

The request by police for handwriting samples from a person accused of crime is not viewed as a critical stage of the pretrial proceedings because any threat to a

---

[13]384 U.S. 757 (1966).

fair trial can be brought out and corrected at trial. Unlike the lineup, there is nothing suggestive to witnesses, and numerous additional handwriting samples can be made for comparison analysis. The high court's opinion in *Gilbert* v. *California*[14] states this principle as follows:

> 1. The taking of the exemplars did not violate petitioner's Fifth Amendment privilege against self-incrimination. The privilege reaches only compulsion of an accused's communications, whatever form they might take, and the compulsion of responses which are also communications, for example, compliance with a subpoena to produce one's papers, and not compulsion which make a suspect or accused the source of real or physical evidence. (*Schmerber* v. *California*, 384 U.S. 757) One's voice and handwriting are, of course, means of communication. It by no means follows, however, that every compulsion of an accused to use his voice or write compels a communication with the cover of the privilege. A mere handwriting exemplar, in contrast to the content of what is written, like the voice or body itself, is an identifying physical characteristic outside its protection. (*United States* v. *Wade*, 388 U.S. 218) No claim is made that the content of the exemplars was testimonial or communicative matter.
>
> 2. The taking of the exemplars was not a critical stage of the criminal proceedings entitling petitioner to the assistance of counsel. Putting aside the fact that the exemplars were taken before the indictment and appointment of counsel, there is minimal risk that the absence of counsel might derogate from his right to a fair trial. If, for some reason, an unrepresentative exemplar is taken, this can be brought out and corrected through the adversary process at trial since the accused can make an unlimited number of additional exemplars for analysis and comparison by government and defense handwriting experts. Thus, the accused has the opportunity for a meaningful confrontation of the state's case at trial through the ordinary processes of cross-examination of the state's expert (handwriting) witnesses and the presentation of the evidence of his own experts (handwriting).

A person's handwriting is a means of communication, but when the identifying physical characteristics of the handwriting are of primary importance rather than the content of the writing, forcing a person to write down does not violate the privilege against self-incrimination. Handwriting exemplars are nontestimonial, identifying physical characteristics outside the protection of the Fifth Amendment.

Fingerprinting

Fingerprint impressions are classic evidence of identity often found at crime scenes in some form, latent, partial, plastic, and so forth. Fingerprints used for

[14]388 U.S. 263 (1967).

comparison, unless taken from police records, must be taken by procedures that qualify as reasonable under the provisions of the Fourth Amendment. Otherwise, evidence based on the impressions will be inadmissible at trial. Most fingerprint impressions compared with fingerprints found at crime scenes are part of police records, the impressions having been taken for the purpose of identification at the time of arrest. When fingerprints are not available for comparison, the safeguards of the Fourth Amendment apply to any intrusion to secure them.

Because fingerprinting discloses many unique characteristics useful in identification common to criminal investigation, the taking of fingerprints can be classified as a search for identification evidence. In *Davis* v. *Mississippi*,[15] the U.S. Supreme Court held that detention for the sole purpose of obtaining fingerprints made such evidence invalid because it was secured in the course of an unreasonable search. However, the court's opinion implied police could make such an intrusion lawful by (1) seeking prior court approval and (2) restricting the request to a convenient fingerprinting session unaccompanied by any form of interrogation.

Documentary Evidence

A "writing" means handwriting, typewriting, printing, photostating, photographing, and every other means of recording upon any tangible thing, any form of communication or representation, including letters, words, pictures, sounds or symbols, or combinations thereof.

A handwriting must be authenticated before it may be received in evidence, or before secondary evidence of its content may be received in evidence. If a portion of the writing material to the dispute has been altered, or appears to have been altered after the writing was made, the person offering the writing must account for the alteration, or the appearance of being altered. He may do this by showing that: (1) the alteration was made by someone else without his consent, (2) it was made with the consent of parties affected by it, (3) it was otherwise properly or innocently made, or (4) the alteration did not change the meaning or language of the instrument.

Authentication requires the production of evidence which will show the writing is what it is supposed to be. If it is offered as genuine, there must be proof of its integrity. If it is offered as a forgery, there must be proof it is a forged writing. The evidence necessary for authentication depends on the circumstances under which the document is presented. Some documents are self-authenticating while others require proof of signing of the signature or of a comparison of signatures.

A writing may be authenticated by evidence that (1) the opposing party has at some time admitted its authenticity or that (2) the opposing party has acted as though the document was authentic.

---

[15]394 U.S. 721 (1969).

Writings more than thirty years old can be authenticated by comparison with writings of known equal age, generally respected and acted on as genuine by persons with an interest in knowing whether the suspect writing is genuine. Authentication can also be made by evidence that the writing was received in response to a communication sent to the claimed author, or that it refers to or states matters unlikely to be known by anyone other than the alleged author. Authenticity may also be shown by acknowledgements and seals of public agencies or officials. A writing may be authenticated by the testimony of anyone who saw the writing executed, including a witness who signed it. When the testimony of someone who signed the writing is required and he cannot recollect the execution of the writing or denies it, other evidence may be presented to authenticate the document.

A writing may also be authenticated by evidence that the handwriting is genuine. Opinions about the genuineness of the handwriting may be accepted from qualified nonexpert or expert witnesses who have (1) seen the supposed writer write, or (2) seen a writing purporting to be in the handwriting of the supposed writer on which the supposed writer has acted, or (3) received letters in the due course of mail purporting to be from the supposed writer in response to letters they have duly addressed and mailed to the supposed writer, or (4) obtained personal knowledge of the handwriting of the supposed writer by other means.

The Best Evidence Rule

The best evidence rule applies only to writings. In proving the content of a writing, the writing itself is the best evidence of its content. Copies of writings or testimonial evidence of their content are admissible only after an in-court showing that the writing itself cannot be obtained and brought to court.

Secondary evidence, written or oral, may be admissible under the following conditions:

1. The writing is lost or has been destroyed without fraudulent intent on the part of the person proffering the evidence (the proponent).
2. The writing is not reasonably procurable by the proponent by use of the court's process or by other available means.
3. The opponent had control of the writing and was expressly or implicitly notified, by the pleadings or otherwise, that the writing would be needed at the hearing, and on request at the hearing the opponent has failed to produce the writing.
4. The writing is a record of other writing in the custody of a public entity.
5. The writing has been recorded in the public records, and by statute, the record or an attested or certified copy of it is sufficient.

6. The writing is not closely related to the controlling issues, and it would be inexpedient to require its production.

7. The writing consists of numerous accounts or other writings that cannot be examined in court without great loss of time, and the evidence sought from them is only the general result of the whole. (The court, in its discretion, may require that such accounts or other writings be produced for inspection by the adverse party.)

The usual procedure for handling this aspect of documentary evidence requires the production of a copy of a writing. If a copy cannot be produced, the proponent is often required to show that despite due diligence he has failed to locate a copy of the writing or, if he has located a copy, that he is unable to produce it in court. Then, other secondary evidence can be utilized for authentication.[16]

Parol Evidence Rule

The evidence about the terms and content of a written contract is the writing that has been made and signed by the contracting parties. This is documentary evidence. This integration of the history of negotiating a contract with the written endproduct has led to development of the parol evidence rule. When an agreement is placed in writing, the court will reject oral testimony about arrangements made or things said which would tend to substitute the unwritten for the written contract which has been agreed upon and signed, to the possible prejudice of one of the contracting parties.

However, a written contract can be attacked by any evidence for fraud and illegality.

Viewing the Crime Scene

The court decides whether or not to take a jury to view a crime scene. The court's decision will not be reversed unless it is clearly shown that the court abused its discretion.

Usually a request to view the crime scene will be denied if an adequate representation of the scene by photographs, diagrams, maps, or clear testimony is available.

Neither the judge nor individual members of the jury are allowed to view the scene independently. If the judge or a juror does so, it is grounds for a mistrial. All evidence received by the triers of fact must be received in court or by direction of the judge if he rules the crime scene should be viewed.

[16]Rules 1003–08, Federal Rules of Evidence.

If the crime scene is viewed as a part of the admissible evidence during the trial, the jurors should not try demonstrating tests or experiments except under the direction of the court with the concurrence of counsel.

Maps and Diagrams

Maps and diagrams are admissible as evidence when they are reasonably necessary to understand the testimony of witnesses, and when a foundation of accuracy is laid by the person who prepared the map.

Under some circumstances, an inaccurate sketch will be admissible if it is reasonably related and explanatory of the testimony of the witness who drew it and used it to illustrate his testimony.

Maps are generally used to illustrate testimony relating to the scene of a crime. However, drawings and sketches may be admissible when the subject matter is anatomy, shape or location of a wound, kinds of marks on an item of evidence, graphs, and the like.

Admission of this evidence rests in the discretion of the trial judge and his decision will be reversed only where a clear abuse of discretion is shown.[17]

Photographs

To be admissible, a photograph must be relevant, accurately taken, and a correct representation of the subject portrayed. The admissibility of photographs is discretionary with the court.

Photographs of a victim of crime are regularly admitted even when they are gruesome and likely to prejudice the triers of fact. There must be some nonprejudicial basis, however, for their introduction, such as illustrating a wound, a part of the crime scene, a particular position of the victim, or some other relevant and material fact. The trial court must decide whether the probative value of the photograph outweighs the probable prejudicial effect.[18]

The court may refuse admission to prejudicial photographs when other evidence, and clear and uncontradicted testimony on the disputed issue is available.

Experiments and Demonstrations

Some experts are termed demonstrative experts because they supplement their testimony with exhibits or demonstrations. This is particularly true of witnesses skilled in examining questioned documents. The exhibits of these experts,

---

[17]*Silvey* v. *Harm*, 120 Cal. App. 561 (1932).
[18]*People* v. *Love*, 53 Cal. 2nd 843 (1960).

usually consisting of photographic enlargement of similarities or differences in the suspect handwriting, is demonstrative evidence. The fact finders look at the exhibits in order to understand the rationale for the expert's opinion.

A demonstration must be "in kind" in its relationship to the testimony of the witness—that is, it must support his testimony. In-court demonstrations must be simple and easily understood. Out-of-court demonstrations must be explained with coherence and unity. It is vital that the triers of fact understand the demonstration if it is to be a basis for fact finding.[19]

An excellent in-court demonstration was given during a murder trial in which the fatal wound was inflicted with a knife. The murder weapon, a long and slender knife, had been admitted as evidence during the prosecution's case in chief. The following portions of the testimony in this case accompanied the demonstration that was part of the core testimony associated with the defendant's claim of self-defense:

Direct Examination of Defendant (Defense counsel laid a foundation for the following line of questioning by questions establishing defendant's identity and recall of the event.)

Q: Well, at that time, what happened?
A: Well, I seen a knife when he flashed it. He made a motion toward me, and I grabbed it.
Q: What kind of a motion did he make toward you?
A: Come down from over his head.
Q: And where had his hand been prior to the time he came down toward you with the knife in his hand?
A: Up by the pillow.
Q: Did you get a good look at the knife?
A: No, I didn't.
Q: What occurred then when he made a motion toward you with the knife?
A: I grabbed his hand by the wrist when he came down and I pulled him toward me against the wall, and then I came back over to him, and that is when the knife hit him.
Q: You grabbed the hand that had the knife?
A: Yes.

(Thereupon the witness left the stand and approached the area in back of counsel table, before the jury stand.)

Q: Which hand held the knife?

---

[19]*People* v. *Adamson* 27 Cal. 2d 478 (1946).

A: In his right hand.

Q: If I am Mr. Morris and I have the knife in my right hand, and I strike toward you, what did you do?

A: Well, I was—I reached up and grabbed him by the wrist, right here.

Q: And then what did you do?

A: Reached around toward the wall and leaned on the wall and pulled him.

Q: And then what happened?

A: Grabbed him by the wrist and turned it, and that is when the knife hit him.

Q: What happened when you turned the knife into him?

A: He let go of the knife.

Q: What did you do?

A: I pulled it back out.

Expert witnesses may describe and give the results of out-of-court experiments conducted under conditions corresponding to the scene of the crime. Ballistics evidence is usually based upon the firing of a firearm in a laboratory test, with the recovered test bullet as evidence submitted as the result of the out-of-court experimenting.

A nonexpert witness, as well as an expert, can conduct simple experiments such as firing shots to estimate the range of a shooting event. When it is necessary to know the distance at which an assailant shot his victim, tests with guns of caliber and barrel length similar to the weapon used in a shooting have been fired at clean and nonyielding surfaces. Tests from various ranges show a pattern matching the victim's wound or wounds at some specific distance. The resulting evidence can be used to estimate the distance from gun to victim.

Demonstrations and experiments, in or out of court, tie together exhibits and articles of evidence and join them with the testimony of witnesses. They are effective combinations of compelling evidence.

Videotaping

The admission of videotapes as evidence in America's criminal trial courtrooms has had an intrusive and dramatic impact upon the business-as-usual routine of determining guilt or innocence. Videotaping transports the audience within the courtroom to the scene of a happening. There is an unbelievable credibility in videotaping.

The early use of videotaping in police organizations was open: a camera was set up to film a sobriety test of an arrestee suspected of driving while intoxicated. Subsequently, filming was covert: a concealed camera recorded the seller-buyer transaction between thieves and undercover police officers or the bribing of public officials by federal agents. More recently, law enforcement agents videotaped interrogation sessions, and a few police units are videotaping the scenes of serious crimes.

Videotapes are usually examined for admissibility on whether or not they contain testimonial or nontestimonial evidence—video and/or audio. In *Pennsylvania* v. *Muniz*, 496 U.S. 582 (1990), the U.S. Supreme Court held that most of a videotape of a driving-while-intoxicated (DWI) suspect was admissible, but that one question and response were not admissible.

Muniz was stopped for suspicion of drunken driving, failed roadside sobriety testing, and was arrested. Transported to the booking center Muniz was informed that videotaping was standard practice and was instructed as the taping progressed. During the test, Muniz responded to several queries, and these interactions were duly recorded on the tape. When the videotaping was completed, Muniz was advised of his *Miranda* rights for the first time and signed a statement waiving those rights. At trial both video and audio portions of the tape were admitted into evidence. Muniz was convicted of DWI (alcohol). The Superior Court of Pennsylvania reversed, noting that the entire audio portion of the tape should have been suppressed.

On certiorari, the U.S. Supreme Court vacated the state court's judgment and remanded the case for further proceedings. The majority opinion held that the suspect's Fifth Amendment rights were violated by the admission of that part of the video tape calling for a testimonial response to one question (birthday date). Asking the suspect the date of his sixth birthdate evoked a testimonial answer because the context of the answer allowed the viewer to draw an inference as to the suspect's confused mental state.

On the other hand, routine booking questions such as name, address, height, weight, eye color, and the like elicit nontestimonial responses.

Videotaping is new and compelling, and it is well worth the effort to produce videotapes likely to be admissible in court at trial.

Case Studies

Rochin v. *California*, 342 U.S. 165 (1952).

Schmerber v. *California*, 384 U.S. 757 (1966).

Gilbert v. *California*, 388 U.S. 263 (1967).

Miniproject

Study the *Rochin* case, and briefly list any circumstances in which a videotaping might "shock the conscience."

Discussion Questions

1. How is testimony related to demonstrative evidence?
2. What is associative evidence?

3. What are some problems of identity evidence?

4. What evidence may be taken from the body of the suspect?

5. What is the best evidence rule?

6. What may be demonstrated in court?

7. What are the major aspects of the "parol evidence rule"?

8. What are the basic requirements for the admissibility of photographs as evidence?

9. Discuss problems regarding the admissibility at trial of a videotaping containing testimonial evidence.

Glossary

Autopsic (Evidence)   Evidence as a result of viewing an object or thing.

Ballistics   Science of the motion of projectiles; firearms identification; the scientific examination of evidence found at crime scenes and connected with firearms; firearms; spent bullets, empty cartridge or shell cases, and cartridges and shells.

Exemplar (Handwriting)   A specimen (of handwriting); an example; a model.

Latent (Fingerprint)   Not visible to ordinary visual examinations; must be searched for with special skill and equipment; a latent fingerprint with the possibility of development by evidence technicians and preserved as evidence.

Plastic (Fingerprint)   A finger impression made in a pliable (plastic) substance.

CHAPTER 9

Direct Versus Circumstantial Evidence

CHAPTER OBJECTIVES

- To list and explain the important differences between direct and circumstantial (indirect) evidence.
- To explore the role of circumstantial evidence as corroboration of direct evidence.
- To outline the essential requirements of a "chain" of circumstantial evidence in circumstantial-evidence-only cases.
- To describe reasoning from evidence—inferences and presumptions.

Triers of fact may base their decisions on either or both of two classes of evidence: direct and circumstantial.

Direct evidence means evidence that directly proves a fact, without any inference or presumption, and which in itself, if true, conclusively establishes that fact.

Direct evidence of a person's conduct consists of testimony by a witness who at the time in question and with his physical senses perceived the person's conduct, or some portion of it, and recalls what he perceived. Direct evidence applies to the fact to be proved immediately and directly by witnesses testifying about matters they know personally without the need of any intervening fact or process of deduction. The value of the evidence rests on the truth of the fact asserted by the witness. The direct evidence of one witness who is entitled to full credit is sufficient for proof of any fact, except when additional evidence is required by a special circumstance such as the rule requiring that an accomplice's testimony be corroborated.

All other evidence is circumstantial. The basic clarity of the standard definition of direct evidence has created the "all other" terminology to define circumstantial evidence, and probably explains the use of term "indirect" as a synonym for circumstantial.

The two classes of evidence are often described as direct and indirect evidence. Circumstantial evidence, however, is a more appropriate term. This class of evidence is, in fact, based on analysis and interpretation of circumstances and facts. Circumstantial evidence is evidence of things, of facts and circumstances, of a succession of events, all of which must be investigated and interpreted. Circumstantial evidence is the "language of things," when interpreted and explained, and the tale of an isolated fact when its relations and significance to a disputed fact are clearly shown.[1]

When the question of guilt or innocence rests substantially on circumstantial evidence, each essential fact contributing to the classic "chain of circumstances" must be proven beyond a reasonable doubt; and the total measure of proven circumstances must be not only consistent with a hypothesis of guilt but inconsistent with any hypothesis of innocence.

Inferences

An inference is a deduction drawn by a process of logical reasoning; it is not evidence but the result of reasoning from evidence. An inference is supported by evidence when it can be described as a conclusion that can be logically and reasonably drawn from the impact of the evidence on the trier of fact. The scope or limits of the inference to be drawn may be limited by the nature of the evidence and the reasonableness of the possible inference. When an inference can be made, it is up to the trier of fact to make it by the reasonable and logical deduction of some fact from another fact or group of facts that have been found or otherwise established in the criminal action.

The usual objection to the introduction of an item of circumstantial evidence is lack of relevancy, that—even if true—the inference for which the evidence is offered does not necessarily follow as a logical conclusion. The evidence will usually be admitted if it is shown that the proffered evidence will establish a fact for which the desired inference is a probable or natural explanation or is more probable than other explanations. The odds must be that the inference claimed is the true proposition, or that the proffered evidence makes probable the existence of the fact in dispute. Of course, an item of evidence may be rejected on grounds of legal relevancy. The trial judge may, after weighing values against dangers, rule it out as misleading, confusing, or too remote.

[1]Albert S. Osborn, ed., *Questioned Document Problems*, 2nd ed. (Albany, N.Y.: Boyd Printing Co., 1946), pp. 21, 107.

Presumptions

A presumption is a rule of law by which a judge attaches to one evidentiary fact certain procedural consequencs such as the duty of the opposition to produce contrary evidence. A presumption is a deduction that the law requires a trier of facts to make. A conclusive presumption is a rule of law determining that only one inference can or must be drawn from certain evidence. A rebuttable presumption determines the inference to be drawn only in the absence of evidence to the contrary. It is dangerous to rely completely on rebuttable presumptions instead of gathering and producing positive evidence about these issues. There are presumptions of legitimacy, of continuance of things once proved to exist, of death, of death in bigamy cases, survivorship in the death of two or more persons in a common disaster, foreign law, and ownership from possession. More important in criminal investigations and prosecutions are the presumptions of innocence; sanity and capacity; identity, from a name; chastity; honesty; intent, from voluntary acts; malice, from intentional acts; and guilt, from preparations, flight, attempt to escape, withholding evidence, or false statements.

The Role of Circumstantial Evidence In Corroborating Direct Evidence

As each item of circumstantial evidence is proffered, it must withstand the objections of the opposing party. Preliminary facts may have to be established to show that a fair inference can be drawn from the proffered evidence either alone or when connected with other evidence. Counsel seeking admission of such evidence may be forced to show legal sufficiency. He may have to show that the "chain" of proof is sufficient to establish, *prima facie*, the fact in issue, guilt, or innocence.

The direct evidence of witnesses can be and sometimes needs to be corroborated by circumstantial evidence, for instance, testimony of a witness who observed the defendant a short distance from the scene before or after the crime. This is direct evidence of the observation, but only inferential evidence of the defendant's presence at the scene or of his guilt. In one murder case, the accused was seen throwing away some then unknown articles. This was direct evidence that the articles found in that spot were thrown away by the accused. The articles were a bloodstained hammer and a jacket. To connect the accused with the crime charged, the recovered articles had to be "circumstantially" connected with the scene of the crime at the time of the crime (as loot or debris), or with the dead victim (as blood or weapon). The recovered articles did "circumstantially" connect with the time and place of the crime, and "circumstantially" as well as directly with the defendant. The weapon was shown to be the murder weapon by testimony of the autopsy surgeon, and a criminalist testified that numerous dog hairs found on the jacket were similar to dog hairs taken from the defendant's dog.

Physical evidence, after being examined and tested in a criminalistics laboratory, may serve as the base for an expert's opinion. This type of evidence is associative, connecting the accused with the crime scene in some manner and indicating his presence at the scene. Fingerprints, footprints, and like traces along with the testimony of the identification technician or the criminalist are examples of this type of evidence.

Testimony that places a suspect near a crime scene, and scientific evidence or traces and things found at crime scenes, corroborate the direct evidence or eyewitnesses. Without the direct evidence of eyewitnesses, such evidence will only contribute to the "chain" of inferential evidence.

The investigation of the tragic death of fourteen-year-old Stephanie Bryan[2] illustrates the web of direct and circumstantial evidence that may ensnare a defendant.

> Stephanie Bryan, a shy fourteen-year-old honor student at Willard Junior High School in Berkeley, California, disappeared on April 28, while walking home from school along Ashby Avenue. Stephanie was carrying several books, including a French textbook and a purse which contained a wallet and a pair of glasses. She was wearing, among other garments, a navy blue cardigan sweater over a white slip-on sweater, a blue cotton skirt, several petticoats, nylon panties and a brassiere. About 4:15 P.M. on the day Stephanie disappeared, several motorists saw a man struggling with a young girl in a car that had stopped suddenly at the side of Tunnel Road in Contra Costa County, near the Broadway Tunnel, a few miles north of the Claremont Hotel. The girl appeared to be very frightened and was screaming. She was in the back seat of the car, and the man, who was leaning over the front seat, was beating her and pulling her down and away from the rear window. She was wearing a navy blue cardigan garment over something white.
>
> On May 2, four days after Stephanie's disappearance, her French textbook was found beside Franklin Canyon Road in Contra Costa County. Except for the fact that its cover was slightly dampened by dew, the book was clean and dry, although it had rained in the area on April 29 and 30.
>
> Nothing further was learned about Stephanie's disappearance until July 15, when her purse and wallet were found in Alameda at the home of defendant, Abbott. His wife discovered the articles in a cardboard box in the basement and, after reading the identification cards that were in the wallet, she went upstairs and excitedly asked her husband and others who were present if Stephanie Bryan was not the name of the girl whose

[2]*People v. Abbott*, 47 Cal. 2d 362 (1956).

disappearance had been reported in the newspapers. Abbott said that the purse probably belonged to some friend of Mrs. Abbott. A guest suggested that the police be called, and this was done. The police searched Abbott's home the following day, and found Stephanie's glasses, brassiere, and the rest of her books buried in the basement under eight inches of sand.

At the time of these events, Abbott was twenty-seven years old and attending the University of California at Berkeley. He was a regular customer at a doughnut shop located less than a block from the school Stephanie attended. This shop was frequented by pupils from that school, and Stephanie occasionally made purchases there. When questioned by the police, Abbott said that on April 28, the day of Stephanie's disappearance, he left his home in Alameda in the morning and drove to a mountain cabin in Trinity county that was owned by his wife's family. He said that he arrived at the cabin sometime after 8:30 that evening and remained there until May 1. Abbott described in detail the route he said he had taken from his home in Alameda to the cabin in Trinity County.

On July 20, a search party discovered Stephanie's body in a shallow grave about three hundred feet from the cabin in Trinity County. Her panties, which had been "cut or torn" through the left side and the crotch, were knotted around her neck. The rest of the clothing Stephanie was wearing on the day of her disappearance was on her body, except for her brassiere, which, as we have seen, was found in Abbott's basement.

Because of extensive decomposition, it was impossible to determine by a physical examination whether Stephanie had been sexually attacked. Her body had been buried in a state of rigor mortis, and the victim's arms and hands were raised in front of her face. There were multiple compound fractures of the skull and two holes about two inches in diameter through the skull. The head injuries were the principal cause of Stephanie's death. Particles of soil had become enmeshed in her cardigan sweater, and it could be inferred that the soil was wet when she was buried. It had rained and snowed near the cabin for several days prior to April 30, but there had been very little rain in the area during May, June, or July.

A search of Abbott's car led to the discovery of two hairs which were indistinguishable from Stephanie's and six hairs which were very similar to hers. Eighteen fibers matching those in four of her garments were also found. There was blood deep in the floor mat in the back of the car, but no blood on the surface, indicating that the mat had been washed.

The cardboard box in which Stephanie's purse and wallet were found (in the basement of Abbott's residence) contained old clothes which Abbott usually wore at the mountain cabin. His boots were encrusted with red mud which was the same as a sample of soil taken from Stephanie's grave at a point nine inches below the surface. Several fragments of bloodstained cleansing tissue, which had been carried by a pack rat from the grave site to a nearby nest, were of the type used by Abbott.

At the trial, Abbott testified that he was not in Berkeley on April 28, that he started for the cabin from his home about 10:45 A.M. and, en route, stopped at a restaurant about 3:00 P.M., where he was served by a twenty-five- or thirty-year-old waitress with dusty blonde hair. He testified that he also stopped at the Wildwood Inn for a drink about 8:30 P.M., and that he then drove two miles to the mountain cabin, built a fire, and went to bed.

Abbott's account of his activities on April 28 was in conflict not only with the evidence connecting him with Stephanie's disappearance and death set forth above but with other testimony as well. He was seen at the state controller's office in Oakland at 1:30 P.M. and at the beauty shop where his wife worked about 2:30 P.M. A witness testified that he saw Abbott at the doughnut shop on the afternoon in question and that he saw him leave about 3:20 P.M. and enter his car, a Chevrolet sedan. Five persons testified that they witnessed the struggle between a man and a young girl on Tunnel Road near the Broadway Tunnel. One of them identified Abbott as the man in the car. Another stated that a picture of Abbott published in a newspaper resembled the man. A third said that the man was about thirty years of age and had a receding hairline like Abbott's. The other two witnesses described the car in which the incident occurred as similar to Abbott's. Tunnel Road leads to the Orinda Crossroads, and from this point, several roads lead to Highway 40, which may be used to reach the area in Trinity County in which the mountain cabin (owned by the family of Mrs. Abbott) is located.

Abbott was seen near the cabin on the morning of April 29, and he was at Wildwood Inn, a nearby tavern, from 2:00 P.M. until midnight of that day. Abbott's brother and sister-in-law joined him at the cabin about 3:00 A.M. on April 30. They all left at the same time on the afternoon of May 1, Abbott driving alone in his car. Their return route took them over Franklin Canyon Road where Stephanie's French textbook was discovered about 7:30 A.M. the next morning. During this portion of the trip, Abbott's car was behind the one in which his brother and sister-in-law were riding. Abbott arrived home about eight or nine o'clock that evening.

On May 2, Abbott returned to the area in Contra Costa County through which he had traveled the day before on his way home from the mountain cabin. The records of an oil company showed that he had purchased gasoline at a station located near the place where Stepanie's book had been found earlier that morning. Abbott admitted being in the vicinity between 11:00 A.M. and 1 P.M., and said he had gone there to purchase used tires. He was unable to name or describe any place where he had stopped to look at tires, and he did not purchase any. The area is about twelve miles north of the campus of the university where Abbott had classes scheduled at ten, eleven, and one o'clock.

The Chain of Circumstantial Evidence

Circumstantial evidence in cases in which there is no direct evidence to identify the defendant as the guilty person must be clear, convincing, and conclusive, excluding all rational doubt of guilt. This inferential relationship of various and related items of evidence can be as convincing in its nature and substance as direct evidence from a credible witness. When the facts and circumstances disclosed by each item of circumstantial evidence form an evidence structure which excludes any reasonable inference of innocence, a clear and strong conclusion as to guilt can be achieved.

A strong circumstantial-evidence case will contain evidence that the accused had the "motive" or "disposition" to commit the crime, the possession of the means to commit it, and was present at the scene at or about the time of the crime. Evidence of "motive" may be shown in a number of ways. The accused can be revealed as a person who "profited" from the crime (fraud, fire, murder of unwanted spouse), or as a person who was jealous, revengeful, or had a sexual motivation. Evidence of the means to commit a specific crime may be shown by

1. Possession or ownership of the murder weapon.
2. Possession of contraband in cases of the sale of contraband.
3. Possession of access tools necessary for the commission of the crime (burglary and safe burglaries).

Evidence of opportunity—presence at the crime scene—may be shown by:

1. Paint transfers connected with the scene of the crime.
2. Bloodstains of victim on the accused.
3. Debris on the accused traceable to the crime scene.
4. Admissions of presence.
5. Possession of loot traceable to the crime scene.
6. Absence of an alibi.

Similar acts by a defendant in the past may support an inference about the defendant at the time of a criminal trial. Evidence about past crimes cannot be admitted just to show that a person with a criminal record is more likely to be guilty of the crime charged than an individual without a prior criminal history. Such evidence can be admitted, however, to show (1) motive, (2) intent, (3) identity, (4) absence of mistake, and (5) a common scheme or plan.

Motive   Evidence that the defendant had attempted on other occasions to have intercourse with the victim is admissible to establish a motive for the subsequent murder.[3] When the motive for the charged crime is concealment of a prior crime, evidence of the prior crime is admissible.[4]

Intent   Evidence that the accused shot the victim on a prior occasion is admissible in a trial based on a second shooting of the same victim to show an intent to murder.[5] However, not every case of specific intent will allow the admission of prior unlawful acts.[6]

Identity   When an identification by police witness was questioned by the defense, the fact that the defendant had previously been arrested for robbery by the same police witness was admissible.[7]

Absence of Accident or Mistake   Evidence about prior sales of obscene material to minors was admissible to show that the defendant's sale to a minor in the case charged was no accident or mistake.[8]

Common Scheme or Plan   Evidence about other thefts may be admissible where these acts show a similarity in pattern, a *modus operandi*, to the crime presently charged.[9] In a prosecution for assault and robbery, evidence was admissible about a prior robbery during which the defendant obtained the name and address of the present victim by threats.[10]

A 1956 illegal gambling case shows how valuable circumstantial evidence can be.[11] Sam Goldstein was charged, in a two-count information, of unlawfully keeping a place for taking wagers on horse races, and unlawfully accepting such bets. Goldstein was observed conducting the typical operation of a bookmaker. When he was arrested, the arresting officers seized betting records in a search incidental to the arrest. Goldstein was convicted on both counts and appealed.

The court's opinion in this case sums up the evidence and its likely impact on the jury as follows:

> The evidence points convincingly to the guilt of defendant. Within a period of two and one-quarter hours on February 16, 1955, eight to ten persons went into defendant's newsstand, did not stop in the front room but went into the rear room. Defendant immediately followed each one into that

---

[3]*People* v. *Malguist*, 26 Ill. 2d 22, 185 NE 2d 825.
[4]*Ables* v. *State*, 201 Tenn. 491; 300 SW 2d 890.
[5]*Moss* v. *State*, 364 SW 2d 389 (Tex.).
[6]*People* v. *Kelly*, 66 Cal. 2d 232, 424 P. 2d 947.
[7]*San Fratello* v. *State*, 154 So. 2d 327 (Fla.).
[8]*State* v. *Locks*, 94 Ariz. 134, 382 P. 2d 241.
[9]*Pabst* v. *State*, 169 So. 2d 329 (Fla.).
[10]*State* v. *Yoshino*, 45 Hawaii 206, 364 P. 2d 638.
[11]*People* v. *Goldstein*, 139 Cal. App. 2d 146, 293 P. 2d 495 (1956).

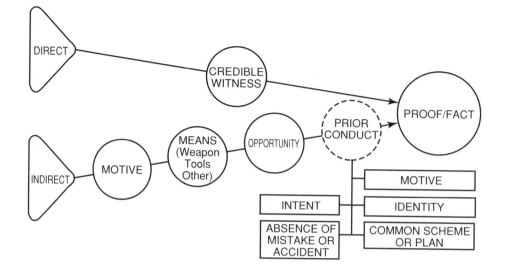

FIGURE 9-1. Direct and indirect evidence.

room. He returned to the front room ten or fifteen seconds later, each time putting his pen into his shirt pocket. The other person immediately left the premises. No one of the eight to ten persons made a purchase. The only window in the rear room was covered by a green shade. Shortly after 2:00 P.M. that day the officers found six betting markers with a series of letters written on them, all in defendant's handwriting, in the rear room. All the betting markers, with one exception, were written partly with ink; the one exception was written with ink and partly with a pencil. When asked what they were, defendant replied they were a form of double bookkeeping for tax evasion purposes, and when asked to explain, said, "I can't; you will have to talk to my lawyer." The officers found a newspaper of February 16, 1955, open to the entries "at the current tracks" in the rear room. The betting markers shows bets on horses running at Santa Anita and Hialeah on February 16, 1955.

The fact that all the evidence was circumstantial does not lessen its weight, for circumstantial evidence is as adequate to convict as direct evidence. That the officers did not observe any activity in the rear room, did not know who any of the persons were who went into that room, that the six papers were not dated, that neither "owe sheets" nor a "scratch sheet" were found on the premises, that no one saw anyone place a bet, and that Officer Marshall supposed a code of the kind indicated by the six papers could be applied "to a business operation, or purchases, and so forth," do not weaken the force of the evidence on which the verdict rests.

The offense charged in Count 1 was complete when it was shown that the accused occupied a place with paraphernalia for the purpose of registering bets on February 16, 1955. The offense denounced is the occupancy of the place with the necessary equipment for registering bets, not the actual taking of bets. The evidence to the effect that notations on the slips of paper, admittedly in the handwriting of defendant, were records of bets on horses which ran on February 16, 1955, together with the other circumstances related, established that defendant registered bets on that day. There is no doubt the jury was justified in concluding that defendant was guilty as charged in both counts.

Case Studies

Virgin Islands v. *Rosado*, 699 F.2d 121 (1983).

California v. *Yu*, 191 Cal. Rptr. 859 (1983).

United States v. *Mitchell*, 427 F. 2d 644 (1970).

Discussion Questions

1. What are the similarities and differences between inferences and presumptions?
2. Is the opinion of an expert concerning associative evidence circumstantial or direct evidence?
3. What is the role of circumstantial evidence in corroborating direct evidence?
4. How much circumstantial evidence is needed in cases without direct evidence to identify the defendant as the person responsible for the alleged crime?
5. When can evidence of past crimes be admitted as circumstantial evidence?
6. What is the role of circumstantial evidence in revealing the accused's presence at the crime scene? In demonstrating an accused had possession of the means to commit the alleged crime?

Glossary

Modus Operandi (M. O.)   Method of operation; used in the identification of criminals by their crime techniques or habitual criminal conduct.

CHAPTER 10

The Exclusionary Rule

CHAPTER OBJECTIVES

- To present a chronological arrangement of case law, describing the steady growth of the exclusionary rule as a legal process to control police misbehavior and illegal conduct.
- To describe the use of the Fourteenth Amendment and its due process clause to restrain state agents and align their evidence-gathering methods with standards set for federal agents.
- To discuss pertinent cases and provide outlines of the decisions related to excluding evidence tainted by illegal or improper searches and seizures, interrogations, and lineups.
- To explore the legal mechanics of suppressing tainted evidence subject to exclusion by judicial ruling.
- To evaluate potential revisions of the exclusionary rule.

The exclusionary rule is designed to discourage law enforcement agents from violating constitutional guarantees while gathering evidence. The rule does this by rejecting any illegally obtained evidence. Police have not hesitated to violate procedural rules in gathering evidence for the ultimate purpose of using such evidence in court to prove, with the aid of the prosecutor, the guilt of the accused person. Their work, however, is wasted when the tainted evidence is suppressed before trial or is not admitted into evidence at trial. The exclusionary rule compels respect for constitutional guarantees by removing the incentive for disregarding them.

Before the growth of the exclusionary rule, there was no effective way of restraining agents of law enforcement while gathering evidence for use in court. Under the rule of common law, illegally obtained evidence was admissible. If it could be shown that the evidence was pertinent to the issue, the court did not take notice of how it was obtained.

The exclusion of logically relevant evidence in criminal prosecutions is justified by the public policy expressed in the Constitution. The exclusionary rule has been slow in its emergence and application to the states and their courts, and is under constant attack from police and prosecuting attorneys. The concepts of home rule and state criminal justice as well as the ageless problem of resolving the conflict between the government power and the protection of citizens from misuse of that power were heavy handicaps in developing the rules for suppressing illegally obtained evidence.

Some jurisdictions have expressly prohibited state courts from interpreting state constitutions in a way which gives greater rights to individuals than is provided in the U.S. Constitution and its interpretation by the U.S. Supreme Court.[1]

The exclusionary rule has shaped the conduct of all agents of law enforcement into a new pattern of reasonableness and fundamental fairness in connection with searches and seizures, confessions, and other critical stages of a criminal case, from the focusing of a case through arrest to trial. This rule has also preserved the moral force of law and the integrity of the judiciary. Law enforcement agents are asked to act out the adversary role in a way that will earn the respect of the community. If they fail to do so, the "imperative of judicial integrity" demands that their conduct be negated by the courts.

The basic merit of the exclusionary rule is that it affords every person—innocent and possibly guilty—the constitutional guarantees enacted to protect all citizens of the United States, and it now does so in both federal and state courts.

In developing the exclusionary rule, the U.S. Supreme Court acted initially under its authority over U.S. court proceedings and over federal agents who used these courts to prosecute violations of federal law. The Court hesitated to extend federalism into the local criminal justice field by forcing state courts and state officials to abide by the federal rules of procedure. The failure of state authorities to use some other effective methods to compel state agents to comply with the provisions of the Constitution in gathering evidence, and the continual refusal of most state appellate courts to reject illegal evidence, led to the Supreme Court's action in *Weeks, Mapp, Gideon, Wade,* and *Miranda.* These five cases established procedural safeguards to protect three essential areas of individual liberty: the rights to privacy, to an attorney, and to protection against self-incrimination.

Federal Agents and Proceedings

In 1914, in *Weeks* v. *United States,*[2] the U.S. Supreme Court held that the private papers of an accused, which had been seized by federal officers during a warrantless search of his home, were inadmissible as evidence in the federal courts because they had been obtained through an illegal search and seizure in violation of the Fourth Amendment.

[1]California Constitution, Article I, Section 28 (by initiative; Proposition 8, 1982).
[2]232 U.S. 383 (1914).

This decision established the exclusionary rule as the best means for discouraging lawless searches and seizures by federal agents. The majority opinion noted that exclusion is implicit in the right to privacy created by the Fourth Amendment and, that if the constitutional guarantees against unreasonable searches and seizures are to have significance, they must be enforced. If such guarantees had been effectively enforced by means other than excluding evidence before 1914, there would have been little justification for initiating this judicial rule. However, experience had demonstrated that administrative, criminal, and civil remedies were not effective in suppressing lawless searches and seizures by federal agents.

A few of the states became "exclusionary" in conformity with the Weeks doctrine. In these exclusionary states, law enforcement agents who had obtained evidence during an unreasonable search could not use it in their state courts, but they could turn it over to federal authorities for prosecution under federal law. This became known as the "silver platter" doctrine. The doctrinal justification for this procedure was that the federal courts could admit this evidence because federal agents had had nothing to do with the illegal search and seizure. The rationale was given that the turnover from state to federal agents legitimized the legal evidence.

In their opinion in *Elkins* v. *United States*,[3] in 1960, the Court rejected this silver platter doctrine and stopped the traffic in illegal searches aimed at nullifying state and federal laws. The Court's majority opinion in *Elkins* said that the act of a federal court sitting in an exclusionary state and admitting evidence lawlessly seized by state agents not only frustrated state and federal policy but did so in a particularly inappropriate way: "For by admitting the unlawfully seized evidence the federal court serves to defeat the state's effort to assure obedience to the Federal Constitution."

In a comment by Mr. Justice Frankfurter in a 1943 case, *McNabb* v. *United States*,[4] the Court indicated its attitude toward federal criminal justice and of police interrogations:

> Judicial supervision of the administration of criminal justice in the federal courts implies the duty of establishing and maintaining civilized standards of procedure and evidence. Such standards are not satisfied merely by observance of those minimal historic safeguards for securing trial by reason which are summarized as "due process" of law and below which we reach what is really trial by force.

In *McNabb*, the arresting officers delayed Benjamin McNabb's arraignment after his arrest and secured a confession from him during this period of detention which violated a federal law requiring prompt arraignment of arrestees. The

[3]364 U.S. 206 (1960).
[4]318 U.S. 322 (1943).

Court's opinion pointed to legislative recognition that police must act with reasonable promptness to show legal cause for the arrest to safeguard both innocent and guilty arrestees. Its comment about this law was: "It aims to avoid all the implications of secret interrogations of persons accused of crime. It reflects not a sentimental but a sturdy view of law enforcement. It outlaws easy but self-defeating ways in which brutality is substituted for brains as an instrument of crime detection."

In 1957, the court was confronted with a case similar to *McNabb*. In this case, *Mallory* v. *United States*,[5] a unanimous Court reaffirmed its position in *McNabb*. Andrew R. Mallory was a nineteen-year-old youth of limited intelligence. He was arrested in the early afternoon hours in Washington, D.C., and accused of forcible rape. He was questioned for about a half hour and asked to submit to a lie detector test. He was given the test about four hours later, and after slightly less than two hours of testing, Mallory confessed. At about midnight, he finished dictating his confession to a typist. He was not told of his right to counsel and that he might keep silent, nor was he warned that any statement made by him might be used against him. He was arraigned before a U.S. commissioner the following morning. In a subsequent trial, Mallory was convicted of rape.

In its review, the Court conceded that a brief delay was justified under the federal law specifying arraignment of arrestees "without unnecessary delay,"[6] but concluded that the delay must not be designed to give federal agents an opportunity to extract a confession. The court ruled against the concept of investigative arrests or detention: "Whomever the police arrest they must arrest on 'probable cause.' It is not a function of the police to arrest, as it were, at large and to use an interrogating process at police headquarters in order to determine whom they should charge before a committing magistrate on 'probable cause.'"

State Agents and Proceedings

In 1961, the country's highest court gave up its campaign to encourage state authorities to use methods other than exclusion to protect the constitutional right to privacy, justly concluding this right had not been adequately protected from the intrusions of state agents in the "nonexclusion" states. In the landmark decision in *Mapp* v. *Ohio*,[7] the U.S. Supreme Court held that the constitutional prohibition against unreasonable searches and seizures under the Fourth Amendment was enforceable against the states under the due process clause of the Fourteenth Amendment.

For a long time, the Court believed exclusion vital to this protection in federal proceedings but was reluctant to extend its supervision to state courts.

[5]354 U.S. 449 (1957).
[6]Federal Rules of Criminal Procedure, Section 5(a).
[7]367 U.S. 643 (1961).

As early as 1949, in *Wolf* v. *Colorado*,[8] the justices expressed this reluctance in the following words:

> There are, moreover, reasons for excluding evidence unreasonably obtained by the federal police which are less compelling in the case of police under state or local authority. The public opinion of a community can far more effectively be exerted against oppressive conduct on the part of police directly responsible to the community itself than can local opinion, sporadically aroused, be brought to bear upon remote authority pervasively exerted throughout the country.

Freedom from arbitrary intrusion by state agents, however, was not achieved by the remedies suggested for states by the Wolf doctrine. The legal stumbling block to imposing minimum standards on the states by U.S. Supreme Court action was the doctrine that the first eight amendments to the Constitution were directed only to the federal government and its agents and were not adopted to limit state governments or state agents.

In 1833, Mr. Chief Justice Marshall delivered the opinion of the court in *Barron* v. *Baltimore*.[9] The following segment of his opinion indicated the court's concept of federalism at that time:

> The Constitution was ordained and established by the people of the United States for themselves, for their own government, and not for the government of the individual states. Each state established a constitution for itself, and in that constitution provided such limitations and restrictions on the powers of its particular governments as its judgment dictated. The people of the United States framed such a government for the United States as they supposed best adapted to their situation, and best calculated to promote their interests. The powers they conferred on this government were to be exercised by itself; and the limitations on power, if expressed in general terms, are naturally and, we think, necessarily applicable to the government created by the instrument.

The 1961 Court, in *Mapp*,[10] cleared away this road block by reasoning that the due process clause of the Fourteenth Amendment, adopted after the Civil War, was meant to impose the Bill of Rights limitations on state governments as well as on the federal government.

The facts in *Mapp* were as follows: Three Cleveland police officers came to Mapp's home in that city after receiving information that "a person [was] hiding out in the home, who was wanted for questioning in connection with a

---

[8]338 U.S. 25 (1949).
[9]*Barron* v. *Baltimore*, U.S. Supreme Court Reports 7 Peters 243 (1833).
[10]*Mapp* v. *Ohio*, 367 U.S. 643 (1961).

recent bombing, and that there was a large amount of policy paraphernalia being hidden in the home." Miss Mapp and her daughter by a former marriage lived on the top floor of the two-family dwelling. When they arrived at the house, the officers knocked on the door and demanded entrance, but Miss Mapp, after telephoning her attorney, refused to admit them without a search warrant. They advised headquarters of the situation and began surveillance of the house.

The officers again asked to be admitted about three hours later after four or more additional officers had arrived. When Miss Mapp did not come to the door immediately, at least one of the several doors to the house was forcibly opened and the policemen gained admittance. A police officer testified, "We did pry the screen door to gain entrance." Miss Mapp demanded to see the search warrant. A paper, claimed to be a warrant, was held up by one of the officers. She grabbed the "warrant" and placed it in her bosom. After a struggle in which the officers recovered the piece of paper, they handcuffed Miss Mapp because she had been "belligerent" in resisting their official rescue of the "warrant" from her person. Miss Mapp, in handcuffs, was then forcibly taken upstairs to her bedroom where the officers searched a dresser, a chest of drawers, a closet, and some suitcases. They also looked into a photo album and through some of her personal papers. The search spread to the rest of the second floor including the child's bedroom, the living room, the kitchen, and a dinette. The basement of the building and a trunk found there were also searched. Some obscene materials, for possession of which she was ultimately convicted, were discovered in the course of that widespread search.

At the trial, no search warrant was produced by the prosecution, nor was the failure to produce one explained or accounted for. At best, "there is, in the record, considerable doubts as to whether there ever was any warrant for the search of defendant's home." The Ohio Supreme Court affirmed the conviction. The United States Supreme Court noted probable jurisdiction and reviewed the action of the lower courts.

The Court's review of the right to privacy in this case noted that this right was enforceable against the states through the due process clause of the Fourteenth Amendment by the same sanction of exclusion that was used against the federal agents saying:

> Moreover, our holding that the exclusionary rule is an essential part of both the Fourth and Fourteenth Amendments is not only the logical dictate of prior cases, but it also makes very good sense. There is no war between the Constitution and common sense. Presently, a federal prosecutor may make no use of evidence illegally seized, but a state's attorney across the street may, although he supposedly is operating under the enforceable prohibitions of the same amendment. Thus the state, by admitting evidence unlawfully seized, serves to encourage disobedience to the Federal

Constitution which it is bound to uphold. Moreover, as was said in Elkins "the very essence of a healthy federalism depends upon the avoidance of needless conflict between state and federal courts."

Control of police power, preservation of judicial integrity, and reiteration of the right to privacy were the objectives of this landmark decision. These goals are apparent in the concluding words of the majority opinion:

> The ignoble shortcut to conviction left open to the state tends to destroy the entire system of constitutional restraints on which the liberties of the people rest. Having once recognized that the right to privacy embodied in the Fourth Amendment is enforceable against the states, and that the right to be secure against rude invasions of privacy by state officers is, therefore, constitutional in origin, we can no longer permit that right to remain an empty promise. Because it is enforceable in the same manner and to like effect as other basic rights secured by the Due Process Clause, we can no longer permit it to be revocable at the whim of any police officer who, in the name of law enforcement itself, chooses to suspend its enjoyment. Our decision, founded on reason and truth, gives to the individual no more than that which the Constitution guarantees him, to the police officer no less than that to which honest law enforcement is entitled, and to the courts, that judicial integrity so necessary in the true administration of justice.
>
> The judgment of the Supreme Court of Ohio is reversed and the cause remanded for further proceedings not inconsistent with this opinion. Reversed and remanded.

The exact nature of the supervisory power of the U.S. Supreme Court over the administration of criminal justice in state courts is best illustrated by the Court's standards for protecting constitutional rights. The Court's standards for protecting these rights in federal proceedings are now matched by the standards in state proceedings. The unity of the Court's standards for admitting evidence, when there is a dispute as to whether it was secured during an illegal search and seizure, is illustrated by the concluding words of the majority opinion in the case of *Ker* v. *California*.[11]

> We have no occasion here to decide how many of the situations, in which by the exercise of our supervisory power over the conduct of federal officers we would exclude evidence, are also situations which would require the exclusion of evidence from the state criminal proceedings under the constitutional principles extended to the states by Mapp. But where the conduct effecting an arrest so clearly transgresses those rights guaranteed by the Fourth Amendment as does the conduct which brought about the

[11]374 U.S. 23 (1963).

arrest of these petitioners, we would surely reverse the judgment if this were a federal prosecution involving federal officers. Since our decisions in Mapp has made the guarantees of the Fourteenth Amendment co-extensive with those of the Fourth Amendment we should pronounce precisely the same judgment upon the conduct of these state officers.

The Court's concern for minimum standards next found the inequality of legal representation offensive and violative of the constitutional admonition that every person accused of crime has the right to be represented by legal counsel. The Court recognized the widespread practice that allowed an attorney for those who could afford one, but ignored the constitutional right to legal assistance if the accused was unable to hire an attorney. In *Gideon* v. *Wainwright*,[12] the Court found the vehicle for extending these minimum standards through the Sixth Amendment, and ruled that every defendant who desires an attorney should have one, even if counsel must be appointed at state expense for indigent defendants.

In 1967, in *Wade* v. *United States*,[13] the Court again extended its supervision over state agents and proceedings. In *Wade*, the critical stage at which an accused is entitled to legal assistance was moved forward to the time of the post-indictment lineup. Again, seeking to deter violations of accused persons' constitutional rights the Court warned police and prosecutors that courtroom identification of a defendant would be barred unless the defendant's counsel was present at this prior identification. Wade was as much entitled to the aid of legal counsel while being viewed by eyewitnesses as at the trial itself. The danger the Court sought to avoid was and is the possibility of identification by suggestion. The Court recognized that the main source of unjust convictions is mistaken identification and has sought to standardize the lineup, or other identification procedures, by providing that defense counsel may be present to independently criticize any suggestive procedures.

In 1972, a differently balanced Supreme Court, in *Kirby* v. *Illinois*,[14] limited any extension of *Wade's* critical stage doctrine at which an accused is entitled to an attorney at postindictment lineups, ruling that accused persons are not entitled to counsel until prosecution against them has been initiated, and differentiating between postarrest and postcharge lineups.

The reasoning behind the Supreme Court's determination to outlaw pretrial practices by state agents that violate constitutional privileges and protection, and to exclude any evidence obtained by such actions, may be traced through the court's firm stand in *McNabb* and *Mallory*—cases in which conduct by federal agents was ruled likely to coerce confessions—and an 1896 case—*Brown* v. *Walker*.[15] This case involved that clause of the Fifth Amendment which declares

[12]372 U.S. 335 (1963).
[13]388 U.S. 218 (1967).
[14]406 U.S. 682 (1972).
[15]161 U.S. 591 (1896).

that no person "shall be compelled in any criminal case to be a witness against himself." The majority opinion contained the following background data on the privilege against self-incrimination:

> The maxim, *Nemo tenetur seipsum accusare*, had its origin in a protest against the inquisitorial and manifestly unjust methods of interrogating accused persons, which has long obtained in the continental system, and until the expulsion of the Stuarts from the British throne in 1688, and the erection of additional barriers for the protection of the people against exercise of arbitrary power, was not uncommon even in England. While the admissions or confessions of the prisoner, when voluntarily and freely made, have always ranked high in the scale of incriminating evidence, if an accused person be asked to explain his apparent connection with a crime under investigation, the ease with which the questions put to him may assume an inquisitorial character, the temptation to press the witness unduly, to browbeat him if he be timid or reluctant, to push him into a corner, and to entrap him into fatal contradictions, which is so painfully evident in many of the earlier state trials, notably in those of Sir Nicholas Throckmorton and Udal, the Puritan minister, made the system so odious as to give rise to a demand for its total abolition. The change in the English criminal procedure in that particular seems to be founded upon no statute and no judicial opinion, but upon a general and silent acquiescence of the courts in a popular demand. But, however adopted, it has become firmly imbedded in English as well as in American jurisprudence. So deeply did the inequities of the ancient system impress themselves upon the minds of the American colonists that the states with one accord, made a denial of the right to question an accused person a part of their fundamental law; so that a maxim, which in English was a mere rule of evidence, became clothed in this country with the impregnability of a constitutional enactment.

In federal prosecutions, the issue of voluntary confessions is controlled by the Fifth Amendment's privilege against self-incrimination. This is the basic requirement set forth in *Bram* v. *United States*.[16]

The high court's ultimate dissatisfaction with constitutional violations of an accused's rights before trial climaxed in *Miranda* v. *Arizona*.[17] It extended the doctrine of the *Mapp* case to the Fifth Amendment and imposed its standards on state agents and courts through the "due process clause" of the Fourteenth Amendment and implemented the Sixth Amendment's guarantee of legal help.

Miranda's requirements are more than the mere provision that the accused has a procedural right not to have a coerced confession used against him at trial. In many ways, *Miranda* is similar to *Mapp*. The Court, through *Miranda*, seeks to

[16]168 U.S. 532 (1897).
[17]384 U.S. 436 (1966).

prevent illegally secured confessions by forewarning police against actions which will result in the confession being excluded from evidence. *Miranda's* trio of warnings (notice of the right to silence, of any statement being used against its maker, and of the right to counsel) put the span of time between the focusing of police attention on a suspect to his arraignment in court in the same category as the arrest-to-arraignment period of threat which developed the *McNabb-Mallory* rule for federal agents and proceedings.

Derivative Use of Illegal Evidence

The rule of exclusion for evidence seized during an illegal search was expanded in 1920 in the U.S. Supreme Court's decision in *Silverthorne Lumber Company* v. *United States*.[18] This decision supported the exclusionary rule by plainly stating that the essence of the provision forbidding illegal acquisition of evidence in violation of the Fourth Amendment is that not only shall such evidence be rejected in court, but that it shall not be used at all.

Frederick W. Silverthorne and his father were indicted, arrested, and detained by U.S. agents. During this initial detention period, U.S. agents went to the office of the Silverthorne Lumber Company, operated by the defendants, and without a shadow of authority, searched the premises and seized all the books and papers they found there. The Silverthornes made a timely application to the U.S. district court for the return of the unlawfully seized books and papers, and the prosecutor was forced to return the original books and papers. But first the prosecutor made photographs and copies of the seized evidence. Subsequently, the prosecutor served the Silverthorne firm with a subpoena to produce the original books and papers in court. Their refusal resulted in a court order of compliance, and their continued refusal to obey this order led to a judgment of contempt and a fine of $250. In response to a writ of error filed by the Silverthornes, the judgment was reversed, and Mr. Justice Holmes delivering the Court opinion. The proposition involved in this case is summed up in this opinion as follows:

> The government now, while in form repudiating and condemning the illegal seizure, seeks to maintain its right to avail itself of the knowledge obtained by that means which otherwise it would not have. The proposition could not be presented more nakedly. It is that although, of course, its seizure was an outrage which the government now regrets, it may study the papers before it returns them, copy them, and then may use the knowledge that it has gained to call upon the owners in a more regular form to produce them; that the protection of the Constitution covers the physical possession but not any advantages the government can gain over the object of its pursuit by doing the forbidden act. *Weeks* v. *United States*, 232, U.S.

[18]251 U.S. 385 (1920).

383 (1914), to be sure, had established that laying the papers directly before a grand jury is unwarranted, but it is taken to mean two steps are required instead of one. In our opinion such is not the law. It reduces the Fourth Amendment to a form of words.

The *Silverthorne* opinion recognized the exigencies of criminal investigation by pointing out that any knowledge of the illegally gathered facts obtained from an "independent source" could be used to prove those facts. There is no doubt the source must have no connection with the warrantless search or its fruits, in this case, the examination of the seized books and papers. The Court warned in *Silverthorne* that "The knowledge gained by the government's own wrong cannot be used by it in the way proposed."

Further, in a 1925 prosecution for conspiracy to violate a drug possession law, evidence obtained in an illegal search was held not admissible in the prosecution's case in chief nor in rebuttal during cross-examination of the defendant. The facts in this case, *Agnello* v. *United States*,[19] were as follows: Frank Agnello and others were convicted of conspiracy to sell cocaine in violation of federal law. Among the items of evidence proffered by the government in its case in chief was a can of cocaine that had been seized by U.S. agents in Agnello's bedroom some time after his arrest. At the time of the search, Agnello was in custody elsewhere, and the place searched was not the place where Agnello had been arrested. This evidence was excluded on the ground that the search and seizure had been made without a search warrant. On direct examination, Agnello was not asked and did not testify about this can of cocaine. In cross-examination, however, he was asked if he had ever seen this evidence ("Did you ever see narcotics before?"), and he answered no after the trial judge overruled defense counsel's objection.

The court held that this line of questioning, after the prosecutor had failed in his efforts to introduce the unlawfully seized evidence in its case in chief, was nothing more than an attempt to smuggle illegal evidence into the court record. After Agnello's expected denial of the above question, the prosecutor attempted to introduce the can of cocaine illegally seized in Agnello's bedroom. The judgment against Agnello was set aside, and a new trial ordered on the grounds he had done nothing to waive his constitutional protection or justify cross-examination about the evidence obtained by the unlawful search, and the admission of such testimony was an error that prejudiced Agnello's rights.

The doctrine barring derivative evidence tainted by illegal origin from federal courts was further expanded when the U.S. Supreme Court ruled, in *Nardone* v. *United States*,[20] that once the accused established that any evidence was unlawfully procured, the trial court must give the accused an opportunity to prove that a substantial portion of the case against him was based on such unlawfully procured evidence.

[19]269 U.S. 20 (1925).
[20]308 U.S. 338 (1939).

After Nardone's original trial, his conviction was reversed because illegally intercepted telephone messages were a vital part of the prosecution's proof of guilt. Nardone was again convicted in a new trial, and the Court agreed to review his appeal to determine whether the trial judge had improperly refused to allow the accused to ask the prosecution about the uses to which it had put the information contained in the illegal wire-tapping which had caused Nardone's original conviction to be reversed. The court's opinion noted that, as in the Silverthorne case, facts improperly obtained do not "become sacred and inaccessible." If knowledge of them is gained from an independent source they may be proved like any others, but the knowledge gained by the government's own wrong cannot be used by it simply because it is used derivatively.

In reversing Nardone's second conviction, the Court's majority indicated the sensible way of handling this problem: "The burden is, of course, on the accused in the first instance to prove to the trial court's satisfaction that wire-tapping was unlawfully employed. Once that is established—as was plainly done here—the presiding judge must give opportunity, however closely confined, to the accused to prove that a substantial portion of the case against him was the fruit of the poisonous tree. This leaves ample opportunity to the government to convince the trial court that its proof had an independent origin. And if such a claim is made after the trial is under way, the judge must likewise be satisfied that the accused could not, at an earlier stage, have had adequate knowledge to make his claim."

Collateral Use Doctrine

An exception to the exclusionary rule has become known as the collateral use doctrine. This rule allows the introduction of illegally obtained and otherwise inadmissible evidence for the limited purpose of impeaching the credibility of a defendant in a criminal action when he assumes the role of a witness. In a 1954 case, *Walder* v. *United States*,[21] Walder was indicted in the U.S. district court for purchasing heroin. Claiming that the heroin capsule had been obtained through an unlawful search and seizure, Walder moved to suppress it. The motion was granted, and shortly thereafter on the government's motion, the case against him was dismissed. In January 1952, Walder was indicted again, this time for four other illicit transactions in narcotics. The government's case consisted principally of testimony by two drug addicts who claimed to have procured the illicit stuff from Walder under the direction of federal agents. The only witness for the defense was the defendant himself. He denied any narcotics dealings with the two government informers and attributed the testimony against him to personal hostility.

During direct examination, Walder was questioned and testified as follows:

[21]347 U.S. 62 (1954).

Q: Now, first, Mr. Walder, before we go further in your testimony, I want you to tell the Court and jury whether, not referring to these informers in this case, but whether you have ever sold any narcotics to anyone?

A: I have never sold any narcotics to anyone in my life.

Q: Have you ever had any narcotics in your possession, other than what may have been given to you by a physician for an ailment?

A: No.

Q: Now, I will ask you one more thing. Have you ever handled or given any narcotics to anyone as a gift or in any other manner without the receipt of any money or any other compensation?

A: I have not.

Q: Have you ever even acted as, say, have you acted as a conduit for the purpose of handling what you knew to be a narcotic from one person to another?

A: No, sir.

On cross-examination, in response to a question by government counsel referring to this direct testimony, Walder again said that he had never purchased, sold, or possessed any narcotics. Over the defendant's objection, the government then questioned him about the heroin capsule unlawfully seized from his home, in his presence, during a prior arrest in February 1950. The defendant stoutly denied that any narcotics had been taken from him at that time. (This denial squarely contradicted an affidavit filed by the defendant in the earlier proceedings in connection with his motion to suppress the evidence unlawfully seized.) The government then put on the stand one of the officers who had participated in the unlawful search and seizure and also the chemist who had analyzed the heroin capsule that had been seized.

The trial judge admitted this evidence, but carefully charged the jury that it was not to be used to determine whether the defendant had committed the crimes charged, but solely for the purpose of impeaching the defendant's credibility. The defendant was convicted.

The Court's opinion shows a basic aversion to perjury while upholding the exclusionary rule. The opinion concludes with the following paragraphs:

1. The Government cannot violate the Fourth Amendment—in the only way the government can do anything, namely through its agents—and use the fruits of such unlawful conduct to secure a conviction (*Weeks* v. *United States, supra*). Nor can the Government make indirect use of such evidence for its case (*Silverthorne Lumber Company* v. *United States*, 251 U.S. 385), or support a conviction on evidence obtained through leads from the unlawfully obtained evidence (*Nardone* v. *United States*, 308 U.S. 388). All these methods are outlawed, and convictions obtained by means of them are

invalidated, because they encourage the kind of society that is obnoxious to free men.

2. It is one thing to say that the Government cannot make an affirmative use of evidence unlawfully obtained. It is quite another to say that the defendant can turn the illegal method by which evidence in the Government's possession was obtained to his own advantage, and provide himself with a shield against contradiction of his untruths. Such an extension of the Weeks' doctrine would be a perversion of the Fourth Amendment.

Take the present situation. Of his own accord, the defendant went beyond a mere denial of complicity in the crimes of which he was charged and made the sweeping claim that he had never dealt in or possessed any narcotics. Of course, the Constitution guarantees a defendant the fullest opportunity to meet the accusation against him. He must be free to deny all the elements of the case against him without thereby giving leave to the Government to introduce by way of rebuttal evidence illegally secured by it, and therefore not available for its case in chief. Beyond that, however, there is hardly justification for letting the defendant affirmatively resort to perjurious testimony in reliance on the Government's disability to challenge his credibility.

The situation here involved is to be sharply contrasted with that presented by *Agnello* v. *United States*, 269 U.S. 20 (1925). There the Government, after having failed in its efforts to introduce the tainted evidence in its case in chief, tried to smuggle it in on cross-examination by asking the accused the broad question, "Did you ever see narcotics before?" After eliciting the expected denial, it sought to introduce evidence of narcotics, located in the defendant's home by means of an unlawful search and seizure in order to discredit the defendant.

In 1971, the U.S. Supreme Court decided *Harris* v. *New York*,[22] which extended the court's attitude in *Walder* to *Miranda* violation confessions, admissions, or statements. Harris was not properly advised of his rights under *Miranda* and did give incriminating statements as a result of interrogation by police. At his trial, the prosecution did not attempt to introduce the statements taken in violation of *Miranda*. During the defense case, Harris's testimony was different from the statements he had made to the police. He was cross-examined concerning the statements he had given in violation of *Miranda* and the Court allowed impeachment with the introduction of the relevant extrajudicial statement:

It is one thing to say that the government cannot make an affirmative use of evidence unlawfully obtained. It is quite another to say that the defendant can turn the illegal method by which evidence in the government's

---

[22]401 U.S. 222 (1971).

possession was obtained to his own advantage, and provide himself with a shield against contradiction of his untruths. Such an extension of the Weeks doctrine would be a perversion of the Fourth Amendment.[23]

In 1990, the Court further extended the collateral use doctrine to allow the prosecution to use a statement taken in violation of the *Jackson* prophylactic rule.[24] The *Jackson* rule established that once a defendant invoked his Sixth Amendment right to counsel, any subsequent waiver of that right is presumed invalid if secured pursuant to police-initiated conversation, and any statements obtained therefrom could not be admitted in the case in chief.

In *Harvey*, two months after the defendant was appointed counsel, he made a statement to a police officer. The prosecutor agreed it was police-initiated conversation and declined to use the statement in his case in chief. At trial the defendant testified. On appeal, the Court relied on the rationale of *Harris* to uphold the prosecutor's ability to use the defendant's statements taken in violation of *Jackson* to impeach his in-court testimony.

The Court in both *Harris* and *Harvey* stated that a defendant has no right to commit perjury and that it is proper to utilize the traditional truth-testing devices to aid the jury in assessing his credibility.

Motion to Suppress

The procedure for suppressing illegally obtained evidence is usually controlled by detailed statute. If these procedures are not followed the illegally obtained evidence may be admitted as evidence against the defendant.

Jurisdictions vary in the details of procedure, but each state provides a procedure for raising and resolving the issue of whether or not the evidence should be excluded. At least twenty states generally follow the federal procedure. Rule 41 of the Federal Rules of Criminal Procedure provides the following exclusive method of suppressing evidence:

Motion for Return of Property and to Suppress Evidence. A person aggrieved by an unlawful search and seizure may move the district court for the district in which the property was seized for the return of the property and to suppress for use as evidence anything so obtained on the ground that (1) the property was illegally seized without warrant, or (2) the warrant is insufficient on its face, or (3) the property seized is not that described in the warrant, or (4) there was not probable cause for believing the existence of the grounds on which the warrant was issued, or (5) the warrant was illegally executed. The judge shall receive evidence on any issue of fact

---

[23]*Harris* v. *New York*, 401 U.S. 222 (1971), p. 224.
[24]*Michigan* v. *Harvey*, 494 U.S. 344 (1990).

necessary to the decision of the motion. If the motion is granted the property shall be restored unless otherwise subject to unlawful detention, and it shall not be admissible in evidence at any hearing or trial. The motion to suppress evidence may also be made in the district where the trial is to be held. The motion shall be made before trial or hearing unless opportunity therefore did not exist or the defendant was not aware of the grounds for the motion, but the court in its discretion may entertain the motion at the trial or hearing.

Scope and Definition. This rule does not modify any act, inconsistent with it, regulating search, seizure and the issuance and execution of search warrants in circumstances for which special provision is made. The term 'property' is used in this rule to include documents, books, papers, and any other tangible objects.

California's procedure is both exclusive and comprehensive.[25] In a felony case, a motion may be made at the preliminary examination, tested on a motion to set aside the information, and aligned with a petition for a writ of prohibition to the appellate court. It may be repeated with an evidentiary hearing on a written motion made to the trial court prior to trial, and an appeal by either party to the ruling of the court. If the motion is granted in favor of the defendant and the prosecution appeals, the defendant may be released on his own recognizance. The court—if additional evidence is produced—may also allow the question of suppression to be raised again at the trial. However, without good cause the issue is lost unless raised at the pretrial hearing, or if raised, has been denied at such hearing.

Attacking the Exclusionary Rule

Whenever evidence gathered by police has been excluded at the subsequent prosecution, there has been the outcry that the court is letting the guilty criminal go free. In 1922, when the Chicago police had coerced a confession from a defendant and the court excluded that confession and would not allow it in evidence at the trial of the defendant, a high police official made the following comment to the newspapers: "Ninety-five percent of the work of the department will be nullified if the [court] policy is permitted to prevail. Few, if any, prisoners confess except after lengthy examination. We are permitted to do less every day, pretty soon there won't be a police department."[26]

The official was obviously a bit premature and perhaps overreacting. There is, however, considerable sentiment and substance to the argument that the criminal should not go free merely because the policeman blunders. Few in or

[25]California Penal Code, Section 995 and 1538.5.
[26]*People* v. *Rogers*, 136 N.E. 470, 474 (1922).

outside of law enforcement advocate that there be no limit to police authority and activity, but most contend there are ways other than exclusion to preserve our individual rights and lawful police activity.

The attack on exclusion was given prestige and direction in 1964 by Warren E. Burger in a law review article:

> I suggest that the notion that suppression of evidence in a given case effectively deters the future action of the particular policeman or of policemen generally was never more than wishful thinking on the part of the Courts.[27]

Justice Burger further commented that the spectacle of freeing the guilty because of the exclusionary rule destroys public respect for the law and the courts.

In 1967, the President's Commission on Law Enforcement and Administration of Justice gave additional substance to the numerous but scattered complaints of the police and prosecution agencies:

> In the Federal system, as well as in many States, the existing rule, now the subject of reconsideration by the Supreme Court, is that search warrants may be used only to seize contraband or the fruits or instrumentalities of crime. If evidence is seized illegally, it cannot be used in court. In the words of a Supreme Court decision: "They may not be used as a means of gaining access to a man's house or office and papers solely for the purpose of making search to secure evidence to be used against him in a criminal or penal proceeding" (*Gouled* v. *United States*, 255 U.S. 298 (1921), p. 309). If evidence is seized illegally, it cannot be used in court.
>
> These limitations on proof of guilt are not universal; many countries operate effective and humane criminal systems without putting so great a burden on the prosecution. America's adherence to these principles not only demands complex and time-consuming court procedures but also in some cases forecloses the proof of facts altogether. Guilty criminals may be set free because the court's exclusionary rules prevent the introduction of a confession or of seized evidence. Crimes may never even be detected because restrictions on the methods of investigation insulate criminal conduct from the attention of the police.[28]

Again, in 1971, Justice Burger, as the chief justice of the United States Supreme Court, stated in an opinion:

> Inadvertent errors of judgment that do not work any grave injustice will inevitably occur under the pressure of police work. These honest mistakes

---

[27]Burger, "Who Will Watch the Watchman?" *American University Law Review*, 1, no. 12 (1964).
[28]The President's Commission on Law Enforcement and Administration of Justice, *The Challenge of Crime in a Free Society* (Washington, D.C.: U.S. Government Printing Office, 1967), pp. 125–26.

have been treated in the same way as deliberate and flagrant Irvine-type violations of the Fourth Amendment. For example, in *Miller* v. *United States*, 357 U.S. 301, 309–310 (1958), reliable evidence was suppressed because of a police officer's failure to say a "few more words" during the arrest and search of a known narcotics peddler.

Freeing either a tiger or a mouse in a schoolroom is an illegal act, but no rational person would suggest that these two acts should be punished in the same way.

I submit that society has at least as much right to expect rationally graded responses from judges in place of the universal "capital punishment" we inflict on all evidence when police error is shown in its acquisition.[29]

In 1973, a select committee appointed directly by the governor of California drew together the arguments opposing the exclusionary rule and made a recommendation to the governor:

> In line with the recommendations of Chief Justice Burger and several other experts in the field, we recommend enactment of law which abolishes the exclusionary rule and creates a better remedy, permitting the victim of an unlawful search or seizure to collect damages from the agency which employed the offending officer.
>
> This better remedy stops the suppression of reliable evidence and freeing criminals for police mistakes. It makes the public entity liable for damages from an unlawful search or seizure. It provides priority to obtain prompt redress and provides attorney's fee so everyone will be able to afford to pursue a valid claim. It retains punitive damages and criminal prosecution where appropriate against persons guilty of malicious, fraudulent, oppressive, or criminal conduct. It returns the emphasis to the ascertainment of the truth.[30]

The California Governor's Select Committee summarized the arguments against the exclusionary rule:

Obstacles to Effective Deterrence

1. There is no penalty against the officer or agency.
2. Exclusion may occur months or years later.
3. The law is complex and confusing.
4. Officers can't be expected to understand and comply with rules when even Supreme Court judges can't agree on what the rules are.

---

[29]*Bivins* v. *Six Unknown Federal Narcotic Agents*, 403 U.S. 388, 418–419 (1971); See also *Irvine* v. *California*, 347 U.S. 128 (1954).

[30]*Report of the Governor's Select Committee on Law Enforcement Problems: Protecting the Law Abiding, Controlling Crime in California* (Sacramento, Calif.: State Printing Office, 1973), p. 52

5. There is no effect on the bulk of police work which is not directed toward prosecution.

6. Many decisions are so unreasonable that they do not inspire respect and compliance.

7. Because most exclusions involve inadvertent violations, officers tend to excuse all violations as trivial and technical.

Other Defects of the Exclusionary Rule

1. It suppresses the truth.
2. It frees guilty criminals.
3. It destroys respect for law and the courts.
4. It offends justice by benefiting guilty persons but not their innocent victims.
5. It causes great delays in justice.
6. It makes capricious distinctions between equally guilty defendants.
7. It diverts the trial from the issue of determining guilt.
8. It creates overwhelming trial and appellate work loads.
9. Motion to suppress may pressure a prosecutor into a bad plea bargain.
10. Officers may confer immunity for serious crimes.
11. It does not differentiate between honest mistakes and flagrant violations.
12. It does not differentiate between releasing murderers and releasing drunks.
13. It implies that releasing a murderer is less serious than a police mistake.

The Committee's solution and the claimed advantage of their solution are also summarized as follows:

A Better Solution

1. Abolish the exclusionary rule.
2. Make the public entity liable for ordinary damages for unlawful searches and seizures, plus attorney's fees.
3. Provide court trial, to avoid possible jury sympathy for police officers and bias against guilty victims.
4. Encourage use of search warrants by excluding liability for searches pursuant to a warrant.
5. Set a minimum award of $250.
6. Provide priority so victims can obtain prompt redress.
7. Retain punitive damages and criminal prosecution, where applicable, against any officers guilty of malicious, fraudulent, or oppressive conduct.

Advantages of the Alternative

1. The individual does not bear the burden of actions taken for public benefit.
2. Criminal trials are returned to their proper purpose.
3. Financial responsibility should stimulate police training and supervision to avoid liability.
4. It provides a remedy to innocent victims and treats guilty victims the same as innocent ones instead of exalting the guilty.
5. It *stops freeing the guilty.*
6. It *returns emphasis to ascertainment of the truth.*

In 1984, the U.S. Supreme Court granted an exception to the *Miranda* doctrine (384 U.S. 436, 1966), ruling that overriding considerations of public safety may justify the police in questioning a suspect in custody without first advising him or her of their right under *Miranda.* Since this is the first time in eighteen years that an exception to the *Miranda* doctrine has been granted by this court, the facts of this case[31] and the reasoning of the majority as cited in their opinion raises questions as to the stability of the *Miranda* doctrine and—possibly—other exclusionary rules.

The facts of this case are

On Sept 11,1980, at approximately 12:30 A.M., Officer Frank Kraft and Office Sal Scarring were on road patrol in Queens, N.Y., when a young woman approached their car. She told them that she had just been raped by a black male, approximately six feet tall, who was wearing a black jacket with the name "Big Ben" printed in yellow letters on the back. She told the officers that the man had just entered an A.&P. supermarket located nearby and that the man was carrying a gun.

The officers drove the woman to the supermarket and Officer Kraft entered the store while Officer Scarring radioed for assistance. Officer Kraft quickly spotted respondent, ordered him to stop and put his hands over his head.

Although more than three other officers had arrived on the scene by that time, Officer Kraft was the first to reach respondent. He frisked him and discovered that he was wearing a shoulder holster, which was then empty. After handcuffing him, Officer Kraft asked him where the gun was. Respondent nodded in the direction of some empty cartons and responded, "The gun is over there." Officer Kraft thereafter retrieved a loaded .38-caliber revolver from one of the cartons, formally placed respondent under arrest and read him his *Miranda* rights from a printed card. Respondent

[31]*Quarles v. New York,* 104 S. Ct. 2626 (1984).

indicated that he would be willing to answer questions without an attorney present. Office Kraft then asked respondent if he owned the gun and where he had purchased it. Respondent answered that he did own it and that he had purchased it in Miami, Fla.

Excerpts from the majority opinion spell out this "public safety" exception to the *Miranda* rule:

We conclude that under the circumstances involved in this case, overriding considerations of public safety justify the officer's failure to provide *Miranda* warnings before he asked questions devoted to locating the abandoned weapon.

In the subsequent prosecution of respondent for criminal possession of a weapon, the judge excluded the statement, "the gun is over there," and the gun because the officer had not given respondent the warnings required by our decision in *Miranda* v. *Arizona*, 384 U.S. 436 (1966), before asking him where the gun was located. For the reasons which follow, we believe that this case presents a situation where concern for public safety must be paramount to adherence to the literal language of the prophylactic rules enunciated in *Miranda*.

The Fifth Amendment guarantees that "no person ... shall be compelled in any criminal case to be a witness against himself." In *Miranda* this Court for the first time extended the Fifth Amendment privilege against compulsory self-incrimination to individuals subjected to custodial interrogation by the police.

In this case we have before us no claim that respondent's statements were actually compelled by police conduct which overcame his will to resist. Thus the only issue before us is whether Officer Kraft was justified in failing to make available to respondent the procedural safeguards associated with the privilege against compulsory self-incrimination since *Miranda*.

The New York Court of Appeals was undoubtedly correct in deciding that the facts of this case come within the ambit of the *Miranda* decision as we have subsequently interpreted it. We agree that respondent was in police custody because we have noted that "the ultimate inquiry is simply whether there is a 'formal arrest or restraint on freedom of movement' of the degree associated with a formal arrest." Here Quarles was surrounded by at least four police officers and was handcuffed when the questioning at issue took place. As the New York Court of Appeals observed, there was nothing to suggest that any of the officers were any longer concerned for their own physical safety. The New York Court of Appeals majority declined to express an opinion as to whether there might be an exception to the *Miranda* rule if the police had been acting to protect the public, because the lower courts in New York had made no factual determination that the police had acted with that motive.

We hold that on these facts there is a "public safety" exception to the requirement that *Miranda* warnings be given before a suspect's answers may be admitted into evidence, and that the availability of that exception does not depend upon the motivation of the individual officer involved. In a kaleidoscopic situation such as the one confronting these officers, where spontaneity rather than adherence to a police manual is necessarily the order of the day, the application of the exception which we recognize today should not be made to depend on post hoc findings at a suppression hearing concerning the subjective motivation of the arresting officer. Undoubtedly most police officers, if placed in Officer Kraft's position, would act out of a host of different, instinctive, and largely unverifiable motives—their own safety, the safety of others, and perhaps as well the desire to obtain incriminating evidence from the suspect.

Whatever the motivation of individual officers in such a situation, we do not believe that the doctrinal underpinnings of *Miranda* require that it be applied in all its rigor to a situation in which police officers ask questions reasonably prompted by a concern for the public safety. The *Miranda* decision was based in large part on this Court's view that the warnings which it required police to give to suspects in custody would reduce the likelihood that the suspects would fall victim to constitutionally impermissible practices of police interrogation in the presumptively coercive environment of the station house. The dissenters warned that the requirement of *Miranda* warnings would have the effect of decreasing the number of suspects who respond to police questioning. The *Miranda* majority, however, apparently felt that whatever the cost to society in terms of fewer convictions of guilty suspects, that cost would simply have to be borne in the interest of enlarged protection for the Fifth Amendment privilege.

The police in this case, in the very act of apprehending a suspect, were confronted with the immediate necessity of ascertaining the whereabouts of a gun which they had every reason to believe the suspect had just removed from his empty holster and discarded in the supermarket, with its actual whereabouts unknown, it obviously posed more than one danger to the public safety: an accomplice might make use of it, a customer or employee might later come upon it.

In such a situation, if the police are required to recite the familiar *Miranda* warnings before asking the whereabouts of the gun, suspects in Quarles's position might well be deterred from responding. Procedural safeguards which deter a suspect from responding were deemed acceptable in *Miranda* in order to protect the Fifth Amendment privilege; when the primary social cost of those added protections is the possibility of fewer convictions, the *Miranda* majority was willing to bear that cost. Here, had *Miranda* warnings deterred Quarles from responding to Officer Kraft's question about the whereabouts of the gun, the cost would have been something more than merely the failure to obtain evidence useful in

convicting Quarles. Officer Kraft needed an answer to his question not simply to make his case against Quarles but to insure that further danger to the
public did not result from the concealment of the gun in a public area.

We conclude that the need for answers to questions in a situation pos-
ing a threat to the public safety outweighs the need for the prophylactic
rule protecting the Fifth Amendment's privilege against self-incrimination.
We decline to place officers such as Officer Kraft in the untenable position
of having to consider, often in a matter of seconds, whether it best serves
society for them to ask the necessary questions without the *Miranda* warnings and render whatever probative evidence they uncover inadmissible,or
for them to give the warnings in order to preserve the admissibility of evidence they might uncover but possibly damage or destroy their ability to
obtain that evidence and neutralize the volatile situation confronting them.

In recognizing a narrow exception to the *Miranda* rule in this case, we
acknowledge that to some degree we lessen the desirable clarity of that
rule. At least in part in order to preserve its clarity, we have over the years
refused to sanction attempts to expand our *Miranda* holding.

As we have in other contexts, we recognize here the importance of a
workable rule "to guide police officers, who have only limited time and
expertise to reflect on and balance the social and individual interests
involved in the specific circumstances they confront." But as we have pointed out, we believe that the exception which we recognize today lessens the
necessity of that on-the-scene balancing process.

The exception which we recognize today, far from complicating the
thought processes and the on-the-scene judgments of police officers, will
simply free them to follow their legitimate instincts when confronting situations presenting a danger to the public safety.

It is so ordered.

The search for a balance between the power of government and the right of
the individual against unlawful intrusion, and the further right of citizens to the
protection by government from intrusions of criminals, is continuing and ongoing.

Case Studies

Silverthorne v. *United States*, 251 U.S. 385 (1920).

Mapp v. *Ohio*, 367 U.S. 643 (1961).

Nardone v. *United States*, 308 U.S. 338 (1939).

Discussion Questions

1. Why was the U.S. Supreme Court reluctant to extend federal rules on invasion of privacy to state courts and proceedings dealing with state agents?

2. Why did the Court outlaw the "silver platter" routine?

3. Explain the "fruit of the poisoned tree" concept of derivative evidence. Why should evidence justly classified solely as fruits of lawless procedures not be used at all?

4. What is meant by the denial of a defendant's "license for perjury" in the collateral use of evidence tainted by illegality?

5. Outline several benefits accruing to the administration of justice as a result of the exclusionary rule and the growing acceptance of pretrial motions to suppress.

6. Outline the arguments against the exclusionary rule.

7. What are the alternatives to the exclusionary rule?

8. What innovative action is likely to achieve the objectives of the exclusionary rule without its many disadvantages?

9. Explain the rationale for the "public safety" exception to the *Miranda* doctrine.

Glossary

Affidavit   Sworn written statement.

Fruits of the Poisoned Tree Doctrine   Doctrine barring the use of derivative evidence tainted by illegal origin.

Irvine-Type Violations   Purposeful violations of the Constitution by police officer.

Nemo Tenetur Seipsum Accusare   No one is bound to accuse himself.

CHAPTER 11

Evidence: Arrests, Searches, and Seizures

CHAPTER OBJECTIVES

- To list and describe the controls of police behavior in arrest situations and searches and seizures.
- To detail the procedure and requirements for warrants (arrest, search).
- To emphasize the role of the issuing magistrate in seeing that summary police action does not interfere with the rights of citizens.
- To develop the reliable informant concept as relevant to evidence of probable cause.

Lawful searches are governed by the doctrine of reasonableness and probable cause embodied in the Fourth Amendment. Unreasonable intrusions by police are likely to invalidate evidence necessary to prove the guilt of a person responsible for a criminal act. The Fourth Amendment protects people and their property from unreasonable search and seizure. To make this protection effective, the law presently prohibits the use of evidence, seized illegally, against the victim of the unreasonable search and seizure.

Under reasonable circumstances, a police officer may interfere with a person's freedom of action and detain him for investigation or arrest him as the person responsible for a specific crime. A police officer may justify a reasonable intrusion to conduct a protective search or to search for and seize fruits and instrumentalities of crime or mere evidence connected with a crime or criminal. Evidence, however, may be tainted by illegality if the police unreasonably interfere with the constitutional liberties of the person stopped, arrested, "frisked," or searched when the articles or objects of evidence are seized.

Court decisions no longer permit extensive searches incidental to lawful arrests, searches to justify arrests, or sham or pretext arrests to justify searches.

The critical area is reasonableness. A uniform rule permitting a search in every case of a valid arrest would greatly simplify the work of police investigators and clarify a nebulous area of admissibility of evidence. However, a uniform approach to a complex problem precludes consideration of the reasonableness of any particular search. A single uniform standard for searches and seizures accompanying arrests would jeopardize the protection the Fourth Amendment was designed to provide each of us. Whenever it happens, a search is a once-only happening to be reviewed not on any broad rule of uniformity but rather on its merits as a particular event brought about by police action which the police involved must justify.

If there is any movement toward uniformity, it is in the concept that the officer must obtain a search warrant. A police officer who searches for and seizes evidence without a search warrant must show exceptionally compelling reasons for his actions. With each decision, the Supreme Court shows more clearly its desire to place an impartial judge between the police officer and the privacy of the individual.[1]

The Fourth Amendment[2] has two major clauses. One concerns reasonableness and the other probable cause. The first clause of the Fourth Amendment establishes a standard of reasonableness applicable to all searches and seizures, and arrests. The second clause establishes the level of reasonableness in situations best termed "warrant areas"—where the intrusion is made not for the protection of the officer, but for the purpose of collecting evidence for use at the trial of the arrestee.

Probable Cause

Probable cause is the standard against which a particular decision to search for and possibly seize evidence is measured to see if it meets the constitutional requirement of reasonableness. A simple assertion of police suspicion is not in itself a sufficient basis for a magistrate's finding of probable cause.[3]

All the definitions of probable cause require, in substance, that there be reasonable grounds for belief of guilt—a belief that is supported by evidence and inclines the mind to assume guilt but which may leave some room for doubt. Probable cause exists when the person taking or planning action knows of facts or circumstances sufficient to justify a man of reasonable caution in believing that an offense has been or is being committed. Quite often, it is difficult to distinguish between mere suspicion and probable cause. Many situations

[1]*Chimel* v. *United States*, 395 U.S. 752 (1969); *Katz* v. *United States* 389 U.S. 347 (1967); *United States* v. *U.S. District Court*, 407 U.S. 297 (1973).

[2]"The right of the people to be secure in their persons, houses, papers, and effects, against unreasonable searches and seizures, shall not be violated, and no warrants shall issue, but upon probable cause, supported by oath or affirmation, and particularly describing the place to be searched, and the persons or things to be seized."

[3]*Apinelli* v. *United States*, 393 U.S. 410 (1969).

confronting police investigators are ambiguous. Some errors in judgment are not unexpected. These mistakes, however, must be the errors of reasonable men acting on facts to arrive at their conclusions of probability.[4]

Belief in the existence of probable cause is best based on the direct observations and knowledge of the police officer involved, but hearsay evidence may be the basis for believing probable cause exists. A police officer may rely on information received through an informant if the informant's statement is corroborated by other matters the officer knows about.[5]

There is movement toward a "good faith" exception to the exclusion of evidence because of an otherwise unlawful search and seizure of evidence.

Reasonableness

Reasonableness is determined by balancing the need to search against the invasion of privacy that the search entails. Wherever a man may be, he is entitled to know that he will remain free from unreasonable searches and seizures. The Fourth Amendment was aimed at the abhorred practice of breaking in and searching homes and other buildings and seizing people's personal belongings without warrants issued by magistrates. The issue of reasonableness is determined by asking whether the invasion is justified by the evidence of criminality. The facts available to the police officer at the time of the search and seizure must be sufficient to warrant the action taken and its urgency.[6]

The right to search without a search warrant with appropriately given consent, to contemporaneously search persons lawfully arrested, or to search premises entered in "hot pursuit" of a suspect, are exceptions to the rule that the Fourth Amendment requires adherence to judicial processes, and that searches without judicial process are in themselves unreasonable under the Fourth Amendment.[7] Vehicles usually have a special status in relation to search warrants because of their mobility, but only when they are suspected of transporting contraband.[8] Exigent circumstances may also substitute for probable cause in very limited types of situations.[9]

Courts scrutinize the claims of police about consent. Consent to enter and search premises must be affirmatively shown to have been secured freely and voluntarily. Any trace of coercion ruins reliance on consent as authority for a search and seizure.[10] Quite often, consent may be secured from a person not in control of the premises or not authorized by the resident involved to grant

---

[4]*Brinegar* v. *United States*, 338 U.S. 160 (1949).

[5]*Jones* v. *United States*, 362 U.S. 257 (1960).

[6]*Chimel* v. *California*, 395 U.S. 752 (1970).

[7]*Katz* v. *United States*, 389 U.S. 347 (1967); *Warden* v. *Hayden*, 387 U.S. 294 (1967).

[8]*Carroll* v. *United States*, 267 U.S. 132 (1925).

[9]*People* v. *Sirhan*, 7 Cal. 3d 710 (1972); *Rice* v. *Wolff*, 513 F. 2d 1280 (1975).

[10]*Bumper* v. *North Carolina*, 391 U.S. 543 (1968).

consent to a search.[11] When any doubt exists, application for a search warrant is more than justified to avoid tainting the evidence likely to be seized. Courts do not approve of unrealistic claims that the person who consented to the search had "apparent authority."

The factual situations spelling out the degree of reasonableness required in making arrests and conducting hot-pursuit and arrest-based searches have remarkable variety. Each case must be judged on its individual circumstances. Factors found important in court decisions should serve as guidelines to police in learning to recognize what is reasonable in an particular situation.

A search which is reasonable when it begins may violate the Fourth Amendment by virtue of its intolerable intensity or scope.

Two cases illustrate police searches that were so intense that the courts considered them unreasonable: (1) The contents of an entire cabin were seized after a search incidental to the arrest, and (2) the stomach of the arrestee was pumped out to recover two capsules of illegal drugs.

The seizure of the entire contents of a small house by FBI agents, in *Kremen* v. *California*,[12] may have been warranted by the remote rural area in which the house was located and the investigative necessity of processing a great deal of the collected evidence in a scientific crime laboratory. On its merits, however, it was ruled that this search was unreasonable.

The scope of the search must be strictly tied to, and justified by, the circumstances that rendered it permissible when the search began. It cannot be founded on subjective viewpoints sensitive to the evidentiary needs of investigators. It must be founded on a constitutional frame of reference—the reasonableness clause of the Fourth Amendment. For this reason, there is little or no justification for searching an arrestee's home or office, if either is the place of arrest. In the ordinary arrest it should be sufficient to search the arrestee and the area immediately within his control to provide physical protection to police from an accessible weapon or to prevent destruction of evidence within the reasonable reach of the arrestee.[13] If there is reason to believe there is other evidence in the general area, police should secure the area, obtain a search warrant, and then conduct a search of the area.

In *Rochin* v. *California*,[14] however, there is little disagreement that the stomach-pumping was unreasonable. The facts in Rochin were as follows: Police officers investigating the illegal sale of habit-forming drugs were alerted to the activities of Rochin by information from underworld sources. Two officers forced the door of Rochin's room. Rochin was found there, sitting on the bed. The officers then asked Rochin about two capsules of suspect drugs visible on a nightstand alongside Rochin's bed. ("Whose stuff is this?") Rochin seized the

[11]*Stoner* v. *California*, 376 U.S. 483 (1964).
[12]353 U.S. 346 (1957).
[13]*Chimel* v. *California*, 395 U.S. 752 (1970).
[14]342 U.S. 165 (1952).

capsules and put them in his mouth. The officers attempted to extract the cap-sules, but Rochin had apparently swallowed them. The officers then handcuffed Rochin and took him to a nearby hospital where a doctor, at the request of the two police officers, forced an emetic solution through a tube into Rochin's stom-ach, against his will. Two capsules of an illegal drug, morphine, were recovered when the emetic solution caused Rochin to vomit. Rochin was charged with ille-gal possession of morphine. He was convicted, and appealed his conviction.

The ground for his appeal was that an unreasonable search had invalidated the evidence on which his conviction was based. The opinion of the court labeled stomach pumping a major and unreasonable intrusion. "The proceedings by which this conviction was obtained," the opinion states, "do more than offend some fastidious squeamishness or private sentimentalism about combatting crime too energetically. This is a conduct that shocks the conscience."

Lawful Arrests

Arrest is defined as the taking of a person into custody for the purpose of bring-ing him before a court in a criminal action (infrequently, in a civil action) in the manner authorized and specified by law. An arrest is made by an actual restraint or by submission.

The law of arrest, which is important to searches and seizures, developed from common law doctrines. In the United States, it is mainly authorized by statute. Either a peace officer or a private person may arrest. However, a duty to arrest in appropriate circumstances is imposed on peace officers—the "sworn" employees of criminal justice agencies.

Peace officers are usually defined by local law as persons employed by law enforcement or other criminal justice agencies with a sworn duty to enforce statutes enacted to control crime and to provide for the apprehension and pun-ishment of criminally liable persons. A peace officer may arrest with or without a warrant for felonies or misdemeanors (or traffic violations and other acts termed minor offenses and below the grade of misdemeanor) committed in his presence or for a felony (but not a misdemeanor) committed out of his presence when he has reasonable grounds for believing the arrestee is the wanted felon. An arrest-ing officer with reasonable grounds for his belief that the person he arrests has committed a felony is protected even if it later appears that no felony was, in fact, committed.

A peace officer may legally make an arrest with a warrant as long as he acts without malice, reasonably believes that the person arrested is the subject of the warrant, and makes the arrest at the time of day or night permitted by federal or local law or authorized in the warrant by endorsement of the issuing magistrate. Generally, felony arrest warrants can be served without any restrictions as to time of day, or day of the week. Misdemeanor warrants are normally restricted to daytime service, and Sunday service may be prohibited.

The legality of an arrest without a warrant depends upon its reasonableness. An arrest without a warrant lacks the safeguards provided by an objective predetermination that probable cause exists. Instead, the far less reliable procedure of an after-the-event justification is substituted. This procedure is likely to be subtly influenced by the familiar shortcomings of hindsight judgment. An officer who arrests without a warrant should act only on the basis of information as reliable and detailed as he would need if he *were* seeking a warrant.[15]

A misdemeanor arrest without a warrant lacks reasonable cause unless something happens in the arresting officer's presence to justify his belief that a crime has been or is being committed by the arrestee. Arresting officers in misdemeanor cases, therefore, must react to personal observation and knowledge. No amount of second-person information or report is allowed—no matter how credible the information or reliable the informant. In this connection, an offense is committed within the presence of an officer if he perceives the activity of the arrestee with his own eyes or with any of his five senses.

Felony arrests may be legal even without activity in the arresting officer's presence, but the officer must have reasonable cause to believe the suspect has committed a felony. Reasonable belief need not be based on the officer's personal knowledge. It may be based on secondhand sources of known trustworthiness and reliability supported by the officer's expertise.

Federal agents act under the authority of Title 18, *United States Code*, the "Crimes and Criminal Procedure" section of federal law. The arrest powers granted to FBI agents are typical of the authority granted to federal agents. These agents may serve warrants and make arrests without warrant for any offense against the United States committed in their presence, or for any felony that may be prosecuted under the laws of the United States if they have reasonable grounds to believe that the person to be arrested has committed or is committing such a felony.[16]

In a trade-off from common law doctrine, private persons may arrest for acts committed in their presence that are misdemeanors or felonies under local law. Some states allow private persons to make arrests for felonies not committed in their presence if a felony has, in fact, been committed, and the person making the arrest knows or reasonably believes, the person arrested committed it.

There are people who are immune to arrest. For instance, out-of-state witnesses are immune from criminal arrests for crimes committed prior to their return to the state as a testifying witness. Legislators and militiamen are immune from civil arrest within the narrow limits associated with their work.

[15]*Beck* v. *Ohio*, 379 U.S. 89 (1964).
[16]Title 18, *United States Code*, Section 3052.

The Arrest Warrant

A warrant of arrest is simply a court order commanding that the individual named therein be taken into custody and brought before the court. The warrant usually contains the following:

1. *Officers Designated to Execute the Warrant*   Federal arrest warrants are usually directed to federal agents. Local warrants are generally directed to state peace officers.

2. *Name of Person to Be Arrested*   The name of the person to be arrested, if known, is specified in the warrant. If the real name of the person is unknown, an alias, nickname or a fictitious name is allowed. "John Doe" and "Jane Doe" warrants are not allowed in some jurisdictions, but when they are accompanied by some descriptive words which describe the specific individual sought, they are generally issued. This is normally required when any fictitious name is used.

3. *Designation of Crime*   The warrant describes the accusation of crime. It is sufficient to designate it in general terms as robbery, arson, or grand theft.

4. *Signature of Magistrate*   To be valid, a warrant of arrest must be personally signed by the magistrate. It usually bears the impress of the court seal as well.

5. *Return*   Space for the return is provided on the warrant. This is the report to the issuing judge of action taken. The arresting officer must enter the time, date, and place he received the warrant and made arrest (if any) and sign his name and title. He is responsible for delivering the completed warrant to the issuing judge at the time he delivers the arrestee, if an arrest has been made.

An arrest warrant is sought by application to an appropriate judicial officer. The person seeking the warrant must appear before the judicial officer and justify his application under oath. An affidavit to secure a criminal arrest warrant must contain (1) information which, if true, directly indicates the commission of the crime charged, and the person committing it and (2) reliable data about the source of this information.[17] The application is usually made in the form of a complaint and, like an indictment or information, it is an accusatory pleading. If the application (complaint) satisfies the presiding judge at the hearing that the offense complained of has been committed, and if there are reasonable grounds for believing the defendant committed it, the judge must issue a warrant to arrest the defendant.

An application for an arrest warrant can be made on the basis of information and belief, as well as on personal knowledge. The complainant must believe

---

[17]*Jaben v. United States*, 381 U.S. 214 (1965).

the facts stated in his application and given under oath, and indicate that the information has been actually received from a trustworthy and reliable source.

Bench Warrants

A bench warrant is slightly different from a warrant of arrest. It is issued by a judge with jurisdiction over the individual named in the warrant. It can be issued to compel the appearance of a witness or the presence of the defendant. It is used, after indictments or the filing of informations, to apprehend an accused who is not in custody. It is also issued, on the application of the prosecuting attorney, or by the judge on his or her own motion, for the arrest of a defendant who has been released on bail, but who has failed to appear for judgment.

The Search Warrant

A search warrant is an order in writing, in the name of the people, signed by a magistrate, and directed to a peace officer, commanding him to search for specified personal property in a particular place and to bring it before the magistrate. If the warrant is void, searches and seizures pursuant to it are illegal, and articles of evidence obtained as a result are not admissible against the person involved.

A search warrant may be issued when the following conditions exist:

1. The property was stolen or embezzled.
2. The property or things were used in committing a felony.
3. The property or things are possessed by someone who intends to use them in committing a public offense, or have been delivered to someone for concealment.
4. The property or things to be seized consist of items or evidence that tend to show a felony has been committed or tend to show that a particular person has committed a felony.

A search warrant is also obtained by application to an appropriate judicial officer. The application for a search warrant requires a deposition or affidavit showing probable cause for believing that something falling within one of the categories mentioned above is in a certain place. This application must provide the magistrate with sufficient facts to show that reliance on such information is reasonable. The facts may be known by the police officer seeking the warrants, or based on knowledge he received from others. When the information comes from an informant, there must be some evidence of the informant's personal knowledge and reliability. The magistrate must be satisfied that the fact alleged in the application support the conclusion that one of the grounds for issuing a search warrant exists and that there is probable cause for believing it exists. The magistrate can, if he wishes, examine the applicant and any witnesses produced under oath. Probable cause is determined on the basis of whether or not the applicant has reasonable cause for believing the truth of the alleged facts. The "totality of circumstances" has been held to be the proper standard for determining probable cause of issuance of a search warrant based on information from an informant.[18]

The search warrant must meet the following criteria:

1. *Particularity*   The warrant must contain a description of the place or person to be searched and property sought with some particularity. The words "or other evidence" cannot be used to justify seizure of evidence not specifically described.

2. *Procedure of Service*   The search warrant must be directed to a peace officer (others may assist him). Conditions of forcible entry may be specified. Service at night may be approved when the magistrate, upon a showing of good cause, believes such service is justified. A time limit is usually set within which the warrant must be executed. The seizure of property under authority of a search warrant requires that an officer taking the property give a detailed receipt to the person found in possession. If no person is found in possession, he should leave a receipt where the property was found.

3. *Return*   The peace officer executing the search warrant must make a return (report) under oath and deliver to the magistrate an inventory of all property seized. This must be done publicly or in the presence of the person from whom the property was taken. The inventory usually is a duplicate copy of the required receipt, and the return is frequently the police arrest or offense report. The use of such reports does not taint this procedure but rather enhances it because they contain the stories of the incidents written in the course of official business.

The Reliable Informer Concept

The reliable informer concept justifies police action when police may lack personal knowledge.

In 1806, the Supreme Court expressed the view that oaths and affirmations to secure warrants either for arrest or for search and seizure must state facts with a sufficient definiteness that civil damages could be assessed against the person swearing or a criminal penalty imposed upon one falsely signing such statements.[19] Chief Justice Marshall noted this point by writing: "If the charge against him (Burford) was malicious, or grounded on perjury, whom could he sue for the malicious prosecution? Or whom could he indict for perjury?"

---

[18]*Illinois* v. *Gates*, 76 L. Ed. 2d 527 (1983).
[19]*Ex parte Burford*, 3 Cranch 448 (1806).

In 1959, in *Draper* v. *United States*,[20] the Supreme Court held that there was probable cause for arresting Draper without a warrant, and for making a search incidental to the arrest, on the basis of information the arresting officers had received by telephone from a reliable informant. The only personal knowledge the arresting officer had at the time of the arrest was that the suspect met the description given by the informant and was alighting from a train as the informant said he would be, and was within the time span mentioned by the informant. When stopped, arrested, and searched he was found to be in possession of illegal narcotics as stated by the informant.

In 1960, in the case of *Jones* v. *United States*[21] the U.S. Supreme Court ruled that an affidavit is not to be deemed insufficient by virtue of the fact that it sets out, not the affiant's observations, but those of another, as long as a substantial basis for believing the hearsay is presented. In his affidavit in this case, the police investigator, Detective Didone of the Metropolitan (Washington, D.C.) Police Department swore there was a basis for accepting the informant's story: The informant had previously given accurate information; his story was corroborated by other sources of information; and the suspect Jones was known by police to be a narcotics user.

In 1967, in *McCray* v. *Illinois*, McCray was arrested, searched, and convicted for the illegal possession of heroin found in the course of a search. The arresting officers justified the search on the basis of information from an informant whose reliability had been established. In sustaining the informer privilege in this case the Court commented that the arresting officers acted "in good faith upon credible information supplied by a reliable informant."[22]

Although a great deal has been written about the doubtful character of the so-called reliable informant and his dubious motives for informing, it is the informer's record for reliable performance on which he is evaluated. A reliable informant, who gives the police information on which to base probable cause for summary action or for an affidavit for a warrant to arrest or search, is necessarily a steady source of information. The informant's reliability is personally known to the police officer, and the officer is prepared to state that the informant in question has given similar information on past occasions, and that this information has proven to be accurate.

Arrest-Based Searches

Traditionally, officers and agents of law enforcement agencies have believed that searches and seizures incidental to or accompanying a lawful arrest are reasonable. Probable cause and reasonableness of this type of intrusion was believed to

[20]358 U.S. 307 (1959).
[21]362 U.S. 257 (1960).
[22]386 U.S. 300 (1967).

flow from the circumstances which led to and justified arrest. This belief has generally been in harmony with prevailing rules of decisional law. Majority opinions in cases recently reviewed by the U.S. Supreme Court have both supported and limited this right to search and seize. The basic conflict is between searches and an accused's constitutional rights (primarily his right to be let alone).

In each case in which there is a search for evidence at the time of arrest, the circumstances must indicate both a bona fide arrest and a search merely incidental to the apprehension.

When a valid arrest is made the scope of the search is now limited to the person of the arrestee and the area within the immediate control of the prisoner at the time of arrest, from which he might gain possession of a weapon, or of destructible evidence. A weapon, if discovered, can be seized because the prisoner might use it to assault the officer or to escape. Articles of evidence are seized to prevent their concealment or destruction. This is the doctrine of *Chimel* v. *California*.[23]

All too often, limitations such as those imposed on police officers by *Chimel* are misunderstood by investigators. As a result, legally significant evidence is tainted beyond hope by procedures which the court has said are forbidden by the Fourth Amendment.

In this decision, the Court noted that the doctrine that a warrantless search "incidental to a lawful arrest" may generally extend to the entire area considered to be in the "possession" or "control" of the person arrested developed from the case of *United States* v. *Rabinowitz*,[24] but the Court said that this doctrine was wrong. "That doctrine," the majority opinion states, "at least in the broad sense in which it was applied by the California courts in this case, can withstand neither historical nor rational analysis." Further, quoting its decision in *Terry* v. *Ohio*, the Court outlined its position on these searches:

1. We emphasized that the police must, whenever practicable, obtain advance judicial approval of searches and seizures through the warrant process.

2. The scope of a search must be strictly tied to and justified by the circumstances which rendered its initiation permissible.

3. The practice of searching a man's house when he is arrested in it is founded on little more than a subjective view regarding the acceptability of certain sorts of police conduct and not on the considerations of the Fourth Amendment.

4. There is ample justification, however, for a search of the arrestee's person and the area within his immediate control. This is the area from within which he might gain possession of a weapon or destructible evidence.

[23]395 U.S. 752 (1970).
[24]339 U.S. 56 (1950).

5. There is no comparable justification, however, for routinely searching rooms other than that in which an arrest occurs, or—for that matter—for searching through all the desk drawers or other concealed areas in that room itself.[25]

In 1973, the U.S. Supreme Court, in two cases decided on the same day, set guidelines for an arrest-based search.[26] Arrests in both cases were based upon traffic offense stops[27] which the Court defined as custodial arrests (full-custody arrests). Both arresting officers conducted a full search of the prisoners. The search in each case resulted in the discovery of contraband, which in turn led to a felony possession conviction. The Court commented that the effect of these decisions is to authorize police to fully search the person of an arrestee if the arrest has been valid and the arrestee has been placed in custody, despite the fact the arrest may be for a minor offense. The Court held all arrests to be alike. The Court described this as a custodial arrest, distinguishable from an investigative stop as in *Terry* v. *Ohio*,[28] and the search is not confined to the frisk necessary for the self-protection of the officer.

> A custodial arrest of a suspect based upon probable cause is a reasonable intrusion under the Fourth Amendment; that intrusion being lawful, a search incident to the arrest requires no additional justification. It is the fact of the lawful arrest which establishes the authority to search, and we hold that in the case of a lawful custodial arrest a full search of the person is not only an exception to the warrant requirement of the Fourth Amendment but also a "reasonable" search under that Amendment.[29]

English and American law has always recognized the right, on the part of arresting officers, to search the person of an accused who has been legally arrested to discover and seize fruits or evidence of crime.[30]

When a man is legally arrested for an offense, whatever is found on his person, or in his control, which may be used to prove the offense may be seized and held as evidence in the prosecution.[31]

---

[25]395 U.S. 752 (1970), p. 762.

[26]*United States* v. *Robinson*, 414 U.S. 218 (1973); *Gustafson* v. *Florida*, 414 U.S. 260 (1973).

[27]Operating a vehicle after revocation of license (Robinson); no license in possession of operator (Gustafson).

[28]392 U.S. 1 (1968).

[29]*United States* v. *Robinson*, 414 U.S. 218 (1973).

[30]*Weeks* v. *United States*, 232 U.S. 383 (1914).

[31]*Carroll* v. *United States*, 267 U.S. 132 (1925); *United States* v. *Robinson*, 414 U.S. 218 (1973).

Entry

The laws of many states differ on the exact circumstances under which a police officer may break and enter a dwelling, but there is some uniformity when the purpose of the entry is (1) to arrest for a felony, (2) to prevent the flight of the person to be arrested, (3) to prevent such a person from destroying evidence, or (4) considered necessary by the police officer because his life or the life of someone inside is endangered. Entry, however, requires notice. Such action by federal agents to execute a search warrant must follow the provisions of Title 18, *United States Code*, which allows an agent to break and enter forcibly "if, after notice of his authority and purpose, he is refused admittance or when necessary to liberate himself or a person aiding him in the execution of the warrant. State agents are more likely to obtain court approval of their entry when they can testify that they expressly announced their purpose in demanding admission or can cite facts indicating their certainty that the person involved already knew their purpose.[32]

Sometimes, the method of entry may suggest that notice or demand is unnecessary, as when officers enter through an unlocked door. However, the opening of an unlocked door is a breaking and notice and demand is required. In one case, *Sabbath* v. *United States*,[33] U.S. Customs agents knocked on the door of an apartment, waited a few moments, and then entered the apartment. The case was reversed because of the agents' failure to announce their authority and purpose. Failure to give notice by raiding police to occupants of a residence has resulted in raids being carried out in the wrong premises. In addition, the entry of armed unidentified persons into a home might be resisted forcibly by some householders, with unlimited possibilities for tragedy.

Stop and Frisk

When a police officer observes unusual conduct which leads him reasonably to conclude, in the light of his experience, that criminal activity may be afoot and that the person he is dealing with may be armed and presently dangerous; when, in the course of investigating this behavior, he identifies himself as a policeman and makes reasonable inquiries; and when nothing in the initial stages of the encounter serves to dispel his reasonable fear for his own or other's safety, he is entitled, for the protection of himself and others in the area, to conduct a carefully limited search of the outer clothing of such a person in an attempt to discover weapons that might be used to assault him. Such a search is reasonable under the

---

[32]*Miller* v. *United States*, 357 U.S. 301 (1958).
[33]391 U.S. 585 (1968). See also *People* v. *Rosalas*, 68 Cal. 2d 299 (1968).

Fourth Amendment, and any weapons seized may properly be introduced in evidence against the person from whom they were taken.[34]

The stop-and-frisk routine is less than an arrest. It is a "stop" only, and the search is a superficial patdown for weapons. A police officer is alerted to suspicious conduct and stops the suspect, "frisking" him because it is usually reasonable, under the circumstances, to fear the suspect is armed and may attack his questioner. To justify this type of intrusion, the police officer must be able to point to specific and definite facts which, together with rational inferences from those facts, reasonably warrant the intrusion. The Court, in *Terry* v. *Ohio*,[35] established the objective standard to be followed in these cases: "Would the facts warrant a man of reasonable caution in the belief the action taken was appropriate?"

Such a procedure, referred to as a "stop and frisk," comes within the purview of the Fourth Amendment because it involves the limitation of one's freedom. While the Court allows the officer to curtail the suspect's freedom and to conduct a superficial patdown for safety, the stop and frisk is nonetheless tantamount to an arrest and search. To justify even this limited intrusion, the police officer must be able to point to specific and definite facts that, together with rational inferences from those facts, reasonably warrant the intrusion.

Traditionally, officers were limited to seizing weapons after conducting a patdown search pursuant to a stop and frisk. Recently, the Court ruled that probable cause to seize contraband can be developed through an officer's sense of touch during a patdown search for weapons. In *Minnesota* v. *Dickerson*, 113 S. Ct. 2130 (1993), an officer observed the defendant leave a building known to be a "crack house" and take evasive action upon seeing the police. The officer stopped the defendant and frisked him upon the reasonable suspicion he was carrying drugs and was also armed and dangerous. During the patdown search, the officer felt a small lump in the defendant's pocket and examined it with his fingers. After reaching the conclusion it was a lump of crack cocaine, the officer reached into the pocket and retrieved the package.

While the Court found this search to be illegal, it did so because of the strictures laid down by *Terry*. A *Terry* patdown is limited to a search for weapons. Once the officer in *Dickerson* concluded the defendant's pocket contained no weapon, his continued exploration of the defendant's pocket by sliding, squeezing, and manipulating the lump was unrelated to the *Terry* frisk, and therefore the evidence was not lawfully seized.

Dickerson will be important to law enforcement, though, because it does establish that through training, experience, and other surrounding circumstances, an officer can establish probable cause that a detainee is carrying contraband and lawfully seize it.

---

[34]*Terry* v. *Ohio*, 392 U.S. 1 (1968); *People* v. *Waters*, 30 Cal. App. 3rd 354 (1973).
[35]392 U.S. 1 (1968).

Case Studies

Chimel v. *California*, 395 U.S. 752 (1969).

Illinois v. *Gates*, 76 L. Ed. 2d 527 (1983).

Terry v. *Ohio*, 392 U.S. 1 (1968).

Discussion Questions

1. Why is it important for a policeman to have up to date knowledge of arrest and search-and-seizure laws?
2. What may an officer do to investigate a suspicious individual short of arrest?
3. How extensively may an officer search while making a lawful arrest? When making a limited protective search for weapons?
4. What is probable cause?
5. What are the laws pertaining to a citizen's arrest?
6. What is a search warrant? How is it obtained? What is its importance?
7. What role should informants play in arrest and search?

Glossary

Ex Parte   On one side only; no adverse party in proceedings.

Peace Officer   A "sworn" police officer, sheriff's deputy, or state investigator; usually named by job title in state statutes giving peace officers power to carry out their sworn duty.

Return (Search Warrant)   A report of police action when executing a search warrant, including an inventory of property seized and a description of the place in which such property was found.

CHAPTER 12

Confessions
and Admissions

CHAPTER OBJECTIVES

- To define confessions and admissions.
- To list and describe the controls on police behavior during police interrogations.
- To detail the circumstances indicating whether a confession or admission is voluntary or involuntary, with the exclusion of involuntary statements.
- To express the thesis that involuntary confessions are basically untrustworthy.
- To describe involuntary confession aspect of plea negotiations and the acceptance of guilty pleas and to cite procedural safeguards against judicial compulsion.
- To point out the contribution of *Miranda* v. *Arizona* toward upgrading police interrogation standards.

A confession is a statement—verbal, written, or both—by a person accused of crime saying that he is guilty of the specific crime with which he is charged. An extrajudicial confession is a statement made out of court to any person. A judicial confession is usually a plea of guilty made in court or at a coroner's inquest. A plea of guilty accepted at a prior arraignment, hearing or trial is considered an extrajudicial confession at a subsequent trial.

A reading of appellate opinions in the "confession cases" can lead to a broad knowledge of interrogation techniques that may violate an accused's rights. Many of these cases, reversing previous lower court decisions, set forth the doctrine that involuntary confessions should not be admitted into evidence against the person making them, not only because no one should be compelled to incriminate himself,[1] but also because of the unreliability of any coerced confession.

An admission is less than a confession. The facts admitted as true only raise the inference of guilt when viewed in connection with other evidence or circumstances. The term "damaging" is used frequently to modify the word "admission." This illustrates how these statements do little more than connect some aspect of the crime with the person making the admission.

The Jackson-Denno Hearing

It is up to the trial judge to determine whether a confession is voluntary. The standard of proof for admitting confessions places a heavy burden on the prosecution. On the issue of voluntariness, the role of the trial judge has been outlined by the U.S. Supreme Court in *Jackson* v. *Denno*.[2] In this landmark case the court ruled: It is both practical and desirable that, in cases to be tried thereafter, a proper judicial determination of voluntariness be made before allowing the confession to be presented as evidence to the jury which is adjudicating guilt or innocence.

Jackson shot and killed a police officer following a robbery in a New York City hotel. He was badly wounded in the robbery. His confession was made to police and to an assistant prosecutor shortly after he was admitted to the hospital for treatment but before surgery. He was convicted of first-degree murder on a web of evidence based in part on his confession. His petition for relief was reviewed by the United States Supreme Court. Jackson contended that he was in pain during the police interrogation, was refused water, and was told he would not be let alone until he had answered all the questions of the police. The evidence showed that the hospital staff had administered demerol and scopolamine, and that Jackson had lost a great deal of blood. The state denied that the drugs had had any effect on his statements and presented evidence to indicate the prisoner was denied water because of his impending operation. Under the New York rules, a confession could be submitted to the jury with instructions to disregard it if they found the confession to be involuntary, or to determine its reliability and weigh it accordingly if they found the confession voluntary. The jury in Jackson's case returned a verdict of guilty. The U.S. Supreme Court reversed this conviction, saying that New York's procedure did not afford a reliable determination of the voluntariness of the confession, and that it was not clear whether the jury had

---

[1]"No person shall be held to answer for a capital, or otherwise infamous crime, unless on a presentment or indictment of a Grand jury, except in cases arising in the land or naval forces, or in the Militia, when in actual service in time of War or public danger; nor shall any person be subject for the same offence to be twice put in jeopardy of life or limb; nor shall be compelled in any criminal case to be a witness against himself, nor be deprived of life, liberty, or property, without due process of law; nor shall private property be taken for public use, without just compensation." Amendment V, U.S. Constitution.
[2]378 U.S. 368 (1964).

found the confession to be voluntary or involuntary. The danger, the Court pointed out, was that the jury might believe the confession and find it difficult to understand the policy forbidding reliance on a coerced-but-true confession.

The Issue Of Voluntariness

A confession is judged to be involuntary when it is induced by (1) promise and hope of reward or benefit, (2) coercion (violence, threats or fear), or (3) judicial compulsion.

Promise and Hope of Reward; Coercion   In attempting to lay the foundation before introducing a confession as evidence, the attorney conducting the direct examination will usually probe this area of promises and hope of reward, and coercion, with three or four simple questions:

Q: Either before or during the questioning of the defendant were any promises of reward or benefit made to persuade him to confess?
A: No.
Q: Was there any force or threats of force made against him or his family if he failed to answer your questions?
A: No.
Q: Were his answers freely and voluntarily made?
A: Yes.

Promises on which the accused person can depend must be made by a person in authority, and almost any employee of a criminal justice agency has been defined as a person in authority. An accused individual's belief or hope that confessing will gain some advantage is often one of the factors that lead him to admit guilt even though his hope is not induced by the promise of a public official. Such belief or hope does not make a confession involuntary when it originates in the mind of the accused, or is suggested by a friend, relative, or legal counsel. It is not uncommon for a guilty individual to react this way to the threat inherent when police investigation focuses on his criminal activities.

In one case, statements made by a convicted defendant to a probation officer during a presentence interview were held to be involuntary when proffered as evidence. The convicted defendant in the case[3] had pled guilty to a single charge of robbery, after being indicted on several felony charges. He made damaging admissions to a probation officer during a presentence interview, but he then withdrew his guilty plea and pled not guilty to all three felony charges in the indictment. The probation officer testified at the subsequent trial about the

[3]*People* v. *Quinn*, 61 Cal. 551 (1964). See also *People* v. *Siemsen*, 153 Cal. 387 (1908).

content of the admissions and said that all convicted persons interviewed by him were informed that they would not be recommended for release on probation if they did not tell the truth. The defendant was convicted on all three charges. However, the California Supreme Court reversed the action of the trial court, saying the defendant's admissions were involuntary and, therefore, inadmissible as evidence against him.

On the issue of coercion, the question in each case is whether the defendant's will was overborne at the time he confessed.[4]

A determination regarding the voluntariness of a confession must be viewed in totality of the circumstances.[5] The probability of truth or falsity of the confession is not in issue during this inquiry. The attention of the judge conducting the inquiry should be focused: that the confession was not freely self-determined. Simply stated, absent police conduct causally related to the confession, there is simply no basis for concluding that any state actor has deprived a defendant due process of law. While it is true that as interrogators turn to more subtle forms of psychological persuasion, the courts will look toward the mental condition of the defendant as a significant factor in the voluntariness calculation, but a defendant's mental condition alone, apart from any relation to official coercion, is not enough to make a confession involuntary.[6]

Judicial Compulsion—Guilty Pleas   Judicial compulsion is inherent in the sentencing function of the judiciary. It is not any express pressure upon any one accused person. It is the result of the judicial role. For this reason, it must be shown that judicial confessions (pleas of guilty) are not influenced by fear or hope of leniency, or lack of knowledge of all the implications of such action. Because this inherent judicial compulsion is a thing of value in plea negotiation, it must be shown that the plea did not result from misrepresentation or overpersuasion during plea negotiations. Finally, there must be some evidence that the accused understood the crime charged and the possible sentence, and that the plea was not the result of ignorance or misunderstanding.

Beginning in the late 1960s and culminating in the early 1970s, cases throughout the country brought plea negotiation out into open court where the promises made became part of the court record. Illustrative of these cases was *People v. West.*[7] Dale West entered a *nolo contendere* plea as the result of a plea bargain, and subsequently appealed on the basis that his plea had been coerced and not "voluntary" because of the promises involved in the bargain. The California Supreme Court took the opportunity to fully discuss the propriety (and necessity) of plea bargaining:

[4]*Lynumn v. Illinois,* 372 U.S. 528 (1963).
[5]*Arizona v. Fulminante,* 111 S. Ct. 1246 (1991).
[6]*Colorado v. Connelly,* 479 U.S. 157 (1986))
[7]3 Cal. 3d 595 (1970).

We undertake here to confirm the legality of the plea bargain and set up procedures for its acceptance or rejection in the strong light of full disclosure. In a day when courts strive to simplify trial procedures and to achieve speedier dispatch of litigation, we believe that the recognition of the legal status of the plea bargain will serve as a salutary time saver as well as a means to dispel the procedural obscurantism that now enshrouds it. The grant of legal status to the plea bargain should enable the court in each case to reach a frank, open and realistic appraisal of its propriety.

The Effect and Procedures

1. A plea of guilty or *nolo contendre* is not rendered "involuntary" merely because it is the product of plea bargaining between defendant and the state.
2. Counsel should disclose any plea bargain to the court, and the terms of that agreement should become part of the record of the case.
3. The court may accept a bargained plea of guilty, or *nolo contendere* to any lesser offense reasonably related to the offense charged in the accusatory pleading.[8]

The questions trial judges often ask at hearings about the accuracy of a guilty plea illustrate the requirement being enforced in many courts—voluntariness and accuracy.[9]

Before an accused person enters a plea of guilty, the sentencing judge asks the defendant about the voluntariness of his plea and his understanding of its nature and consequences. The following line of questioning explores this area in a murder-robbery case:

COURT: (Addressing the defendant.) You come up here with your attorney. Your attorney has indicated you want to withdraw your plea of not guilty as to the charges, and we'll take them one at a time. Do you want to withdraw your plea of not guilty as to the first count?

DEFENDANT: Yes, sir.

COURT: That's the count charging you with the murder of Vernice Bowen. You do withdraw your plea of not guilty?

DEFENDANT: Yes, I do.

COURT: Counsel, do you concur in the withdrawal of the plea of not guilty as indicated?

MR. SMITH (defense attorney): Yes, your Honor.

---

[8]*People* v. *West*, 3 Cal. 3d 595 (1970), p. 611.
[9]Donald J. Newman, *Conviction: The Determination of Guilt or Innocence Without Trial* (Boston, Mass.: Little, Brown & Co., 1966), p. 27.

COURT: All right, I'll grant you permission to withdraw your plea of not guilty. You understand the nature of the charges against you in this court?

DEFENDANT: Yes, sir, I do.

COURT: You've discussed this all with Mr. Smith, have you?

DEFENDANT: Yes, I have.

COURT: Your attorney has explained your constitutional rights to you, has he?

DEFENDANT: Yes, sir.

COURT: Are you changing your plea freely and voluntarily, without threat or fear to yourself or to anyone closely related to or associated with you?

DEFENDANT: Yes, your Honor.

COURT: Has anyone made you any promise of a lesser sentence, or probation, reward or immunity, or anything else, in order to induce you to change your plea?

It is at this point in the court's questioning of the defendant that any promises made pursuant to a plea bargain are explained to the defendant there in open court and on the record. The defendant is asked if he is under the impression that there have been any other or different promises made in connection with his plea or change of plea. If the defendant believes there were other commitment he has the opportunity then to express that belief. If such commitments were made they are confirmed then on the record; if the defendant's understanding of the commitments made is mistaken, the court will not accept his plea, or a change of plea, until he has had an opportunity to fully confer with his attorney and decide whether he wishes to accept the commitments offered in exchange for his plea or change of plea. If the defendant does enter his plea of guilty based upon commitments which the court later determines cannot be kept, he is allowed by the court to withdraw the plea of guilty and enter a not guilty plea without prejudice attaching from his prior guilty plea.[10]

COURT: You understand that the matter of sentence is to be determined by the jury or by the court in this case?

DEFENDANT: Yes, I do.

COURT: You are charged with murder. Are you changing your plea to guilty? Is that going to be—

MR. SMITH: Yes, your Honor.

COURT: Are you changing your plea to guilty because in truth and in fact you are guilty, and for no other reason, Mr. T_____?

DEFENDANT: Yes, sir.

[10]*People* v. *West*, 3 Cal 3d 595 (1970), and citations to other jurisdictions extensively set forth in that decision.

COURT: Do you waive a further reading of the indictment as to count one?

MR. SMITH: Yes, your Honor.

COURT: What is your plea, Mr. T _____?

DEFENDANT: Guilty.

(The court repeated this process for the other counts in this indictment and then took up the question of the degree of guilt.)

COURT: All right. The court will find that the degree of murder as to count one is first degree.

DISTRICT ATTORNEY: Your Honor, I think on that matter, if the defense is willing, we'd be willing to stipulate to that.

COURT: I think so. I understood there would be a stipulation that it was first degree, is that right?

MR. SMITH: So stipulated.

DEPUTY DISTRICT ATTORNEY: The People so stipulate; does the defendant?

COURT: Mr. T _____, I think since you've entered your plea, you've got to concur also that this is murder in the first degree.

DEFENDANT: Yes.

MR. SMITH: Your Honor, it is my understanding that murder in the first degree is stipulated to, since the robbery count would be first-degree robbery, and this is a murder committed in the course of a robbery or attempted robbery.

COURT: Well, I don't know if the district attorney wants to be limited to that or not.

DEPUTY DISTRICT ATTORNEY: My feeling is that I would assume that the defense attorney has explained to his client, and I would appreciate it if the court would inquire of the defendant whether he fully understands what we are now talking about, and it has been explained to him, so that he would stipulate.

COURT: I think so. This has been explained to you, about murder in the first degree if it's committed while committing a robbery? You understand that, is that right, Mr. T _____?

DEFENDANT: Yes.

COURT: With that in mind, do you agree that this is murder in the first degree?

DEFENDANT: Yes, I do.

DEPUTY DISTRICT ATTORNEY: Your Honor, may we go back to count number three? There's a further matter charged there, and I think that should be established as to degree.

COURT: Yes, (addressing the defendant). I think in the third count I neglected to ask you if at the time of the commission of the offense—it says: "said defendant was armed with a deadly weapon, to wit, a .410 gauge shotgun." Do you admit that you were so armed?

DEFENDANT: Yes, I do.

Standards For Police Interrogation

The case of *Miranda* v. *Arizona*[11] is the controlling case on the standards of police interrogation. In dealing with statements obtained through interrogation, the court did not purport to find all such confessions inadmissible. The majority opinion of the court in this case points out that any statement given freely and voluntarily without any compelling influences is, of course, admissible in evidence. "Volunteered statements of any kind are not barred by the Fifth Amendment and their admissibility is not affected by our holding today." Police are not required to stop a person who enters a police station and states that he wishes to confess to a crime, or to silence a person who calls the police to offer a confession or any other statement he desires to make.

The majority opinion also spells out circumstances which will safeguard the integrity of the confessions secured by interrogation. This segment of the opinion states that unless other fully effective means are devised to inform accused persons of their right of silence and to assure a continuous opportunity to exercise this right, the following measures are required: Before questioning, the person must be told that (1) he has a right to remain silent, that any statement he does make may be used as evidence against him and (2) he has a right to the presence of attorney, either retained or appointed.

The defendant may waive these rights, provided the waiver is made voluntarily, knowingly, and intelligently. If, however, he indicates in any manner and at any stage of the process that he wishes to consult with an attorney before speaking, there can be no questioning. Also, if the individual indicates in any manner that he does not wish to be interrogated, the police may not question him. The mere fact that he may have answered some questions or volunteered some statements on his own does not deprive him of the right to refrain from answering any further inquiries until he has consulted with an attorney and thereafter consents to be questioned.

The U.S. Supreme Court in 1974 with a newly balanced court reexamined the *Miranda* decision in the case of *Michigan* v. *Tucker*.[12] The case itself was not a direct assault on Miranda because it involved an interrogation which was held after *Escobedo* v. *Illinois* had required advice and before *Miranda* v. *Arizona*[13] had

[11]384 U.S. 436 (1966).
[12]417 U.S. 433 (1974).
[13]378 U.S. 478 (1964); 384 U.S. 436 (1966).

set down rules for such advice, which included informing the suspect he could have an attorney appointed for him if he couldn't afford to hire one. There was also a question of the fruits of such interrogation being admitted at the trial of Thomas Tucker.

Neither the arguments of counsel nor the decision of the court in *Michigan* v. *Tucker* reflected a concern under the Sixth Amendment's right to counsel, but instead concentrated upon the Fifth Amendment's right against compulsory self-incrimination. The emphasis of the court was the evil which preceded the *Miranda* decision: "Not whether a defendant had waived his privilege against compulsory self-incrimination but seemingly whether his statement was voluntary ... examining the circumstances of interrogation to determine whether the processes were so unfair or unreasonable as to render a subsequent confession involuntary."

A coalition of justices appointed to the Supreme Court after the *Miranda* decision (Chief Justice Burger, Justices Rehnquist, Powell, and Blackmun), and Justices Stewart and White, who dissented to the *Miranda* opinion, here placed a limiting interpretation on the philosophy of and the rules set out in the *Miranda* case.

The major thrust of *Michigan* v. *Tucker* and the rationale for its decision are shown by the following extracts from the majority opinion:

> It was not until this Court's decision in Miranda that the privilege against compulsory self-incrimination was seen as the principal protection for a person facing police interrogation. This privilege was thought to offer a more comprehensive and less subjective protection than the doctrine of previous cases. ...
>
> Thus the Court in Miranda, for the first time, expressly declared that the Self-Incrimination Clause was applicable to state interrogations at a police station, and that a defendant's statements might be excluded at trial despite their voluntary character under traditional principles.
>
> To supplement this new doctrine, and to help police officers conduct interrogations without facing a continued risk that valuable evidence would be lost, the Court in Miranda established a set of specific protective guidelines, now commonly known as the Miranda rules. The Court declared that "the prosecution may not use statements, whether exculpatory or inculpatory, stemming from custodial interrogation of the defendant unless it demonstrates the use of procedural safeguards effective to secure the privilege against self-incrimination."
>
> The Court recognized that these procedural safeguards were not themselves rights protected by the Constitution but were instead measures to insure that the right against compulsory self-incrimination was protected. ...
>
> The suggested safeguards were not intended to "create a constitutional straightjacket," but rather to provide practical reinforcement for the right against compulsory self-incrimination.

A comparison of the facts in this case with the historical circumstances underlying the privilege against compulsory self-incrimination strongly indicates that the police conduct here did not deprive respondent of his privilege against compulsory self-incrimination as such, but rather failed to make available to him the full measure of procedural safeguards associated with that right since Miranda. Certainly no one could contend that the interrogation faced by respondent bore any resemblance to the historical practices at which the right against compulsory self-incrimination was aimed.

The police had "warned [respondent] that he had the right to remain silent," and the record in this case clearly shows that respondent was informed that any evidence taken could be used against him." The record is also clear that respondent was asked whether he wanted an attorney and that he replied that he did not. Thus, his statements could hardly be termed involuntary as that term has been defined in the decisions of this Court. Additionally, there were no legal sanctions, such as the threat of contempt, which could have been applied to respondent had he chosen to remain silent. He was simply not exposed to "the cruel trilemma of self-accusation, perjury, or contempt." Murphy v Waterfront Commission, 378 U.S. 52, 55, 12 L. Ed. 2d 678, 84 S. Ct. 1594 (1964).

Our determination that the interrogation in this case involved no compulsion sufficient to breach the right against compulsory self-incrimination does not mean there was not a disregard, albeit an inadvertent disregard, of the procedural rules later established in Miranda. The question for decision is how sweeping the judicially imposed consequences of this disregard shall be. ...

But we have already concluded that the police conduct at issue here did not abridge respondent's constitutional privilege against compulsory self-incrimination, but departed only from the prophylactic standards later laid down by this Court in Miranda to safeguard that privilege.

Just as the law does not require that a defendant receive a perfect trial, only a fair one, it cannot realistically require that policemen investigating serious crimes make no errors whatsoever. The pressures of law enforcement and the vagaries of human nature would make such an expectation unrealistic. Before we penalize police error, therefore, we must consider whether the sanction serves a valid and useful purpose.[14]

The court implies, but does not decide, that the "valid and useful purpose" may be to deter future police behavior which would deny the guarantee of the Fifth Amendment's right against compulsory self-incrimination. This implication has led to a "totality of the circumstances" test, leaning heavily upon the conduct of the police in securing the confession. Indeed, later, the Court became explicit:

---

[14]*Michigan* v. *Tucker*, 417 U.S. 433 (1974).

"The purpose of excluding evidence seized in violation of the Constitution is to substantially deter future violations of the Constitution."[15] Where suppressing a defendant's statements would serve no purpose in enforcing constitutional guarantees, the Court has refused to further extend currently applicable exclusionary rules by erecting additional barriers to the admission of probative and truthful evidence before juries.

Case Studies

Miranda v. *Arizona*, 384 U.S. 436 (1966).

Culombe v. *Connecticut*, 367 U.S. 568 (1961).

Jackson v. *Denno*, 378 U.S. 368 (1964).

Discussion Questions

1. What is the difference between a confession and an admission? Is the difference important for admissibility rules?
2. Who initially passes on the admissibility of a defendant's confession or admission?
3. What must the court determine before accepting a guilty plea?
4. What is coercion?
5. What are the present standards for police interrogation?

Glossary

Appointed Attorney   Legal counsel provided by a court for defendant without funds to hire private counsel.

Confession Cases   A series of U.S. Supreme Court decisions concerned with illegal or improper police interrogations.

[15]*Colorado* v. *Connelly*, 479 U.S. 157 (1986).

CHAPTER 13

Discovery and Disclosure

CHAPTER OBJECTIVES

- To define pretrial discovery and to establish that the disclosure of evidence gathered by police to defense counsel is within the concept of a fair trial.
- To describe the kind of evidence within the scope of discovery.
- To show that counterdiscovery (defense to prosecutor) is a threat to the defendant's privilege against self-incrimination.
- To discuss the conflict that exists between the police policy of keeping the identity of informants confidential and the rights of a defendant when disclosure of an informant's identity is necessary for a fair trial.

The procedure for making available to participants in a criminal action the data underlying the in-court testimony of witnesses or exhibits of evidence is known as criminal discovery and disclosure. Discovery is a pretrial procedure by which one party requests the production of evidence possessed by the opposition. One of the inequities of common law procedure was that it afforded no adequate machinery for one party to obtain from his adversary any disclosure of facts material to the issue—either by compelling him to make admissions in his pleading, or to testify at or before the trial, or to furnish documents material to the issue for inspection. To remedy these defects, the courts of chancery entertained the bill of discovery, that is, a bill which sought no relief other than the discovery of facts known by the defendant or the discovery of deeds, writings, or other things in the defendant's possession or power.

The concept of a fair trial is inherent in the constitutional provisions that provide procedural safeguards for a person accused of crime. Allowing the accused and his attorney, at their leisure, to look over the evidence against the accused, and allowing them to learn the identity of the police informer and to peruse the records of intercepted communications are among the means by which American courts make certain an investigation and an accusation of criminal behavior will end in a fair trial for the accused.

The need for a truthful verdict in a criminal trial outweighs the community's need for evidence with any surprise value at trial. Because the prosecutor, as representative of the government, also has a duty to the accused to see that justice is done, it is unconscionable to allow him to undertake prosecution and then invoke the government's privileges to deprive the accused of anything that might be material to his defense.[1] This is the rationale for discovery and disclosure in criminal cases. It is a balancing between the rights of accused persons and the interests of the community.

The American Bar Association's *Code of Professional Responsibility* states the prosecutor's responsibility as follows: "A public prosecutor or other governmental lawyer in criminal litigation shall make timely disclosure to counsel for the defendant, or to the defendant if he has no counsel, of the existence of evidence known to the prosecutor or other government lawyer, that tends to negate the guilt of the accused, mitigate the degree of his offense, or reduce the punishment."

Pretrial Discovery

Pretrial discovery offers an opportunity to inspect an opponent's evidence. Not all jurisdictions have established extensive areas of discovery, but in most jurisdictions the defendant can request production of one or more items of evidence in the hands of the prosecutor or police by making an appropriate request in the court that has jurisdiction to try the case. If the motion is granted, the court will order the prosecutor to produce specific evidence for inspection by the defense. If discovery is denied, the justification is usually avoidance of some particular evil. Some states favor granting discovery, only withholding it for cause. Federal courts allow extensive discovery to defendants. There is little doubt that the rules of pretrial discovery are being liberalized in all jurisdictions.

Extensive discovery rights have originated slowly but have gained impetus from judicial beliefs that the objective of a criminal action is the ascertainment of the truth, and that a major role to this goal is a well-informed defense counsel. Legislators have adopted this judicial premise and enacted laws regarding pretrial discovery in many states and at the federal level. Although the rationale for discovery by the defense is the belief that the production of information enhances the possibility of a fair trial, its growth may be credited to recognition of a need for balancing the meager capacity of the defense for investigation with the massive investigatory apparatus of police and prosecutor, and rejection of the "sporting theory" of justice in which surprise was part of the game.

From time to time, the prosecutor has sought to establish rights to discovery. In some areas, this thrust has met with success, particularly when the defense has indicated in some fashion that it intends to use an affirmative defense such as an alibi. In *Williams* v. *Florida*,[2] the U.S. Supreme Court reviewed a Florida alibi disclosure statute and found such statute and concept constitutional.

[1]*United States* v. *Reynolds*, 345 U.S. 1 (1953).
[2]399 U.S. 78 (1970).

However, the attempt to convert pretrial discovery into a real two-way process has foundered on the defendant's right to remain silent and his privilege against self-incrimination. The prosecution's rights to counterdiscovery can hardly be expanded to overcome the absolute right of an accused person not to bring forth evidence that will incriminate him.

In 1885, the U.S. Supreme Court nullified legislation requiring that a citizen produce certain evidence or forfeit certain goods, saying the law was a compulsion in violation of the Fifth and Fourteenth Amendments.[3] More recently, a case involving policemen convicted of a conspiracy to obstruct justice in relation to corrupt practices in traffic law enforcement in New Jersey was reversed by the U.S. Supreme Court. During the investigation, the accused officers were informed of a New Jersey statute providing for forfeiture of their jobs by public employees who invoked the privilege against self-incrimination on an official matter. They were told that if they refused to talk they would lose their jobs. They talked. Their statements were then used against them at their trial. The court's opinion suggested the choice was nothing more than forfeiture of job and livelihood or self-incrimination and said that this option was the antithesis of free choice to speak or be silent. "It was likely to exert such pressure upon the individual as to disable him from making a free and rational choice."[4]

Discovery is available to the defense despite its potential for perjury and the intimidation or elimination of witnesses. These hazards can be neutralized by cross-examination and prompt judicial action. Minimizing the harmful aspects of discovery allows achievement of its main goal—an adequately informed defense counsel.

Police investigators must expect discovery and learn to cope with its problems. It should be expected that the defendant's statements and any police reports, photographs, or sketches that record the criminal act the defendant is charged with will be subject to discovery. This is also true of physical evidence, reports of identification and of laboratory technicians, lists of witnesses, and witness's statements.

Illustrative of the scope of discovery in various states are the items now subject to production and inspection in California. These include

1. Written, typed, or signed statements of the accused.
2. Transcripts of recorded statements of the accused.
3. The right to hear recordings of electronic devices (such as tape recordings) of the accused.
4. Written statements of prosecution witnesses.
5. Transcripts of statements of prosecution witnesses.
6. Written statements or transcripts thereof used by the prosecution to impeach an accused's witness.

[3]*Boyd* v. *United States*, 116 U.S. 616 (1885).
[4]*Garrity* v. *New Jersey*, 385 U.S. 493 (1967).

7. The right to hear recordings of statements of prosecution witnesses.
8. The right to interview witnesses without interference from the prosecution.
9. The names and addresses of eyewitnesses to a crime in the hands of the prosecution.
10. Coroner's and pathologist's reports.
11. Scientific reports, specimens, and samples in the hands of the prosecution.
12. Blood tests.
13. Police reports.
14. Police notes of conversations with prosecution witnesses.
15. Photographs used in identifying an accused.
16. Documents in the hands of the prosecution such as receipts that are material to the crime charged.

Disclosures—Informants

Police investigators depend on a great variety of people for information about crime and criminals. So-called amateur informants supply information about one crime, one criminal, or one criminal group. Citizenship and revenge are the two terminals along the continuum of amateur motivation. On the other hand, the professional informant is a wholesaler of data about the commission of crimes. He is knowledgeable about underworld or subversive activities, and his motivation is plain profit in most cases—except for cases involving national security where there is little doubt of basic patriotism because in these instances the total monies paid out have never been really sufficient to justify the hazards inherent in the role of informer. Although some amateur informants may fear adverse social reactions or civil actions for defamation of character, most informants worry about death or injury—to themselves or to their families.

Disclosing the identity of informants raises many problems similar to pretrial discovery. It also requires a balancing between the rights of the accused and the interests of the community. The accused certainly has a right to prepare and present his defense against the accusation. In a system of criminal justice committed to the resolution of doubt by adversary proceedings, the right to confront witnesses must be guaranteed. There is also a bona fide public interest in protecting the flow of information about crime and criminals to police. Wholesale disclosure will certainly curtail sources of information.

This has led to the "informer's privilege," a privilege which does not extend to the informant who is a participant in the criminal transaction. The accused cannot be made helpless at trial, unable to subject any witness to effective examination. To deny the accused the identity of an informant-participant deprives him of the right of effective cross-examination which is an essential safeguard accompanying the defendant's right to confront the witnesses against him or to produce witnesses in his own behalf.[5]

The role of the informant-participant is not that of a mere informant, but rather that of a material witness to the transaction or criminal act. Refusal to identify such an informant would deprive the defendant of a fair trial because the informant-participant is likely to be a material witness on the ultimate issue of guilt or innocence. The prosecutor must, therefore, disclose the informant's identity or face dismissal of the case or other sanction by the trial judge.[6]

Roviero v. *United States*[7] is a case in which the rights of the individual prevailed and the informer's privilege was rejected. In this case the informant in a drug possession-and-sale case was actually involved in the criminal transaction despite the fact that he did not purchase the drugs. He was a material witness on the issue of guilt or innocence.

The identity of an informant need not be disclosed when the question is whether there was probable cause for an arrest or a search, rather than the fundamental issue of guilt or innocence. When it appears that law enforcement officers making the search or arrest relied on facts supplied by an informant they had reason to trust, there is no constitutional requirement that the informant's identity be disclosed at any preliminary hearing.

This is the doctrine of *McCray* v. *Illinois*.[8] In this case, the two officers making a warrantless arrest on information supplied by an informant testified, in open court, fully and in detail as to what the informant had told them about the defendant and as to why they had reason to believe the informant was reliable and his information was trustworthy. Both officers were under oath, each withstood a searching cross-examination, and the presiding judge was obviously satisfied that truthful statements were made by each officer.

Disclosure—Reports and Records

In 1957, the landmark case of *Jencks* v. *United States*[9] established the right of a defendant to inspect reports shown to relate to the testimony of witnesses.

Jencks, a labor union official, was convicted, in federal court, of falsely swearing to a National Labor Relations Act affidavit about being a non-Communist. The basis of Jencks's appeal involved the government's two principal witnesses, both members of the Communist Party and informants who were paid by a federal investigative agency (FBI) to make oral or written reports while engaged in Communist Party activities. They made such reports to the FBI which

---

[5]*Pointer* v. *Texas*, 380 U.S. 400 (1965).
[6]*People* v. *Lawrence*, 149 Cal. App. 2d 435 (1957).
[7]353 U.S. 53 (1957).
[8]386 U.S. 300 (1967).
[9]353 U.S. 657 (1957).

contained information about Jencks participating in Communist Party activities with the two informants. At trial, both witnesses testified to such activities by Jencks. Counsel for Jencks made timely and appropriate motions that the government be required to produce these reports for defense inspection and use in cross-examination of both informant-witnesses. These motions were denied by the trial judge. Jencks was convicted.

In this case, the Supreme Court said: "We hold that the criminal action must be dismissed when the government, on the grounds of privilege, elects not to comply with an order to produce, for the accused's inspection and for admission in evidence, relevant statements or reports in its possession of government witnesses touching the subject matter of their testimony at trial." In concluding its opinion, the Court noted that the government must decide whether the consequences of allowing the crime to go unpunished are greater than the dangers of possible disclosure of state secrets and other confidential information.

The Jencks doctrine permits the defense to inspect reports related to testimony without first showing that the reports and testimony conflict and allows the defense to inspect the documents to decide whether to use them in the defense case. Only the defense can make a judgment about the value of using such reports to discredit the government witnesses—and thus further the accused's defense—and to make this decision defense counsel must see the reports. "Justice," the court noted, "requires no less."

In 1969, the U.S. Supreme Court reviewed three cases involving disclosure of electronic surveillance records.[10] The petitioners in one of these cases, *Alderman* v. *United States*, were convicted of conspiring to transmit murderous threats in interstate commerce, while petitioners Ivanov and Butenko were convicted of conspiring to transmit information relating to the national defense of the United States to the Soviet Union. The Court review joined all three cases because the questions in each were nearly identical. The Court held that a defendant had "standing" to object to evidence obtained by unlawful electronic surveillance only if he was a party to the overheard conversation or if, whether or not he was present, the conversations occurred on his premises. On the question of whether the evidence against any of the petitioners grew out of illegally overheard conversations or conversations occurring on his premises, the Court found and ordered the following:

1. Surveillance records as to which any petitioner had standing to object should be turned over to him without being screened privately by the trial judge.
2. The trial judges, through lack of time or unfamiliarity, were unable to provide the scrutiny which the Fourth Amendment exclusionary rule requires.

---

[10]*Alderman* v. *United States; Ivanov* v. *United States; Butenko* v. *United States*, 394 U.S. 165 (1969).

3. Petitioners were entitled to a hearing, findings, and conclusions (a) on the question of whether the electronic surveillance violated their Fourth Amendment rights; and (b) whether the nature and relevance of any conversations overheard and recorded during such surveillance related to the convictions in these cases.

Case Studies

McCray v. *Illinois*, 386 U.S. 300 (1967).

Roviero v. *United States*, 353 U.S. 53 (1957).

Williams v. *Florida*, 399 U.S. 78 (1970).

Discussion Questions

1. What is discovery?
2. What is the extent of discovery in your jurisdiction?
3. Should there be discovery? Why?
4. What are the arguments for and against making discovery a "two-way street?"
5. What are the rules concerning the disclosure of an informant's identity?
6. What reasons are given for disclosure of the identity of informants?

Glossary

Informer's Privilege   Right of police to avoid disclosure of identity of informants to protect them from retaliation and to enhance continuance of the flow of information about crime and criminals from informants to police.

CHAPTER 14

Evidence of Electronic Surveillances

CHAPTER OBJECTIVES

- To describe the judicial review of electronic surveillances and the methods used for such surveillances.
- To develop criteria useful in evaluating the admissibility of evidence secured as the result of wiretapping or electronic eavesdropping.
- To describe and evaluate the trend to require prior judicial approval of electronic surveillances.

Evidence gathered through electronic surveillances must be viewed as the fruit of wiretapping and eavesdropping. Both the content of the overheard wire and oral communications and the identity of the participants fall into this category. The use of this type of evidence against accused persons in criminal proceedings has led to a long series of legislative and judicial attempts to resolve the conflict between the constitutional privacy of individuals and the public goal of protecting all citizens against criminal behavior. Federal and state laws of varying-but-similar content are a morass of restrictions and permissiveness. Generally, wiretapping is banned and eavesdropping is suspect, with various levels of privilege accorded agents of law enforcement.

Eavesdropping is an area of conflict. Legislators made wiretapping a crime, but still, judges often held the fruit of such surveillance to be lawful evidence. More recently, courts have held electronic surveillances to be unlawful and have refused to allow the evidence of intercepted communications to be used against the aggrieved persons. Legislators, meanwhile, have enacted an extensive law allowing electronic surveillance. The U.S. Congress, in Title III, *Omnibus Crime Control and Safe Streets Act of 1968*, established procedural guidelines for law enforcement agents conducting such surveillances. This is the area of future conflict.

Constitutional protection against evidence secured by electronic surveillances seems to be based on the right to be let alone. Mr. Justice Brandeis, in a dissenting opinion in an early wiretapping case,[1] noted that the makers of our Constitution undertook to secure conditions favorable to the pursuit of happiness, saying

> They conferred, as against the government, the right to be let alone—the most comprehensive of rights and the right most valued by civilized man. To protect that right, every unjustifiable intrusion by the government upon the privacy of the individual, whatever the means employed, must be deemed a violation of the Fourth Amendment. And the use, as evidence in a criminal proceeding, of facts ascertained by such intrusion must be deemed a violation of the Fifth Amendment.

Mr. Justice Holmes, dissenting in the same case, joined with Brandeis in applying the maxim of "unclean hands" to wiretapping. This maxim, which comes from the courts of equity, is usually applied in civil litigation between private parties. Here the principle prevails in criminal proceedings. The rule is not one of action but of inaction: The court will not come to the aid of, or grant judgment for, the party who proffers evidence when he has violated the law in collecting the evidence. This maxim may be thought of as abstract thinking about ethical conduct in legal process and law enforcement, but when Justice Brandeis associated it with his comment that wiretapping was a "dirty business," he pinpointed a community attitude toward wiretapping that exists today and militates against the use in court of any evidence based on electronic surveillance.

The aggrieved person is entitled to suppression of evidence originating in electronic surveillance that violates the Fourth Amendment's protection against unreasonable searches.[2]

Admissibility—Totality of Circumstances

The admissibility of any evidence obtained through an electronic surveillance depends on the total circumstances of the surveillance. The totality of circumstances to be considered in a case involving electronic surveillance include:

1. The need for using this type of investigative technique.
2. The probable cause for "search and seizure."
3. The point in time during the criminal proceeding when the interception occurred—whether it happened while the case was "focusing," or after indictment and information.

---

[1]*Olmstead* v. *United States*, 277 U.S. 438 (1928).
[2]*Alderman* v. *United States*, 394 U.S. 165 (1969).

To establish the need for electronic surveillance, the situation should indicate that normal investigative methods are inadequate. The continued operations of organized crime have been cited as justification for the use of electronic surveillance by law enforcement agencies. The urgency of the situation must outweigh the dangers that may result from the lack of notice inherent in these interceptions. Such a showing of urgent need to avoid notice—and that the law enforcement objectives of electronic surveillances depend on secrecy—is important because of the inherent dangers to the citizen's privacy in eavesdropping.[3]

The existence and establishment of probable cause are vital to preserving the admissibility of *any* evidence gathered in the course of search and seizure. Electronic surveillances are searches and seizures within the meaning of the Fourth Amendment, and therefore probable cause and a return or inventory of some kind must be affirmatively shown. This requires specific identification of the parties involved; their connection with a specific crime; the specific facility (wire or oral communication) to be monitored and its designation by location or other means; a description of the communications the surveillance is aimed at; and a termination clause indicating whether the "search" is prosecutorial (terminating when its evidence objective is first obtained), or investigative and not to be terminated until the objective of identifying accomplices and co-conspirators has been achieved.

The point in time during the investigation when interception takes place is critical to the admissibility of intercepted wire and oral communications. In the *Massiah* case[4] the time in which an oral communication was electronically intercepted was a deciding issue. In the original indictment, it was alleged that Massiah and a co-defendant named Colson had acted in concert to violate a federal law forbidding the possession of illegal drugs. Massiah retained legal counsel, pleaded not guilty, and was released on bail. Colson, also released on bail, decided to cooperate with the prosecution. His automobile was wired for sound, utilizing a microphone and short-distance radio transmitter. Colson and Massiah, without any notice to Massiah of Colson's new role as government informer, had a conversation in Colson's wired automobile while it was parked on a New York City street. By prearrangement with Colson, a government agent who was equipped with an appropriate radio receiver and stationed a short distance from the parked car overheard the lengthy conversation between the two co-defendants. The agent subsequently testified, at trial, to several incriminating portions of this interception, despite defense objection. Massiah was convicted. His case was reversed on review by the U.S. Supreme Court, with the opinion stating that this action only reflected a constitutional principle established as long ago as *Powell* v. *Alabama*[5]—the principle that the period between arraignment and the beginning of a trial is perhaps the most critical period of the

---

[3]*Berger* v. *New York*, 388 U.S. 41 (1967).
[4] *Massiah* v. *United States*, 377 U.S. 210 (1964).
[5]287 U.S. 45 (1932).

proceedings, and that during this time the accused is as much entitled to counsel as he is at the trial itself.

The *Massiah* case was decided in the same year as the *Escobedo* case,[6] 1964, and is really based on policy underlying the *Escobdo* decision and reinforced in 1966 by the Court's ruling in *Miranda* v. *Arizona*[7]—namely, that a suspect may not be questioned without "informed consent." In the *Massiah* case, the police tried to get around this restriction by, in effect, conducting the interrogation through a third party, but the Court balked at the subterfuge.

The totality of circumstances to be considered in electronic surveillance cases spans possible violations of the rights of an accused person against unreasonable search or seizure, self-incrimination, or denial of legal counsel. The way Fourth, Fifth, and Sixth Amendment rights are affected by the total circumstances of any one case is splendidly illustrated by the final paragraph of the majority opinion in the *Massiah* case. This concluding fragment reads:

> We do not question that in this case, as in many cases, it was entirely proper to continue an investigation of the suspected criminal activities of the defendant and his alleged confederates, even though the defendant had already been indicted. All that we hold is that the defendant's own incriminating statements, obtained by federal agents under the circumstances here disclosed, could not constitutionally be used by the prosecution as evidence against him at his trial.[8]

The total circumstances of an interception also encompass the possibility that the communication may be privileged. Conversations about social, business, and personal affairs are often private and privileged—such as communications between physician and patient, lawyer and client, husband and wife, or others in a confidential relationship. Evidence proffered in these areas must withstand preliminary examination as to the existence of a privilege which would bar admission of the contents of the conversation.

Participant Monitoring to Bolster Credibility

When the issue in dispute hinges on the substance of a conversation, the triers of fact are often faced with the classic courtroom dilemma: Who is telling the truth about a conversation between two persons? When the versions given by the participants conflict, the triers of fact are faced with a credibility problem. If one of the participants is an informant, or some other witness whose credibility is doubtful, a recording device appears to be an ideal instrument to bolster the credibility of the witness.

[6]*Escobedo* v. *Illinois*, 378 U.S. 478 (1964).
[7]384 U.S. 436 (1966).
[8]*Massiah* v. *United States*, 377 U.S. 210 (1964).

The case of *Osborn* v. *United States*[9] shows the rationale followed by the United States Supreme Court in approving this type of electronic surveillance. The use of a recording device in this case had two justifications: (1) The prosecution had made a serious charge against a defense attorney; and (2) a testimonial contest between the only two people who knew the truth was highly undesirable because one was a government informer, the other an attorney previously of good repute.

The court's opinion noted that this case did not involve third-party eavesdropping, the surreptitious surveillance of a private conversation by an outsider, rather it involved one party to a conversation making a record of what was said. The majority opinion (seven to one) held that the use of a recording device was permissible and consequently the recording itself was properly admitted as evidence at trial. The concluding segment of this opinion sums up the court's rationale for this decision:

> The situation which faced the two judges of the District Court when they were presented with Vick's affidavit on November 8, and the motivations which prompted their authorization of the recorder, are reflected in the words of Chief Judge Miller. As he put it, "The affidavit contained information which reflected seriously upon a member of the bar of this court, who had practiced in my court ever since I have been on the bench. I decided that some action had to be taken to determine whether this information was correct or whether it was false. It was the most serious problem that I have had to deal with since I have been on the bench. I could not sweep it under the rug." So it was that, in response to a detailed factual affidavit alleging the commission of a specific criminal offense directly and immediately affecting the administration of justice in the federal court, the judges of that court jointly authorized the use of a recording device for the narrow and particularized purpose of ascertaining the truth of the affidavit's allegations. As the district judges recognized, it was imperative to determine whether the integrity of their court was being undermined, and highly undesirable that this determination should hinge on the inconclusive outcome of a testimonial contest between the only two people in the world who knew the truth—one an informer, the other a lawyer of previous good repute. There could hardly be a clearer example of "the procedure of antecedent justification before a magistrate that is central to the Fourth Amendment as a precondition of lawful electronic surveillance."

A requirement for warrants in participant monitoring is likely to be the rule rather than the exception. However, participant monitoring to bolster credibility without a warrant has not been ruled out.[10] This type of recording is not

---

[9]395 U.S. 323 (1966).
[10]*United States* v. *Riccobene*, 320 F. Supp. 196 (1970).

eavesdropping in any proper sense of the word. It is best described as the use of an electronic device to obtain reliable evidence of a conversation by one of the participants. It is the recorded memory of a witness who participated in the conversation.

Consensual Third-Party Eavesdropping

Each party to a telephone conversation takes the risk that the other party may have an extension telephone and may allow another to overhear the conversation. The communication itself is not privileged and one party may not force the other to secrecy merely by using the telephone. Either party may record the conversation and publish it. In *Rathbun* v. *United States*[11] the Court upheld the admission in evidence of a policeman's testimony about a conversation he had overheard on an extension telephone with the consent of a party to the conversation who was also the subscriber to the telephone service and the extension user.

Listening on an extension telephone doesn't seem to be a great deal different from using a "party line" to overhear a conversation. However, the party line telephone hookup is quite different from a single telephone with an extension paid for by a single subscriber. Listening in on a party line involves more than the possibility of one subscriber taking part in a telephone conversation and allowing someone else to listen in over an authorized extension that the subscriber-participant has paid for.

Although it is true that the telephone party-line service offers an opportunity to overhear conversations between others, misuse of this opportunity has been classed as a forbidden interception within the meaning of Section 605 of the Federal Communications Act. A case illustrating this rule is *Lee* v. *Florida*.[12] Lee sought telephone service for his residence in Orlando, Florida, and the local telephone company advised him that only party line service was available. Lee had no option. He accepted and was given a telephone on a four-party line. A week later the Orlando police had the telephone company install a telephone in a nearby house and hook it up to Lee's party line. The police hookup was installed for the purpose of overhearing and recording Lee's incoming and outgoing calls. The police eavesdropped for more than a week. Neither Lee nor any other participant consented to having the conversations overhead. Several of the recordings were admitted into evidence at Lee's trial for violating Florida's antigambling (lottery) law. The Court ruled that the evidence gained by this interception should be excluded because the federal statute proscribing the divulging of an intercepted communication applies to the states, just as the rule excluding the fruits of illegal searches and seizures was applied to the states in *Mapp* v. *Ohio*.[13]

---

[11]355 U.S. 107 (1957).
[12]392 U.S. 378 (1968)
[13] 367 U.S. 643 (1961).

Antecedent Justification—Electronic Surveillance as Search and Seizure

Lack of physical penetration of the premises is no longer an important factor in electronic surveillances. At one time, "spike" microphones and induction devices were relevant when eavesdropping cases were decided on the basis of trespass. Electronic surveillances that did not involve trespass under local property laws were believed to be outside the protection of the Fourth Amendment,[14] but in *Katz* v. *United States*,[15] the U.S. Supreme Court ruled that the Fourth Amendment protects people and not simply areas. In reviewing the interception of Katz's conversations in a public telephone booth by federal agents, the court concluded the "trespass" doctrine was no longer controlling. Once this concept of privacy is recognized, the court commented, "it will become clear that the protection afforded by the Fourth Amendment cannot turn upon the presence or absence of a physical intrusion into any given enclosure."

The majority opinion of the U.S. Supreme Court in *Katz* v. *United States*,[16] concedes that the law enforcement agents had developed a strong probable cause for their third-party eavesdropping, but the court reversed Katz's conviction in the trial court because of the agents' failure to secure prior court approval of their electronic surveillance. In pointing out the need for a warrant to authorize such an invasion of privacy, the court noted: "Wherever a man may be, he is entitled to know that he will remain free from unreasonable searches and seizures. The government agents here ignored the procedure of antecedent justification that is central to the Fourth Amendment, procedure that we hold to be a constitutional precondition of the kind of electronic surveillance involved in this case."

In 1968, Congress found it necessary to define the circumstances and conditions under which the interception of wire and oral communications may be authorized and the contents of intercepted communications may be used as evidence, and to prohibit unauthorized interception of such communications. The stated purpose of Title III, *Omnibus Crime Control and Safe Streets Act of 1968*,[17] is to safeguard the privacy of wire and oral communications. Potential evidence is the basis for authorizing interception of wire or oral communications under this law, and the federal or local prosecutor is named as the public official who may apply to federal or state courts respectively, for appropriate court orders when such interception may provide evidence of specified crimes justifying the use of this investigative technique. The use of intercepted wire and oral communications is tied to the public duties of law enforcement officials and the in-court use of collected information.

---

[14]*Silverman* v. *United States*, 365 U.S. 505 (1961).
[15]389 U.S. 347 (1967).
[16]389 U.S. 347 (1967).
[17]United States Code, Sections 2510–20.

Under this act, the procedures to be followed in obtaining a court order authorizing the interception of wire or oral communications provides for the judicial antecedent justification called for in *Osborn* v. *United States*[18] and *Katz* v. *United States*,[19] the particularity and overall reasonableness required in the *Berger* v. *New York*[20] opinion, and the general rules suggested to justify an invasion of privacy in these three controlling decisions. However, the law also recognizes an "emergency situation" involving conspiracies threatening the national-security or characteristic of organized crime, and rules are established for after-the-fact judicial review of such emergency interceptions.

Inmates of prisons or jails, however, do not have the rights of a person in other "places": houses, apartments, automobiles, occupied taxicabs, offices, stores, hotel rooms, or telephone booths. In *Lanza* v. *New York*,[21] prison authorities taped a conversation between a prisoner and a visitor (Lanza), and the tape was subsequently used as evidence against Lanza in a trial in New York courts. After conviction, Lanza attacked the interception of his conversation as improper. The court ruled that a public jail is not the equivalent of a person's house or a place in which a person can claim constitutional immunity from search or seizure. An intrusion by jail officers pursuant to a rule or policy with the justifiable purpose of imprisonment or prison security does not violate the Fourth Amendment.[22]

A new dimension in electronic eavesdropping is the use by police and federal agents of a *beeper*. Radio signals (beeps) emanating from this device can be received over a radio set to the same frequency as the signal transmission. Installed on a suspect automobile, police need not keep in close visual contact with the suspect vehicle, as the beeper's signals reveal the route of the vehicle. The use of these electronic devices has now been linked to visual surveillance rather than electronic eavesdropping. In *United States* v. *Knotts*,[23] the United States Supreme Court ruled that the scientific enhancement of the police practice of following an automobile on public streets raised no constitutional issues that visual surveillance would not also raise.

Case Studies

Katz v. *United States*, 389 U.S. 347 (1967).

United States v. *Hearst*, 563 F. 2d 1331 (1977).

United States v. *Knotts*, 75 L. Ed. 2d 55 (1983).

[18]385 U.S. 323 (1966).
[19]389 U.S. 347 (1967).
[20]388 U.S. 41 (1967).
[21]370 U.S. 139 (1962).
[22]*United States* v. *Hearst*, 563 F. 2d 1331 (1977).
[23]75 L. Ed. 2d 55 (1983).

Discussion Questions

1. What danger to privacy is inherent in the uncontested entry of electronic surveillances?

2. Explain the danger to fair trials and due process inherent in the use of "seized" conversations.

3. Describe the "aggrieved person" who can seek to suppress electronic surveillances alleged to violate constitutional safeguards.

4. Is prior judicial approval necessary in participant monitoring of informer-suspect conversations? In consensual third-party eavesdropping? What differences do you see between the two?

5. Are the objectives of participant monitoring different from those of consensual third-party eavesdropping? From nonconsensual third-party eavesdropping?

6. What factors govern the admissibility of electronic eavesdropping evidence of conversations between persons in prisons or jails and their visitors?

Glossary

Antecedent Justification (Police Action)   Prior court approval.

Dirty Business   Term used to describe wiretapping in *Olmstead* v. *United States*.

Doubled (Agent)   Action of "turning" an agent employed by an adverse party into an associate who will provide information about his first employer (adverse party).

In Camera   Not in open court; private; judicial chambers.

Spike Microphone   When driven into the wall of premises, a spike microphone has the capability of picking up sounds on the other side of the wall; similar to induction microphones (which pick up conversations without direct wiring in telephone interceptions), and "shotgun" or "tubular" microphones, which have a long-range directional pickup capability. No physical intrusion into the premises involved is necessary when these eavesdropping devices are used.

CHAPTER 15

The Defense Case

CHAPTER OBJECTIVES

- To focus attention on the defense case.
- To describe common defenses.
- To discuss the *total evidence* concept of evidence of guilt and the evidence necessary to disprove common defenses.
- To emphasize the theme that only the total amount of evidence has real legal significance.

It is wise for a person working within one area of the administration of justice to learn and know about areas other than his own particular specialty. It is particularly valuable for an investigator to know and understand the various affirmative defenses available to a person accused of crime and the evidence that may be admitted at his trial to create, in the mind of the jurors, a "reasonable doubt" of his guilt.

It should be repeated here regarding the burden of proof that the quantity and quality of evidence produced by the defendent need only be strong enough to create a reasonable doubt, while the quantity and quality of the prosecutor's evidence must have the compelling strength to convince the jurors of guilt beyond a reasonable doubt.

The circumstances under which people are accused of crime differ. Sometimes it is difficult for a defendant and his attorney to develop an adequate response to the criminal charge. More often, the nature of the case and the circumstances surrounding it structure the defense case. In any event, the basic affirmative defenses to an accusation of crime include an attack on identification evidence, through claims of alibi, lack of intent or motive, or entrapment; and defenses based on consent of the victim, insanity, or justification.

Identity

Evidence produced on this basic defense may consist of alibi; lack of motive; inability of witnesses to see or to accurately identify on the basis of their perceptions; suggestions by others which influence the identification; and weakness, or absence, of a connecting link in the chain of circumstances supposedly connecting the accused to the event.

The vagaries of identifying witnesses and the inherent suggestibility of lineups have been treated elsewhere in this volume. This is a vast area in which the defense may attack the credibility of the witness, his identification, and police procedures.

Alibi

An alibi is a claim that the defendant was elsewhere at the time of the crime. It is a possibility in every case in which the defendant is not caught in the very act of the crime charged. Witnesses testifying to an alibi may include a mother, a wife, a friendly bartender, or an individual unknown to the defendant previously, but now willing to corroborate his story because of some chance encounter at the time of the crime. Besides people who may testify to seeing the accused, there may be such things as receipts, tickets, or other time-placing items of evidence possessed by the accused which will be admitted to help the jury determine whether he was at the scene of the crime when it happened or whether he was elsewhere. One item of alibi evidence that is seemingly credible and unimpeachable may be, and many times is, sufficient to cast reasonable doubt on the accusing identification.

Lack Of Motive

Lack of motive may be a circumstance in conflict with identification evidence. Evidence of motives, such as greed, revenge, jealousy, family dispute, and sex, may be admissible against an accused as circumstantial evidence of guilt. The reverse is also true—a person without a motive may be inferred to be innocent of the crime.

Lack of motive is often important in cases in which direct evidence is weak, and a chain of circumstantial evidence connects the defendant with the crime. To convict on circumstantial evidence alone, the evidence presented should, to a moral certainty, exclude every theory except that of guilt.[1] Thus, if the defendant can propound a reasonable theory of innocence from the prosecution evidence alone or combined with other circumstances impeaching various of the prosecution circumstances, he should prevail. In jury trials, the triers of fact will be instructed, in these circumstances, to follow the law by the trial judge. He will remind them that the defendant is entitled to an acquittal if the people fail to establish guilt beyond a reasonable doubt.

[1] *State v. Maley*, 153 SE 2d 827 (W. Va.)

Criminal Intent (Mens Rea)

Where an affirmative defense is based on the absence of necessary intent, the accused will generally admit the physical act of the crime while denying a criminal state of mind.

As a general proposition, there must be a union (or uniting) of the physical act and criminal intent (or gross negligence) in order for a crime to be committed. An act without intent or an intent without an act are generally not crimes. Therefore, evidence which will tend to infer intent or lack of it is admissible and most important.

For instance, in a burglary prosecution the elements which must be proven are (1) the identity of the culprit; (2) the fact that a building was broken into; and (3) an intention to steal or commit another felony—assault, rape, or the like. (In some jurisdictions, the element of "entering" a building is also essential.) Thus, evidence that the accused took, or started to take, property from the building; or that he assaulted or had the means to assault; or that he raped or attempted to rape will be admissible evidence that, at the time he broke in, he intended to commit the particular crime. On the other hand, if evidence is produced that the defendant was intoxicated at the time he broke in and that he promptly went to sleep inside the premises without taking or moving any of the property within the building, this would be evidence that he had no intent to steal. If, after gaining entry, he discovered someone there, and immediately fled, this would be admissible evidence from which the jury could infer he had no intent to assault or rape.

Intoxication alone (if to a sufficient degree) will be evidence that the accused could not and did not form a criminal intent. However, if intoxication is offered as a defense, evidence may be admitted, if available, to show that the defendant intended and planned the crime before he became intoxicated.

Intent may also be a vital factor in determining the degree of a crime. Evidence which leads to the inference that a particular state of mind was lacking may reduce the seriousness of a murder charge to second-degree murder or manslaughter.

A particular accused may try to show that he was so ignorant of the law, or of some crucial fact, that there is good reason to doubt he acted with criminal intent. Generally, a mistake of law, even though based on advice of counsel, will not be a defense, nor will evidence of such a mistake be admissible. However, various states have different rules in this field, and there is strong reason to allow evidence of *good faith* reliance on the advice of persons who should reasonably know the law in order to show lack of intent.

Where specific intent is a necessary element, the general rule seems to be that good faith ignorance of the law will negate the existence of that intent. For instance, an honest claim of title and belief in ownership may be a defense to a theft charge (lack of felonious intent) even though the claim is based on a misconception of the law or the defendant's right under the law.

Evidence of an honest mistake or ignorance of fact, based on reasonable grounds, and of such a nature that the conduct would have been lawful had the facts been as they were reasonably supposed to be, will generally be admissible as bearing on the issue of criminal intent. An erroneous belief in the type of crime being committed or the identity of the victim, even though reasonable, will not be a defense.

If the only intent necessary for the commission of a crime is intent to do the act, mistake may not be a defense. However, when the intent necessary is an intention to do wrong, the courts will allow evidence of mistake as an affirmative defense.

Entrapment

The name of this defense is misleading. It probably should be named "seduction." There is nothing in the law which indicates the policeman may not "trap" the criminal. The basis for this defense is evidence that shows the crime or plan originated in the mind of a policeman. Thus, if the plan to break into a building originated in the mind of the burglar, and the policeman went along with it to gain evidence of the crime, there would be no entrapment. On the other hand, if the offense were planned by a police officer who procured its commission by the defendant, and if the defendant would not otherwise have committed the crime except for trickery, persuasion, or fraud by the officer, this will constitute entrapment.

Two questions of fact arise in entrapment defense:

1. Did the agent (police) induce the accused?
2. If so, was the accused ready and willing without persuasion?[2]

In cases where an undercover agent solicits the act (for example, sale of narcotics), the issue or question of entrapment will have to be decided by the triers of fact. The mere fact that the officer gives the defendant an opportunity to commit the crime is not an entrapment. Thus, if the officer gives a seller of narcotics an opportunity to ply his trade, there is no entrapment. Such circumstances are similar to the cases in which the officer plays the role of an unconscious drunk in order to catch "drunk rollers" at their business. There is no entrapment when the police agents play such passive roles.

Entrapment is an affirmative defense. Thus, the defendant has the burden of coming forward with the evidence. The arresting officer's testimony by itself may be sufficient to convict without corroboration because the officer is not a true accomplice.

---

[2]*United States* v. *Sherman*, 200 F. 2d 880 (1952).

Consent

Consent may or may not be a defense to an accusation of crime. This depends on the nature of the crime charged.

Consent is a defense when the crime itself requires that it be against the will of the victim. When rape is charged, the evidence must show that intercourse was against the will of the victim. Lack of consent is an essential element of the crime. In the crime of robbery, if the essential elements include "against the will" of the victim, any proof of consent would require a not guilty verdict as to the crime of robbery.

Other crimes are committed whether or not consent is given. Therefore, in sex crimes against children, evidence of consent would not be allowed because consent has no bearing on this crime. Murder may not be consented to, and evidence that the victim asked to be killed will not be admitted because this is not relevant or material to the charge.

A third category of crimes is more complicated and varying circumstances will determine whether consent is or is not a defense. Participants in a boxing match or a football game may not be the victims of an assault or battery. But prosecution for a fight on the public streets, whether mutually agreed to or not, may not be avoided by evidence of consent because the fight was also a breach of peace or had a tendency to create such a breach. Neither participant can consent to the breach of peace to thwart a criminal prosecution.

Mental Disorder

There are two defenses which may be urged on the basis of a mental disorder at the time of the crime.

Legal insanity will relieve the defendant from legal responsibility for the crime. The term "legal insanity" may be defined in any of three ways depending on where the criminal action took place.

The test for legal insanity most common in the United States is generally this: "At the time of the committing of the act, the party accused was laboring under such a defect of reason, from disease of the mind, as not to know the nature and quality of the act he was doing; or, if he did know it, that he did not know he was doing what was wrong."[3] Many states, while still using this basic test, have modified it in light of modern developments. One such modification is this: "First, did the defendant have sufficient mental capacity to know and understand what he was doing, and second, did he know and understand that it was wrong and a violation of the rights of others. To be sane and thus responsible to the law for the act committed, the defendant must be able to know and understand the nature and quality of his act and to distinguish between right and wrong at the time of the commission of the offense."[4]

---

[3]Daniel M'Naughten's case, House of Lords 1843, 8 Eng. Rep. 718.
[4]*People* v. *Wolff*, 61 Cal. 2d 795 (1964).

A few states have rejected the M'Naughten rule just stated and have fashioned new definitions and tests. The American Law Institute's model Penal Code proposed the following: "A person is not responsible for criminal conduct if at the time of such conduct as a result of mental disease or defect he lacks substantial capacity either to appreciate the criminality (wrongfulness) of his conduct or to conform his conduct to the requirements of law."[5]

An additional test formulated in an 1870 New Hampshire case, *State* v. *Pike*[6] has been adopted in the District of Columbia circuit of the Federal Court. Under this test: "An accused is not criminally responsible if his unlawful act was the product of mental disease or mental defect."[7]

Evidence showing either legal sanity or insanity may arise from the particular facts and circumstances of the crime (evidence showing knowledge of wrongfulness, such as hiding or fleeing); from testimony of persons who had an opportunity to observe the defendant's behavior; and from persons qualified to testify to mental diseases, disorders, and defects.

A second defense, available when the mental disorder is not severe enough to be considered legal insanity, is the capacity of the defendant to hold certain necessary states of mind due to his mental disorder. In *People* v. *Conley*[8] the rule, as it applied to homicide, was stated this way: (1) "If because of mental defect, disease, or intoxication, the defendant is unable to comprehend his duty to govern his actions in accord with the duty imposed by law, he does not act with malice aforethought and cannot be guilty of murder. (2) It has long been settled that evidence of diminished mental capacity whether caused by intoxication, trauma, or disease can be used to show that a defendant did not have a specific mental state essential to an offense."

The doctrine of diminished capacity recognizes that there is a mental disorder, short of legal insanity, which is disabling and should reduce the responsibility even though it does not eliminate it entirely. The facts and circumstances of the offense, the defendant's actions, and the testimony of qualified experts in the field of psychology and psychiatry may be proffered as evidence of such reduced capacity.

Justification

Justification may take several forms as a substantive defense: excuse, duty, necessity, self-defense, and defense of others.

Excuse may be a viable defense to homicide when the killing is committed by accident and misfortune in doing a lawful act by lawful means with ordinary caution and without an unlawful intent, or when done in a heat of passion upon

---

[5]Section 4.01 adopted in substance in Vermont, Illinois, and Missouri and generally known as the Currens Rule, *United States* v. *Currens* 290 F. 2 751 (1961).
[6]49 N. H. 399 (1870).
[8]411 P. 2d 911 (1966).
[7]*Durham* v. *United States*, 214 F.2 862 (1954).

sudden and good provocation. The latter excusable situation may require that no dangerous weapon be used and that the killing is not done in a carnal or unusual manner.

Duty involves the actions of persons or officials pursuant to judgments of a competent court or in the execution of legal process or other legal duty.

Necessity is not statutory but case law developed.[9] It is an attempt to take account legally of very unusual circumstances. Duress is sometimes allied to necessity and is often statutory: A person is incapable of committing the crime if he committed the act (not punishable by death) or made the omission charged under threats or menaces sufficient to show that he had reasonable cause to and did believe his life would be endangered if he refused. As indicated in the statute, the defense of duress is not available to crimes which are serious enough to be punishable by death. One cannot kill because his own life is being endangered, unless he kills the person who is endangering it and then only under the rules of self-defense.

The Total Evidence Concept

The affirmative defenses briefly discussed should give the investigator an idea of an area he must consider before he labels a case completely prepared. Investigators gather and communicate to the prosecuting attorney the bits and pieces of evidence (both testimony and articles or objects of evidence) which point to the defendant as having committed a particular crime. Yet, investigators must also gather and report admissible evidence which will prevent the defendant from successfully asserting any of the affirmative defenses available to him.

Under this "total evidence" concept, a case is ready when there is sufficient legally admissible, available, and credible evidence to prove the offense charged beyond a reasonable doubt, and there is available sufficient legally admissible and credible evidence to overcome the common defenses to crime, from mistaken identification to insanity.

To some extent the total evidence concept rests on the duty and obligation of police investigators. It is the duty of a police investigator to present to the prosecutor and to the court, and to the jury in jury trials, all of the evidence in his possession bearing on the guilt or innocence of the defendant. A police investigator's primary responsibility is to collect all of the evidence he can uncover about the true facts of a criminal event and the guilt or innocence of the person or persons involved.

When an accused person is criminally responsible for the crime charged, this diligence in collecting evidence, and in fulfilling the responsibility of police investigators allows an investigation to be closed with results. When an investigator knows about police procedures that can ruin carefully collected evidence,

---

[9]*People* v. *Lovercamp*, 43 Cal. App. 3d 823 (1974).

and knows about evidence that cannot be admissible when proffered, then all the evidence he collects will have legal significance and will be usable in court to prove the guilt of the person accused of crime.

The burden of proof is not placed on the defendant in criminal cases. The "people" have this burden and must prove guilt beyond a reasonable doubt. Proof is the outcome or effect of evidence. Guilt beyond a reasonable doubt is the result of convincing and compelling evidence—evidence presented in court by the police and prosecutor who represent the "people."

Case Studies

United States v. *Sherman*, 200 F. 2d 880 (1952).

Durham v. *United States*, 214 F. 2d 862 (1954).

Brown v. *United States*, 256 U.S. 335 (1920).

Discussion Questions

1. How are defenses based on alibi and on lack of intent similar? How do they differ?
2. Explain good faith ignorance of the law as a potential defense.
3. What are the legal limits of entrapment? When does this situation become a defense to crime?
4. Cite one or more crimes in which evidence that the victim did not give consent would be required. Cite one in which consent or lack of consent would have no bearing. Try to explain the underlying differences that account for this distinction.
5. Explain the "Currens rule" and the standard it imposes for excusing responsibility for a crime because of mental disease or defect.
6. Define the total evidence concept.

Glossary

Mens Rea   Criminal intent.

CHAPTER 16

Pleading to Appeal

CHAPTER OBJECTIVES

- To introduce students to the procedural framework in felony cases from the time of the defendant's plea, through trial, to judgment and sentence.
- To review the pleas and pretrial options available to defendants.
- To stress the importance of the "weight" of evidence throughout these procedures.
- To discuss the roles of prosecutor and defense counsel at each stage of the proceedings.

The right of an accused in a criminal trial is, in essence, the right to a fair opportunity to defend himself against the state's accusations, to be heard in court in his or her defense.

While justice should be administered with dispatch, the essential ingredient is orderly expedition and not mere speed. When arrest and incarceration are followed by inordinate delay prior to indictment (or filing of an information), a defendant may, under appropriate circumstances, invoke the protection of the Sixth Amendment. The Sixth Amendment provides that "in all criminal prosecutions the accused shall enjoy the right to a speedy and public trial. ... " The amendment is a guarantee to a criminal defendant that the prosecution will move with the dispatch that is appropriate to assure him an early and proper disposition of the charges against him.

The history of the right to a speedy trial and its reception in this country clearly establishes that it is one of the most basic rights preserved by our Constitution. Today, each of the fifty states guarantees the right to a speedy trial to its citizens.[1]

The purposes of the Sixth Amendment's speedy trial provision are (1) to prevent undue and oppressive incarceration prior to trial, (2) to minimize anxiety and concern accompanying public accusation, and (3) to limit the possibilities that long delay will impair the ability of an accused to defend himself.

[1]*Klopfer* v. *North Carolina*, 386 U.S. 213 (1967), 223–226.

Inordinate delay between arrest and trial may impair a defendant's ability to present an effective defense. But the major evils protected against by the speedy-trial guarantee exist quite apart from actual or possible prejudice to an accused's defense. To arrest and detain legally the government must assert probable cause to believe the arrestee has committed a crime. Arrest is a public act that may seriously interfere with the defendant's liberty, whether he is free on bail or not, disrupt his employment, drain his financial resources, curtail his associations, subject him to public obloquy, and create anxiety in him, his family, and his friends. When an arrest occurs, a citizen suffers restraints on his liberty and is the subject of public accusation. Failure to extend the protection of the Sixth Amendment to delays occurring between arrest and the filing of formal charges subverts the purposes of the speedy-trial clause, particularly to relieve an individual from lengthy pretrial imprisonment and—even when released on bail—to relieve the arrestee of the anxiety caused by his arrest and pending trial.

Courts may refuse to apply the speedy trial guarantee to the post arrest but preindictment period. The right to a speedy trial attaches, at the latest, as soon as an individual has been formally charged with a crime, either by indictment or information. On the other hand, a person under arrest is an accused person because an arresting officer has charged him with a crime.

If this be so, the police still are not required to guess at their peril the precise moment at which they have a probable cause to arrest a suspect, risking a violation of the Sixth Amendment (speedy trial) if they wait too long. Law enforcement officers are under no constitutional duty to call a halt to a criminal investigation the moment they have the minimum evidence to establish probable cause, a quantum of evidence which may fall far short of the amount necessary to support a criminal conviction.[2]

A defendant can waive his right to a speedy trial by pleading guilty, failing to demand a prompt trial, failing to present a timely claim (prior to or at trial), and consenting to delay.

The statutes of limitations represent a maximum time beyond which a prosecution cannot be brought. These statutes are public policy decisions of legislators that a trial for a specific offense or grade of crime (capital, felony, misdemeanor) shall be barred after a stated period of time. These statutes provide predictability by specifying a limit beyond which there is the presumption that a defendant's right to a fair trial would be prejudiced.

Such a limitation is designed to protect individuals from having to defend themselves against charges when the basic facts may have become obscured by the passage of time, and to minimize the danger of official punishment because of acts in the far-distant past. Such a time limit may also have the salutary effect of encouraging law enforcement officials to investigate suspected criminal activity promptly.

[2]*Hoffa* v. *United States*, 385 U.S. 293 (1966).

In satisfying the constitutional and statutory commands that an accused be given a public trial, the state and federal courts have differed over what groups of spectators, if any, could properly be excluded from a criminal trial. Without exception all courts have held that an accused is at the very least entitled to have his friends, relatives, and counsel present, no matter with what offense he may be charged. Certain proceedings in a judge's chambers, including convictions for contempt of court, have occasionally been countenanced by state courts, but there had never been any intimation that all of the public, including the accused's relatives, friends, and counsel, can be barred from the trial chamber.[3]

The requirement of a public trial is for the benefit of persons accused of crime, innocent and guilty. Review in the public forum, by the presence of spectators, friends and—possibly—news media representatives, restrains judicial power. The public may see that an accused is fairly treated and not unjustly convicted; and by their presence they tend to keep the judiciary and other triers of fact responsive to their functional responsibility.

Defendant's Pleas and Pretrial Motions

After the prosecutor has filed the accusatory pleading (complaint, indictment or information), a date is set to arraign the defendant, and to accept his or her plea,* if the defendant is ready to plead at that time. Arraignment is conducted in open court and consists of reading the complaint, indictment or information to the defendant or stating to him the substance of the charge, and giving him a copy of the accusatory pleading before he is called upon to plead. A defendant may plead not guilty, guilty or, with the consent of the court, *nolo contendere*. The court may refuse to accept a plea of guilty, and will not accept such plea or a plea of *nolo contendere* without first addressing the defendant personally and determining that the plea is made voluntarily with understanding of the nature of the charge and the consequences of the plea. If a defendant refuses to plead, or if the court refuses to accept a plea of guilty, a plea of not guilty is entered.

While federal rules only allow three major pleas, many states allow an additional range of pleas, particularly double jeopardy and not guilty by reason of insanity. Sometimes the major pleas of guilty or not guilty are termed general pleas and others are termed special pleas. Where the form of pleadings does not offer the defendant a necessary legal remedy, a motion can be filed to achieve the defense goal.

Guilty Plea   The plea of guilty admits, judicially, every essential element of the crime charged to be true. It may require an additional evidentiary showing, or it may stand alone without further determination. State statute and case law vary

---

[3]*In re Oliver*, 333 U.S. 266 (1947).
*An answer to the accusation: guilty or not guilty, or one of the special answers.

concerning evidentiary requirements prior to accepting the plea of guilty. This plea must be made personally by the defendant in open court.

Since the plea of guilty is a judicial confession to the crime, there are certain waivers required of the defendant. The waivers must be made knowingly and intelligently:

1. The defendant must waive his right to be confronted by witnesses.
2. He must waive his right to a jury trial.
3. He must waive his right against self-incrimination.[4]

In addition the court should ensure, by advising the defendant, that the defendant understands the nature of the charge made against him and the consequences of the guilty plea (the possible punishments including any concessions gained through plea negotiations).[5]

Not Guilty Plea   The plea of not guilty denies every element essential to a finding of guilt including the element of identity of the culprit. The burden of proof necessary for a finding of guilt is proof beyond a reasonable doubt. It is this plea which moves the case to trial requiring the prosecutor to meet the burden of proof required by law.

Nolo Contendere   In most jurisdictions a plea of no contest has limited application and may require presentation of evidence before acceptance. Its purpose may be twofold: (1) to protect the defendant in a civil suit from a judicial admission which may be used against him in the subsequent civil law suit; (2) to allow a defendant to enter a plea, tantamount to guilty, when he contends he has no memory of the offense but where the evidence of guilt is overwhelmingly persuasive. This plea is, in effect, a guilty plea and is so deemed by the law.

Double Jeopardy   The issue of former acquittal, conviction, or jeopardy may need to be introduced by a special plea. The defendant has the burden of proof, and it is an issue which must be decided by the court on the law. Based upon the evidence accepted as true the court must apply the applicable law.

Double jeopardy represents a rule of finality. A single fair trial on a criminal charge bars reprosecution; hence the plea of double jeopardy. It developed as a protection against the oppression of attempting repeatedly to convict an individual for an alleged offense. The rule that one acquittal or conviction should satisfy the law is favorable and necessary to protect the liberty of citizens from the power of the prosecutor.

The Fifth Amendment guarantee against being put in jeopardy twice consists of three distinct protections:

[4]*Boykin* v. *Alabama*, 395 U.S. 238 (1969).
[5]*In re Tahl*, 460 P. 2d 449 (Ca. 1969).

1. Protection against a second prosecution for the same offense after acquittal.
2. Protection against a second prosecution for the same offense after conviction.
3. Protection against multiple punishments for the same offense.[6]

Defense counsel should be aware that the claim of double jeopardy is a legal remedy against *persecution* as opposed to *prosecution*. Without the bar against reprosecution after an acquittal, the status of innocence would be meaningless—many juries could acquit, but a single jury could convict; the prosecutor could gain control over punishment (sentencing); many judges might sentence, but a single judge could set an "appropriate" sentence; a prosecutor could keep trying until he found an accommodating jury and/or a willing judge.

In the past, a claim of double jeopardy was raised at arraignment. In most jurisdictions it is now a prearraignment motion or plea in response to the accusatory pleading of prosecution. Nevertheless, it must be pleaded by the defense in proper form and with adequate timeliness, or it is considered waived.

Double jeopardy guarantees against a second prosecution for the same offense. This requires, however, that the initial trial progresses to a certain stage—usually the swearing of the first witness (or acceptance of the first item of evidence) in a nonjury trial, or the swearing of the jurors in a jury trial. If this stage of the trial is reached, followed by a dismissal, acquittal or conviction, then a plea of double jeopardy may be entered for any subsequent trial of the same situation.

Acquittal at an earlier trial also bans a second trial for offenses arising from the same conduct. The double jeopardy guarantee forbids a prosecutor from using a first trial ending in acquittal as a dry run for a second prosecution. The constitutional guarantee protects a person who has been acquitted from having to "run the gantlet" a second time.[7] The claim of double jeopardy after an acquittal is linked to the principle of collateral estoppel, the doctrine that bars relitigation between the same parties of an issue actually resolved at a previous trial.

When a first trial ends in a conviction, double jeopardy bars a second trial for the same offense unless the convicted defendant waives jeopardy by a motion for a new trial, an appeal, or a collateral attack on the circumstances of his or her conviction. However, restrictions on retrials require trial on the offense for which the accused was charged, even when the first trial ended in conviction of a lesser offense than that charged.[8]

Restrictions on reprosecutions after a successful appeal and reversal of the first trial do not bar retrial for equal offenses as in the first trial.

Not Guilty by Reason of Insanity   This plea is usually an affirmative defense requiring the defendant to prove legal insanity by a preponderance of the

---

[6]*North Carolina* v. *Pearce*, 395 U.S. 711 (1969).
[7]*Ashe* v. *Swenson*, 397 U.S. 436 (1970), 446–47; *Green* v. *United States*, 355 U.S. 184 (1957), 190.
[8]*Price* v. *Georgia*, 398 U.S. 323 (1970).

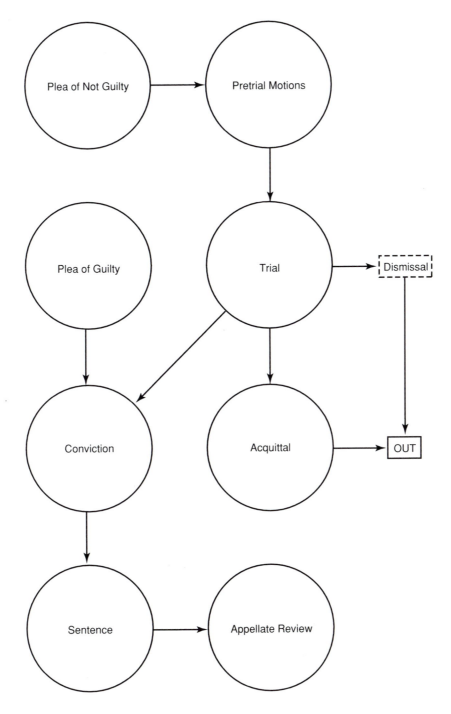

FIGURE 16-1. Procedural framework in felony cases from defendant's plea to appellate review.

evidence. There are, however, jurisdictions which will require only such evidence that creates a reasonable doubt that the defendant was legally sane at the time of the offense.[9]

Present Sanity   A claim may be made of the defendant's incompetency to be tried because of a present mental disorder which blocks the defendant from understanding the proceedings or consulting with counsel and participating in his own defense. No defendant should be tried for a crime if insane or incompetent to stand trial because of mental illness. If at any stage of the action prior to judgment, a defendant is found to be insane or incompetent because of mental illness, the proceedings are suspended and the defendant sent to a state hospital for a reasonable period or until his sanity is restored.

There are set procedures for this determination. The legal action requires a trier of fact (a judge or a separate jury) to present evidence and rule on this evidence with a finding of either sanity or insanity. It is a special proceeding and may, in fact, be a separate jury trial within a jury trial. This trial is quasi-criminal because it requires the defendant to be in a state hospital until his sanity is disproved or restored. The determination of this issue is usually appealable and confinement limited.

At the least, due process requires that the nature and duration of commitment bear some reasonable relation to the purpose for which the individual is committed. Consequently, a person charged by a state with a criminal offense who is committed solely on account of his incapacity to proceed to trial cannot be held more than the reasonable period of time necessary to determine whether there is a substantial probability that he will attain that capacity in the foreseeable future. If it is determined that this is not the case, then the state must either institute the customary civil commitment proceeding, required to commit indefinitely any citizen, or release the defendant. Furthermore, even if it is determined that the defendant probably soon will be able to stand trial, his continued commitment must be justified by progress toward that goal.[10]

In determining how long a defendant should be confined in the state hospital under this procedure the court should consider the nature of the offense; the likely penalty or range of punishment; and the time already confined.[11]

In a succession of cases, courts have developed a requirement of "substantial evidence" as a standard for compelling a competency hearing. Evidence is "substantial" if it raises a reasonable doubt about the defendant's competency to stand trial.[12]

Suppression of Evidence   Illegally obtained evidence must be challenged by defense counsel. The motion to quash a search warrant and generally suppress evidence may greatly hamper prosecution (a successful motion can block the trial). The evidence which defense counsel asks to be considered inadmissible is often that evidence which would lead the defendant to plead guilty, if the motion to suppress is denied.

[9]*People* v. *Wood*, 187 N.E. 2d 116 (New York 1962).
[10]*Jackson* v. *Indiana*, 406 U.S. 715 (1972).
[11]*In re Davis*, 8 Cal. 3d 798, 505 P. 2d 1018 (1973).
[12]*Pate* v. *Robinson*, 383 U.S. 375 (1966); *Moore* v. *United States*, 464 F. 2d 663 (9th Cir. 1972).

A motion to quash a search warrant, and/or asking for the return of items seized in the warrant-authorized search has a time limit. While local procedures vary, this motion must be made early in the process of the defense case and in most states prior to trial.

In some jurisdictions, a warrantless search and seizure may be protested by a motion to quash the results of the search, but it is more likely that the defense will move to suppress the evidence.

Suppression motions may be directed toward physical evidence, confessions or admissions, or statements against interest, or they may, by statute or case law, be limited to only one of these evidentiary issues. In some proceedings the motion may be extended to ask for the return of illegally seized evidence.

Motions to suppress evidence usually stem from the objection to one or more items of evidence which are the products of unconstitutional or unlawful acts by police or prosecution, or their associates, and to any evidence derived therefrom; and show that the defendant has standing to complain. (See Chapter 10.)

Change of Plea   A change of plea from not guilty to guilty is uniformly allowed as if it were an initial plea. The general rule states that a plea of guilty may be withdrawn if the defendant shows "good cause." It is the interpretation of "good cause" that poses the difference between courts. Changing a plea depends upon the attitudes of the judiciary as much as the content of any applicable law.

It has been held that the least influence causing the defendant to plead guilty when he has any defense should be sufficient to permit a change of plea from guilty to not guilty. This is the attitude that "good cause" should be liberally interpreted. On the other hand, a plea of guilty may be withdrawn for mistake, ignorance, inadvertence, or for any other factor overreaching a defendant's free and clear judgment, but the fact of such mistake, fraud, duress, or overreaching must be established by clear and convincing evidence.[13]

If the plea is withdrawn, the original plea of guilty should not be admissible as evidence of guilt at a trial. It is also true that admissions or statements against interests to a probation officer based upon the guilty plea should be inadmissible at the future trial. If the defendant is a witness and testifies to evidence which conflicts with a probation statement, that statement could become admissible for the purpose of impeachment.[14]

The Trial Structure

The trial is a structured proceeding within which each side is given time and opportunity to question the witnesses, rebut* the other's evidence, and argue their case to the jury or to the court when the trial is without a jury.

---

[13]*People* v. *McGarvy*, 142 P. 2d 92 (Ca. 1943).
[14]*Harris* v. *New York*, 401 U.S. 222 (1971).
*Answer.

The trial is conducted to a large extent by the admission and exclusion of evidence. There are, in every jurisdiction, rules which govern the kinds, type, and quality of evidence that is allowed in a particular criminal case. These rules will depend upon the kind of crime committed, the theory of the prosecution and the defense, and the rules which apply to all cases. The rules of evidence govern the admission of oral testimony, physical objects related to the crime or its issues, and documents.

Admissibility and exclusion are determined by the presentation of evidence by the proponent, objections by the opponent, and the trial judge's ruling on the objection. A listing of typical objections, sort of an abstract of the rules of evidence, follows:

"I object ... :"

1. The witness is incompetent. An objection challenges the witness's physical or mental ability to perceive events accurately and correctly relate that perception.

2. The evidence is irrelevant. An objection attacks the substantive value of the evidence—whether the evidence to be produced has rational probative value.

3. The testimony is hearsay. An objection contends that the evidence to be produced is a statement made out of court by someone other than the witness, offered to prove the truth of the matter stated, and not admissible by a legal exception.

4. A question is leading and suggestive. An objection requests that the court prevent the proponent of a witness from cross-examining his own witness; that is, that he proceed by direct examination.

5. A question calls for an opinion by a nonexpert or calls for an inadmissible conclusion. An objection may prevent a witness from expressing an opinion or conclusion.

6. A question has been asked and answered. An objection protects the witness, the court, and the jury from the unproductive repetition of questions to a witness.

7. A question assumes a fact not in evidence. An objection questions the use of facts in a question that have not been part of the evidence produced in court.

8. A question is argumentative. An objection prevents the opposing counsel from arguing with the witness under the guise of cross-examination.

9. The proffered evidence is not the best available evidence. The purpose of objection is to require the proponent to produce the writing itself, rather than introduce the evidence found in a written document by oral testimony.

10. A question is compound and/or complex. An objection requests the examiner to ask questions which contain, in their content, only *one* question rather than multiple questions in one.

11. The question is unintelligible. If the question is not understandable, the court should require the examiner to rephrase his question.

12. There is no proper foundation for the question or evidence. An objection requests the examiner to show the time, place of occurrence, the ability of the witness to perceive, and the fact of actual perception, prior to the witness testifying to an event or other evidence.

13. A question violates the constitutional right against self-incrimination. An objection here refers to the Fifth Amendment requirement which must be expressed or else it is waived.

14. A question seeks to elicit a privileged communication. This is to prevent a witness from testifying who is in a position, with the defendant, that is confidential and protected by law (i.e. husband-wife, doctor-patient privilege).

15. A question calls for a self-serving answer. An objection here is an attempt to exclude a declaration by a witness (or defendant) that is, in substance, to his own interests.

16. The cross examination is beyond the scope. The cross-examination cannot go to evidence unrelated to the evidence revealed on direct examination.

17. No *corpus delicti* has been presented, thus confession is inadmissible. There must be a *prima facie* showing that a crime has been committed before an admission or confession of the defendant may be admissible in evidence.

18. Evidence proffered is cumulative. An objection is an attempt to prevent additional and excessive evidence on one issue of the case.

Unless objected to, evidence is admitted. Even if the proffered evidence violates the rules of evidence, it will not cause a reversal of a conviction based upon it if there was no objection. Absent an objection, the jury may consider the evidence and base a verdict on it. An exception to this general rule of waiver, absent an objection, is if counsel, through incompetence, does not know when to object.

If an answer to an objectionable question has been made before the objection can be made or ruled upon, it is incumbent on the objecting party to request the answer be stricken and the jury be advised by the court to disregard it. If this is done, it will correct the error or prejudice unless the evidence is so obviously and severely prejudicial that an admonition to disregard the evidence would not correct the prejudice.

The rules of evidence strive to keep the evidence presented to such evidence as is logically relevant to the charge made and the issues raised by the charge. They insure, as much as possible, the reliability of the evidence. The rules promote a substance and appearance of fairness to the accused, even at the expense of relevance and truth if this is necessary to maintain that substance and appearance.

The objection made may require argument which will include partial or complete explanation of the evidence offered and the legal authorities for and against admission. If the trial is with a jury, the jury is generally excused from the courtroom during this argument so they will not hear the evidence offered unless it is ruled admissible.

It is important for the objecting party to express the proper reason for the objection and to require the court to rule on the objection so the record will reflect the error if the trial judge is mistaken. Without both of these protections, the issue raised by the objection will not be appealable.

Inexperienced or careless attorneys often approach the judge and participate in whispered conferences which are out of the hearing of the jury and are off-the-record. These off-the-record conferences may concern important legal issues which are resolved outside the record and, therefore, are not the subject of appeal if the judicial ruling is wrong.

Opening Statements   Making an opening statement is almost always correct for the prosecution; however, there is an element of tactics and chance in the defense option of when to make an opening statement or whether to waive the right to open.

It is beneficial for the prosecutor to explain the evidence of his case against the defendant in an organized and logical way prior to presenting that evidence. In most cases, evidence is introduced in bits and pieces and not necessarily in a reasonable or even easily understood manner. Witnesses know only parts of the case, and it may take several or many witnesses to develop the evidence on one issue. The prosecutor has and should take the opportunity to explain to the jury in a way that makes the evidence fit together so that when the juror hears the evidence he knows where to place it in the scheme of the case or at least within the prosecutor's theory of the case. The prosecutor may also gain rapport and credibility with the jury during this initial statement of the evidence.

The considerations of the defense are somewhat different. That the attorney should take every opportunity to speak to the jury on behalf of his client is almost an axiom in the law. Nevertheless there are numerous dangers in making the defense opening statement. The first and most important is the danger of an opening statement made by an attorney who is not completely prepared. If he is unprepared in any phase of the case, the jury can expect to hear in closing argument the variations between the evidence produced and the evidence promised in the attorney's opening statement.

An opening statement puts the defense case in a rigid jacket before the defense case is presented. When the opening statement of the defense is made immediately after the prosecutor's statement, it is made before the prosecution has produced evidence to meet its burden of proof.

A defense attorney need not decide until the prosecutor ends his case, whether to present evidence, whether to present witnesses, or whether to present his defendant as a witness, and if he decides to present evidence he may not want to present everything he thought he would at the beginning of the trial. Thus with the opening statement he may effectively (but not legally) commit the defense to a certain course of action that is unnecessary or unwise after hearing the prosecutor's case.

Legally, neither side is bound to present all the evidence stated in the opening statements, nor is the prosecution theory or defense theory legally circumscribed. However, in the event prejudicial statements of evidence are made in the opening statement with the knowledge that they are not provable or produceable (in bad faith), there may be grounds for a mistrial or a reversal upon conviction.[15]

No matter how prepared the attorney is, or no matter how well he has interviewed his witnesses, there is always the possibility, and often the fact, of witnesses either changing their testimony, forgetting testimony, or remembering things they did not previously reveal to the attorney.

A defense opening statement will give the prosecutor an advanced look at the defense. It may disclose, in advance, defenses previously unknown to the prosecutor and will allow him time to prepare for such defense. It may also alert the prosecutor to the direction of the defense attack on prosecution witnesses and evidence and allow him to alert his witnesses to such defense attack and prepare against it.

Discovery, for the most part, is a one-way street (when it is available at all). Therefore, the prosecutor will be disclosing nothing he hasn't already disclosed to the defense through discovery motions. The defense, however, is not bound to give over its case (with some exceptions, such as an alibi defense), or its witnesses, or its evidence prior to trial, and thus the opening statement when made by the defense is a prosecution discovery tool.

When opening statements are made, the defense attorney usually moves to exclude witnesses so as not to have their memories refreshed by the statement or to give them advanced notice of the planned cross-examination. It is also usual to keep the defense statement as brief and simple as possible so the jury is not confused. The attorney should be accurate; he should not bore or alienate the jury by repetition, personal mannerisms, or undue antagonisms or aggressiveness. The professional, calm, logical approach to this beginning trial process usually produces the best results.

Closing Arguments   Closing argument is the culmination of the attorney's trial work and is his last direct method of influencing the jury. It is the only time (other than the limited opening statement) when the attorney has the stage in the court. The importance of the closing argument to the final jury decision is different with different trials. In some it will be the cement which holds the presented evidence together; in others argument may be unnecessary to the final decision. What the attorney must believe is that argument is of prime importance in every

---

[15]*People* v. *Faulkner*, 257 Cal. App. 2d 56 (Ca. 1967).

case because he can seldom judge with known accuracy what the jury must have in order to decide the case in his favor.

Whether the attorney is a prosecutor or a defender, his goal is the same and his tools are the same. The goal is persuasion, and the tools are those attributes so important to the art of persuasion and debate: emotion, logic, and reason.

Emotion is the least important because it has little staying power and requires a quick verdict, or it is lost. Displaying anger, disgust, shock, and surprise are tools of argument. However, their real and lasting value during the subsequent deliberations of a jury is to impress on the minds of jurors the logic or reason of the attorney's theory of the case. Trial routine tends to be monotonous, which in turn dulls the minds of those who must listen. When the attorney wants the jury alert and receptive to a major point in the trial, emotion is a valuable means to rekindle interest and alertness.

Logic is a means to show the jury the intellectual basis of the attorney's theory of the case. Logic may draw the web of circumstances sufficiently together to form an impressive argument for the acceptance of the attorney's theory of the case. The danger of logic in argument is that it is unexciting and often outright dull, and it tends to be overly scholastic—which may literally put a juror to sleep. It rarely sustains the interest and attention of the listener so it must be used sparingly and only for short periods of time in the argument.

Reason is the best of the three tools of persuasion. The attorney should give the jury reasons for agreeing with his theory of the case. The attorney tells the jury why it should return the verdict he suggests, and at the same time he gives the jury a legal reason they can use to return that verdict. It is important to speak in clear English which can be understood by all, without seeming to be either condescending or overly scholastic or legalistic.

The ideal argument should be organized in such a way as to maintain high interest and alertness, despite the dull material which must be covered to persuade the jury to return a favorable verdict. If well done, the argument becomes a real and effective weapon for the trial attorney.

The right of discussing the merits of the cause, both as to the law and the facts, is unabridged in argument. The range of discussion may be broad. Counsel may be heard in argument upon every question of law. In his addresses to the jury, it is his privilege to descant upon the facts proved or admitted in the pleadings; to arraign the conduct of parties; to impugn, excuse, justify, or condemn motives as far as they are developed in the evidence; and to assail the credibility of witnesses. His illustrations may be as varied as the resources of his genius; his argumentation as full and profound as his learning can make it; and he may, if he will, give play to his wit, or wings to his imagination.[16]

The attorney may actually "feel" his jury, and be able to play to their reactions the way an actor may do with a live audience. Most trial attorneys have at least one time or another during argument seen a yawn or the shake of a disgusted head in the jury box, but the professional advocate moves right on and plays it out to the end as if they had not happened.

---

[16]*Tucker* v. *Henniker*, 41 N.H. 317 (1860).

An attorney should try his case to fit his argument, rather than fitting his argument to the case he has tried. As with most sayings, this should not be taken literally, but it does have important meaning. Its meaning is found in case preparation.

A closing argument prepared *prior to trial* will ensure the following:

1. The attorney knows the case sufficiently well to prepare the argument. He is prepared for trial.

2. The attorney knows which part of the opposition case he can injure or destroy by cross-examination and/or rebuttal evidence and knows which part of the opposition case he should stay away from.

3. The attorney knows what witnesses to present in his case and what evidence must be presented for his theory of the case.

4. The attorney recognizes and can easily incorporate into his final theory the surprise windfalls of a trial.

5. The attorney recognizes and is able to ignore, or to explain away, the surprises which hurt his case.

6. The attorney knows which instructions must be given by the court for his theory of the case.

7. The attorney is prepared to argue at a moment's notice a real advantage over an unprepared attorney.

The attorney need only modify his pretrial argument at the conclusion of the trial, not during the ongoing trial. Revision should be based upon the few unknown windfalls of every trial.

The conclusion of the case is the reason and the result of everything that has preceded it, both during and prior to trial. It should represent the ultimate of the advocate's art. It is the final exposition of the strategy of the case.

The prosecution's closing argument emphasizes the enormity of the crime, the quality of the prosecution's evidence, and the self-serving nature of the defense evidence.

The objective of defense counsel's argument is to try to convince the jury that the defendant is innocent or, at least, try to make the jury want to acquit the defendant. Generally there is a reviewing of the prosecution evidence at its weakest points, and/or the prosecution's summary of it in the prosecutor's closing argument; a statement of the law governing the charge and its relation to the theory of the defense case; and a statement of the critical questions that the jury must decide in light of the law and the facts (this may include the credibility of one witness or the reasonableness of one inference—wherever the defense is strongest.)[17]

---

[17]Anthony G. Amsterdam, Bernard L. Segal, and Martin K. Miller, *Trial Manual for the Defense of Criminal Cases—Student Edition* (Philadelphia: American Law Institute, American Bar Association Committee on Continuing Professional Education, 1974), pp. 435–446.

Instructions on the Law   At various times during the trial, especially at the end, the judge may instruct the jury regarding points of law applicable to the case being tried. The court must explain to the jury any law which may be appropriate when any substantial evidence has been produced in that area of the law. Attorneys are generally required to submit, in writing, the law they wish the judge to explain to the jury. Even when not required to do so, an attorney is well advised to submit instructions which coincide with his theory of the case. It is then the responsibility of the court to decide which of the requested legal instructions he will read to the jury, and which he will not read or explain. There are basic instructions the court is required to give beyond those offered by either attorney. Examples are concepts such as burden of proof, essential elements of the offense, and direct and circumstantial evidence when the case rests substantially on circumstantial evidence.

If the court reads an erroneous instruction of law, or fails to give an instruction required, the mistake may be grounds for reversal upon appeal, depending upon its importance to the case and how it prejudices the defendant's case.

There are books which set out models of jury instructions in virtually every kind of situation.[18] These model instructions are based upon case law interpretation as well as interpretation of statutory provisions, and are a well-regarded authority even though they are not the final authority. Many instructions are submitted, given, or refused, that either modify or change the models. It is then a matter of appellate review and interpretation as to whether the trial court gave the correct explanation of the law to the jury.

It is this combination of evidence and explanation of the law which must serve as the basis for the final decision by the jury. One without the other would be meaningless, and one which is opposed to the other cannot form a successful theory of the case. An attorney who wishes to win his case at trial must know the law, that it will be explained by the court, and be able to produce substantial, credible evidence which will "fit" the law in his favor.

Sentence and Judgment   Defendants found not guilty or who are entitled to discharge for some other reason should have such judgment signed by the judge and entered in the record by the court clerk. A judgment of conviction sets forth the plea, verdict or findings, and the adjudication and sentence.

A real problem confronting the sentencing judge is determining the personal or behavioral elements deserving emphasis in a particular case. For this reason, the judge seeks as much information as possible about the offender and the offense prior to sentencing. Then the appropriate sentence is based upon the offense committed, the circumstances surrounding its commission, and the social and criminal history of the offender. In effect, a sentencing judge attempts to determine the influencing circumstances that led to the crime and, to the extent possible because of the nature of the crime, to individualize the sentence.

---

[18]Committee on Standard Jury Instructions, Criminal, of the Superior Court of Los Angeles County, California, *California Jury Instruction, Criminal*, (St. Paul, Minn: West Publishing Co., 1970).

Presentence investigations are reports by local probation officers. The quality of these reports depends upon the skill and sincerity of the investigating probation officer, his ability to organize collected data, and his ability to present it simply and clearly for judicial guidance. Presentence reports cover a minimum of three major areas as follows:

1. The *present offense* includes details of the offense(s) charged and offense(s) for which the offender was convicted; crime partners, if any; and extenuating circumstances tending to lessen the blame associated with a finding of guilt.
2. A *criminal history* is based on an accurate report of past delinquency adjudications and criminal convictions. If arrests are reported, dispositions must be probed and reported.
3. A *social history* contains significant data, preferably from birth, including the offender's family resources and community or environmental conditions.[19]

Reporting probation officers usually conclude their reports with a recommendation as to the type of sentence. The report will interpret the factors in the offender's current situation as justification, and explain how family and other resources can be utilized to support the program recommended.

Prosecutor's Role in Sentencing

The prosecutor's role in plea negotiations involves quasi-participation in the sentencing process. The prosecutor's willingness to permit a plea of guilty to a lesser charge, to only one count of a multicount indictment or information, and/or to a reduced sentence offers guidance to the judge participating in these plea negotiations. However, the prosecutor also has a role in the sentencing process after a defendant has been convicted at trial and is to be sentenced by the judge (rather than jury participation in sentencing).

Prosecutors may not be consulted by a sentencing judge, but they usually have the opportunity to present a specific recommendation as to the appropriate sentence, or to take a position against leniency.

An advisory committee of the American Bar Association suggests that a prosecutor make no recommendation to a sentencing judge as to an appropriate sentence unless his recommendation is requested by the court, or he has agreed to do so in connection with a negotiated plea. The same committee suggests that prosecutors disclose to the defense and the court, at or prior to sentencing, all information in the files of the prosecutor's office which is relevant to the sentencing. It is also suggested that the prosecutor should correct any apparent incompleteness or inaccurateness in the presentence report.

---

[19] David Dressler, *Practice and Theory of Probation & Parole* (New York: Columbia University Press, 1959), pp. 105–107.

The prosecution as a source of information and/or influence in the sentencing process does provide the sentencing judge with data on the police-prosecution position in regard to specific offenders. The prosecution usually presents a position oriented toward a victim, which can make a significant and meaningful impact on the judicial decision. A study points out that prosecutors are aware that their recommendations of a sentence will place pressure on judges who are otherwise inclined toward leniency. This influence has its place in overcoming the expected arguments of defense counsel for leniency but, in its own right, is effective in bringing about more severe sentences.

A prosecutor's attempts to influence the sentencing decision are usually limited to serious crimes—the operations of organized crime, gangland homicides, atrocious assaults, homicides, sex offenses, child molesting cases, cases involving the so-called wholesalers of the illicit drug traffic, and the corruption of public officials.

Many judges expect the prosecutor to make a recommendation as to an appropriate sentence but will not allow any *ex parte* communication. An *ex parte* communication raises serious legal questions of due process and fair treatment because it is out of the presence and without the knowledge of the opposing party and his counsel.

Role of Defense Counsel at Sentencing

Defense counsel has the opportunity at sentencing to make any representation he wishes. Many probation departments welcome contacts from defense counsel. They view counsel as a resource person who may add to the information they can discover about the convicted defendant. This contact does not involve discussing the probation officer's recommendation, but it is an early opportunity for defense counsel to give information likely to be helpful to his client.

When a presentence report, or a summary, is made available to counsel, he should attempt verification of any information not known to him and/or questioned by his client. It is the attorney's duty to challenge erroneous information or supplement incomplete data. When the presentence report is not disclosed, defense counsel should submit to the court and prosecutor his own written report and recommendations. This report would present favorable information about the defendant likely to be relevant to the sentencing process. When probation is being sought, a sentencing plan should include details of the rehabilitation program suggested as well as information regarding the available community services.

Traditionally, at the time of sentencing defense counsel makes a general oral plea for leniency on broad grounds of humanitarianism or fellowship. Now, many defense attorneys offer a considered analysis of their client as a law violator and a person, together with a sentencing plan. The plan may use nonprison resources and include a firm commitment from one or more community agencies to take the defendant into a treatment program.

To prepare adequate representation for a client at sentencing, a defense attorney must consider

1. The nature of the crime.
2. The blameworthiness of his client for the crime.
3. His client as a certain type of offender—violent, cynical, mercenary, inexperienced, and so on.
4. The predilections of the sentencing judge in regard to certain types of offenders being the proper subject of severe sentences.
5. The types of sentences possible.

In pleading the defendant's case for leniency at sentencing, defense counsel can emphasize initially that the experience of being arrested, confined, tried, and convicted has not only been educational for his client in that he now understands the errors of his behavior, but it has also been a form of punishment which is sufficient to change the offender's behavior in the future. From this take-off point, defense counsel must exploit or counteract an unfavorable presentence report. He may point out the "good" aspects of the crime (for example, client was a follower to the lead of one or more crime partners; the client was provoked). Defense counsel may highlight the favorable aspects of his client's social or criminal history, background, and family resources. The attorney should also be careful to avoid any overt pinpointing of the defendant as one of a class of offenders the sentencing judge has dealt with severely in the past. Defense counsel must make every effort to insure that the sentence will not be disproportionate to the circumstances of the offense and the life situation of the offender.

The proper subject for discussion between attorney and client should be how the defendant should act before the verdict to show he or she is a person worthy of judicial consideration for a lesser sentence in the event the verdict is guilty. The client must begin attempts at rehabilitation as soon as possible so that defense counsel at sentencing, in the event of an adverse verdict, can point out what has been done by the defendant to get and hold a job, to reshape attempts at education, and to enter local treatment programs aligned with an offender's needs. His attorney may then argue convincingly that these recent achievements are illustrative of the client's good intentions and sincere desire for rehabilitation.

It is no more than fundamental fairness in sentencing a convicted defendant to give credit for time actually served prior to conviction or final imprisonment. Some jurisdictions require this credit by statute. Defense counsel is more than justified in asking the sentencing judge to give credit for jail time during the pretrial period, the trial itself, and, if warranted, while defendant was imprisoned while awaiting action on a pending appeal.

Role of Defendant at Sentencing

A defendant has the right to speak to the court in his own behalf. However, in cases in which guilt has been denied at trial, a defendant must remember that his or her statement is part of the court record and any admissions of guilt may prejudice a future appeal, and even result in a more severe penalty.

There is a general and long-standing belief that a mute defendant at sentencing indicates an unspoken contriteness that is favorable to his or her cause. In a few instances, defense counsel may suggest that the defendant speak out briefly on his intent to change, to seek treatment, and to use available resources, but this is usually no more than a reassurance to the court that the defendant joins in the arguments of his counsel and has agreed to the sentencing plan suggested to the sentencing judge by defense counsel.

Appeals

In the post-conviction period a convicted defendant has a fundamental right to an appeal when the judgment of conviction is entered in the court's record after the defendant has been arraigned for sentencing. This is a direct appellate review within the court system in which the case was tried.

The prosecution cannot directly appeal the judgment in a criminal case but can seek legal remedies to set aside trial court orders relating to the criminal proceeding—the granting of a motion to suppress evidence, the granting of a motion to set aside the pleading, and the granting of a post-verdict motion for a new trial.

An initial step in planning an appeal is for defense counsel to obtain a copy of the trial transcript from the court. Transcripts of any evidentiary hearings that were not part of trial, particularly those related to pretrial motions, should also be obtained. These transcripts comprise the factual record of the case.

The scope of direct appellate review focuses on errors in the total criminal proceedings against the defendant that led to his conviction and judgment. Defense counsel, by in-court objections to evidence or judicial rulings believed harmful to the defense, preserves specific issues for claims of error. In addition, the court may question the sufficiency of the evidence to support the verdict. The appellate court may not reweigh the evidence but must determine if there is any evidence which would support the verdict. The burden of proving insufficient evidence after conviction is the appellant's (defendant).

Appeals must be filed within a stated time limit, usually dating from the date judgment was entered. An early application for appeal is advisable. The time periods are short. Counsel may request the release of the defendant on reasonable bail pending the appeal.

Harmless Error

When the nature of an error does not significantly prejudice the rights of a defendant or alter the weight of the evidence, the reviewing court may class it as "harmless error" and refuse to reverse or modify the lower court's decision.

Appellate courts look for errors which lead to a miscarriage of justice in a criminal proceeding. Some errors are so unfair or illegal that they will never be classified as harmless errors (for example, coerced confessions, denial of defendant's right to counsel).[20] Some errors can be classified as harmless despite unfairness or illegality but only when appellate review determines that the evidence of guilt is so strong that the defendant would have been found guilty beyond a reasonable doubt even without the unfairness or illegality.[21] In *Harrington* v. *California*[22] the U.S. Supreme Court concluded that the other evidence of guilt was so overwhelming that there was no reasonable doubt that the jury's verdict would have been guilty without the erroneous admission of defendant's confession. The basic rule is given in *Chapman* v. *California*: no violation will be considered harmless error so long as there is a reasonable possibility of a different verdict if the error had not occurred.[23]

Case Studies

> *Haynes* v. *Washington*, 373 U.S. 85 (1963).
>
> *Hoffa* v. *United States*, 385 U.S. 293 (1966).
>
> *Boykin* v. *Alabama*, 395 U.S. 238 (1969).

Discussion Questions

1. Describe the trial structure.
2. What rights of a defendant are waived by the plea of guilty? Can a guilty plea be withdawn? How?
3. Discuss the plea of not guilty by reason of insanity.
4. What is the usual basis for a pretrial motion to suppress evidence?
5. What are the similarities and differences between the prosecutor's opening statement and the opening statement of defense counsel?
6. What are the goals of closing arguments?

---

[20]*Haynes* v. *Washington*, 373 U.S. 503 (1963).
[21]*Fahy* v. *Connecticut*, 375 U.S. 85 (1963).
[22]395 U.S. 250 (1969).
[23]386 U.S. 18 (1967).

7. Discuss the prosecutor's role in sentencing; the role of defense counsel; of the defendant.

Glossary

Corpus Delicti   Body of the crime.
Ex Parte   One side only; in behalf of one party only.

Selected Bibliography

Cahn, William, *Mock Trial*. Chicago, Ill.: National District Attorneys Association, 1974.

California Evidence Code Manual, Sacramento, Calif.: California Continuing Education of the Bar, 1966.

Dressler, David, *Practice and Theory of Probation and Parole*. New York: Columbia University Press, 1959.

Drinker, Henry S., *Legal Ethics*. New York: Columbia University Press, 1953.

Ehrlich, J. W., *The Lost Art of Cross-Examination*. New York: G. P. Putnam's Sons, 1970.

Kerr, Harry P., *Opinion and Evidence: Cases for Argument and Discussion*. New York: Harcourt Brace Jovanovich, 1962.

McCormack, Charles T., *Handbook of the Law of Evidence*. St. Paul, Minn.: West Publishing Co., 1954.

Mendelson, Irving, *Defending Criminal Cases*. New York: Practicing Law Institute, 1967.

Newman, Donald J., *Conviction: The Determination of Guilt or Innocence Without Trial*. Boston: Little, Brown & Co., 1966.

Perry, Nancy Walker, and Lawrence S. Wrightsman, *The Child Witness*. Newbury Park, Calif.: Sage Publications, 1991.

Richardson, James R., *Scientific Evidence for Police Officers: Scientific Tests and Experiments; Specific Methods of Proof*. Cincinnati: The W. H. Anderson Co., 1963.

Sobel, Nathan R., *Eyewitness Identification: Legal and Practical Problems*. New York: Clark Boardman Co., Ltd., 1972.

Stephens, Otis H., *The Supreme Court and Confessions of Guilt*. Knoxville: The University of Tennessee Press, 1973.

Stryker, Lloyd Paul, *The Art of Advocacy: A Plea for the Renaissance of the Trial Lawyer*. New York: Simon & Schuster, 1954.

Tierney, Kevin, *Courtroom Testimony: A Policeman's Guide*. New York: Funk and Wagnalls, 1970.

Walls, H. J., *Forensic Science*. New York: Praeger, 1968.

Wellman, Francis L., *The Art of Cross-Examination*, 4th ed. New York: Macmillan Publishing Company, 1936.

Weston, Paul B., and Kenneth M. Wells, *Criminal Investigation: Basic Perspectives*, 3rd ed. Englewood Cliffs, N.J.: Prentice-Hall, Inc. 1980.

Zagel, James, *Confessions and Interrogations After Miranda*. Chicago: National District Attorneys Association, 1972.

Glossary

Accomplice   A principal in a crime.

Acquittal   Court or jury certification of the innocence of a defendant during or after trial.

Ad Hoc (Judgment)   Pertaining to, or for the sake of, this case alone.

Admissibility   Determination of whether evidence, exhibits, or testimony will be allowed in trial; inadmissible evidence cannot be allowed and is therefore not presented in court and is not heard or examined by the triers of fact.

Admission   A statement inconsistent with innocence of a crime; defendant admits a damaging fact.

Advocacy   Defending, assisting, or pleading for another; to defend by argument.

Advocate   One who renders legal advice and pleads the cause of another before a court or tribunal; one who speaks in favor of another.

Affidavit   Sworn written statement.

Antecedent Justification (Police Action)   Prior court approval.

Appeal   Judicial review; a postconviction step in judicial proceedings. After the decision of a trial court, the removal of the case (cause) to a higher court with authority to review the decision of the lower court for the purpose of obtaining a retrial.

Appointed Attorney   Legal counsel provided by a court for defendants without funds to hire private counsel.

Autopsic (Evidence)   Evidence as a result of viewing an object or thing.

Bail   Release of a defendant upon his written agreement to appear in court as required. Cash or other security may be required.

Ballistics   Science of the motion of projectiles; firearms identification; the scientific examination of evidence found at crime scenes and connected with firearms; firearms, spent bullets, empty cartridge or shell cases, and cartridges and shells.

Bench   The presiding judge (and his position at the front of the courtroom).

Best Evidence Rule   The best evidence of the content of a writing is the writing itself.

Citation   Reference to an authority; U.S. Supreme Court decisions give the case name, the volume and page numbers (*U.S. Reports*), and the year in which the case was decided.

Common Law   Principles and rules of action derived from ancient usages and customs, or from judgments and decrees of courts enforcing such usages and customs.

Confession   A statement acknowledging guilt; defendant's statement that he committed the crime charged.

Confession Cases A series of U.S. Supreme Court decisions concerned with illegal or improper police interrogations.

Conspiracy (Criminal) A combination of two or more persons for the purpose of committing, by joint effort, an unlawful act or using unlawful means for the commission of a lawful act.

Corporeal Of or pertaining to the human body.

Corpus Delicti Body of the crime.

Criminal Act Act or omission prohibited by law.

Criminal Intent A determination of the mind; an intelligent purpose to do an act prohibited as criminal by law; *mens rea*.

Criminalistics Scientific discipline directed to the recognition, identification, individualization, and evaluation of physical evidence by the application of the natural sciences in matters of law and science. The application of science to the examination of physical evidence; linked to forensic science, the general application of science to the solution of crimes. Evidence technicians represent a subclassification of this field.

Cross-examination Questioning of witness by counsel for opposing party; follows the *direct examination* of a witness by the party calling the witness to court.

Declarant A person who makes a declaration (statement).

De Minimis Insignificant, minute, frivolous.

Dicta, Dictum Judicial opinion not essential to a court's decision on the question under review.

Dirty Business Term used to describe wiretapping in *Olmstead* v. *United States*.

Discovery Disclosure by the prosecution of certain evidence regarding a defendant in a pending trial. There is limited disclosure by the defense. Term is generally identified with defense pretrial request to prosecutor to disclose facts of the police case against defendant.

Diversion Finding alternatives to formal action within the criminal justice system.

Doubled (Agent) Action of "turning" an agent employed by an adverse party into an associate who will provide information about his first employer (adverse party).

En Banc Together, all the judges of a court "sit" and hear a case.

Exemplar (Handwriting) A specimen (of handwriting); an example; a model.

Ex Parte On one side only; no adverse party in proceedings.

Experts Capable of being qualified in court as expert witnesses; men and women of science educated in art or science, or persons possessing special or unusual knowledge acquired from practical experience.

Expert Witness An individual, with reference to a particular subject, who possesses knowledge not acquired by ordinary persons; a man of science or a person possessing special or peculiar knowledge acquired from practice and experience.

Field Interrogation   Questioning of suspicious person stopped by police.

Forensic   Related to courts of justice.

Forensic Science   Application of scientific knowledge to the solution of crimes and in support of the investigation of crime. (See Criminalistics.)

Foundation (Of Testimony)   Establishing the fact that the opportunity of a witness to observe was sufficient to afford a reasonable basis for the proposed testimony.

Fruits of the Poisoned Tree Doctrine   Doctrine barring the use of derivative evidence tainted by illegal origin.

Grand Jury   A certain number of persons selected according to law and sworn to the duty of receiving complaints and accusations of crime in criminal cases, to hear evidence presented by the "state," and to return indictments when they are satisfied a trial is warranted. The term "grand" developed because, at common law, the number of persons on this jury was set at not fewer than twelve nor more than twenty-three, while the original *trial jury* (petit jury, as distinguished from grand jury) was a body of twelve persons.

Guilty   The result of a guilty verdict in a criminal prosecution (jury or judge); the result of judicial acceptance of a guilty plea; the opposite of innocence.

Habeas Corpus   A name for writs seeking to bring a party in custody before a court or judge to examine into the lawfulness of imprisonment. Its sole function is to release from unlawful imprisonment. Technically habeas corpus *ad subjiendum*.

Habeas Corpus *ad testificandum*   Directed to a person having legal custody of a prisoner in a jail or prison and ordering him to bring a prisoner to court to testify. ("You have the body to testify.")

Hearsay   Secondhand evidence; testimony of evidence not based on the personal knowledge of a witness, but information someone else has seen or heard and related to a testifying witness.

Identity   Proof of a person's identity as being the individual alleged in the accusatory pleading.

Impeachment (Of Witness)   Attacking the credibility of a witness.

In Camera   Not in open court; private; judicial chambers.

Infamy   Status of person convicted of crime such as treason and other major felonies. Infamous crimes are those that are scandalous or heinous; usually linked with severe punishment upon conviction.

Informer's Privilege   Right of police to avoid disclosure of identity of informants to protect them from retaliation and to enhance continuance of the flow of information about crime and criminals from informants to police.

Intelligence (Police)   Clandestine or secret collecting and evaluating of information about crime and criminals not normally available through overt investigative techniques.

Inter Alia   Among other items or things; used when the complete wording of a law is not given.

Irvine-Type Violations   Purposeful violations of the Constitution by police officer.

Judicial Instructions   A charge to the jury by trial judge; instructions as to the principles of law in a case and their application to the circumstances of the case being tried.

Juveniles   Persons under a specified age (usually eighteen) who may be processed in a special juvenile court on the issues of neglect and delinquency.

Latent (Fingerprint)   Not visible to ordinary visual examination; must be searched for with special skill and equipment. A latent fingerprint can be developed by evidence technicians and preserved as evidence.

Mens Rea   Criminal intent.

Modus Operandi (M.O.)   Method of operation; used in the identification of criminals by their crime techniques or habitual criminal conduct.

Motion   Application to court for a legal remedy.

Nemo Tenetur Seipsum Accusare   No one is bound to accuse himself.

Nexus   Connection; tie; link.

Nolo Contendere   No contest; designation of a plea in a criminal action having the legal effect of a guilty plea but which cannot be used elsewhere as an admission.

Objection   Opposition to the introduction of certain evidence or questions during a criminal proceeding, or to judicial rulings. Linked with a "request to strike," to remove from record any portion of the opposed evidence or question already before the triers of fact. The objection is granted when the presiding judge *sustains* it; it is *overruled* when denied.

Peace Officer   A "sworn" officer, sheriff's deputy, or state investigator; usually named by job title in state statutes giving peace officers power to carry out their sworn duty.

Per se   By itself.

Physical Evidence   Things and traces (clue materials) found at crime scenes, upon suspects, or at places or upon persons otherwise related to a criminal investigation.

Plastic (Fingerprint)   A finger impression made in a pliable (plastic) substance.

Plea   An answer to the accusation: guilty or not guilty, or one of the special answers.

Preliminary Hearing   A judicial hearing or examination of witnesses to determine whether or not a crime has been committed, and if the evidence presented by the prosecutor is sufficient to warrant the commitment, or bailing, of the accused pending trial.

Presentence Report   A report by a probation officer of an investigation conducted at court direction into the social and criminal history and resources of a convicted defendant, and containing a recommendation to the sentencing judge concerning the best program of corrections for the offender.

Presumption   The inference of one fact from the existence of a related fact.

Prima Facie   On the face of; at first view, uncontradicted.

Privileged Communication   A communication between persons in a confidential relationship who are under a special obligation of fidelity and secrecy, and which the law will not allow to be divulged (or inquired into) for the sake of public policy; husband and wife, attorney and client, and so on.

Protean   Variable; readily assuming different shapes or forms.

Rebuttal   The answer of the prosecutor to the defense case in chief; an opportunity for the prosecution to repair any portion of the prosecution's case damaged by defense evidence.

Rejoinder (Surrebuttal)   The answer of the defense to the prosecutor's rebuttal; opportunity for the defense to repair portions of the defense case damaged by prosecution evidence during the rebuttal stage of a trial.

Return (Search Warrant)   A report of police action when executing a search warrant, including an inventory of property seized and a description of the place found.

Rubric   A form or thing established or settled; formally specified; a class or category.

Spike Microphone   When driven into the wall of a premises, a spike microphone has the capability of picking up sounds on the other side of the wall; similar to induction microphones (which pick up conversations without direct wiring in telephone interceptions), and "shotgun" or tubular microphones, which have a long-range directional pickup capability. No physical intrusion into the premises involved is necessary when these eavesdropping devices are used.

Sporting Theory   A spinoff from the American legal system's trial-by-adversary concept (fight theory), with surprise being part of the strategy of the prosecution.

Standard   Desirable or ideal work performance level; work as expected by supervisors and associates; prevailing practices or authoritative recommendations to upgrade prevailing practices.

Stare Decisis   Rule of precedents; principle that once the law of a specific case has been decided it should serve as a definite and known rule for the future (unless decision in error, or mistake).

Subpoena   A process commanding the person named therein to appear before a court to testify as a witness.

Subpoena *duces tecum*   A process commanding a witness to bring to court a document or other record in his possession or control which is pertinent to trial issues.

Venue   Place or area in which a crime was committed; *situs delicti*. Change of venue is to transfer a pending trial to another county or district.

Voir Dire   In-court preliminary examination of juror or witness when competency, interest, and so on, is in dispute.

INDEX